Dad,
Happy Ch

love She xx.

INTO CHINA

By the same author

INTO JAPAN
JAPANESE CRAFTS

INTO CHINA

John Lowe

JOHN MURRAY

For Judith and Dominic
who bore the heat of the summer
and
Yukiko Nomura
who shared 'noodles over the bridge'

© John Lowe 1986

First published 1986
by John Murray (Publishers) Ltd
50 Albemarle Street, London W1X 4BD

Typeset by Inforum Ltd, Portsmouth
Printed in Great Britain
by The Bath Press, Avon

British Library CIP Data

Lowe, John, *1928–*
Into China.
1. China—Description and travel—1976–
I. Title
915.1′0458   DS712

ISBN 0–7195–4333–9

Contents

6 *Contents*

Illustrations

*All photographs by the author, except for Plate 40,
which is reproduced by permission of
Robert Harding Picture Library Ltd, London*

Acknowledgements

I had long wanted to visit China but it was the encouragement of my son and daughter, Dominic and Judith, that led to a first visit with them in the summer of 1983. They were patient and good-humoured companions and although we enjoyed the journey, it was different from anything we had expected.

In the spring of 1985 I returned to travel through southern China and Tibet which was no less exacting than the first journey, and much longer. This time I shared the fascinations, and the dust and the dirt, with a Japanese friend, Yukiko Nomura. Apart from the pleasure of her company, her ability to read some Chinese was often valuable. It helped my understanding of China to watch her reactions to the oldest oriental culture which had given so much to Japan during the Tang dynasty. She also helped me during the writing of this book to which she has made an important contribution.

I returned by myself to tour northern China in the autumn of 1985. On this and the other journeys I met many other travellers and some Chinese. Several of these meetings are described in the book but mostly I have disguised identities. To all these people, journalists, diplomats, language students, scientific advisers and holiday-makers, I offer my thanks for sharing their knowledge and experience. All the Chinese, from an outspoken one-star general to many men and women in the street, added a personal dimension to a country where it is difficult for the traveller to make any significant contact with the people.

Looking back to my only professional encounter with Chinese studies, in the Ceramics Department of the Victoria and Albert Museum, I thank my colleagues at that time, the late Arthur Lane, Robert Charleston and John Ayers. They taught a poor student the elements of Chinese ceramics and left me with some understanding of Chinese art.

Kyoto, 1986   J.L.

The Chinese Dynasties

Xia *c.* 21st–16th century BC
Shang 16th–11th century BC
Western Zhou 11th century–771 BC
Spring and Autumn Period 770–476 BC
Warring States 475–221 BC
Qin 221–207 BC
Western Han 206 BC–AD 24
Eastern Han 25–220
Three Kingdoms 220–265
Western Jin 265–316
Eastern Jin 317–420
Southern and Northern Dynasties 420–581
Sui 581–618
Tang 618–907
Five Dynasties 907–960
Northern Song 960–1127
Southern Song 1127–1279
Yuan (Mongol) 1271–1368
Ming 1368–1644
Qing (Manchu) 1644–1911
Republic of China 1912–1949
People's Republic of China 1949 – the present

Not all sources, including books published recently in China, agree exactly on the earlier dynastic dates but the above represent a consensus. Since prior to the Yuan dynasty China was continually fragmenting into separate kingdoms a full dynastic chronology would have further subdivisions but the above chart provides all the information necessary for this book.

Introduction

When I think back on my three journeys in China I am reminded of a friend at Oxford who left to start work with a well-known publisher in London. Soon afterwards he was told that he was to take the famous Belgian novelist, Georges Simenon, for a day's tour of Oxford. Diligently, he prepared an itinerary which ensured that Simenon should see as many of the architectural splendours of Oxford as possible in one day. On arrival at Oxford station he showed his master plan to the great novelist. Simenon glanced at it, gave one of those dismissive Gallic shrugs, thrust his hands deep into his raincoat pockets and spent the rest of the day walking in fascination up and down all the meanest streets around the station and along the canal. Those who share Simenon's tastes in sight-seeing may enjoy China best. The great monuments of China's past are splendid but not all that numerous. The present-day life of the streets is fascinating and endless.

I confess that I was disappointed by the general quality of China's cultural sights. At the end of my travels I made a list of the cultural and beautiful places I had visited to which I would award three stars. The criterion was those places which I would go to great trouble to visit again. For such a vast country with such an ancient culture the list was short. The places were the Forbidden City, the Temple of Heaven and the Great Wall, all in and around Beijing. Tibet and Lhasa, despite the vandalisation, fully merit inclusion. I remain strangely haunted by the Muhammadan burial ground in Canton and I would like to take the Guilin river trip at least once a year. The train ride from Kunming to Chengdu is an exciting and magnificent journey, as is the boat ride through the three Yangzi gorges. I would have to return to Xi'an to inspect the terracotta army and I would like to see the cave temples of Luoyang again.

I would like more time for the gardens of Suzhou and the romantic lakeside landscape of Hangzhou. I would return to Datong, not so much to see the Yungang caves but to stand again before the fragile

Buddhist sculpture of the Lower Huayuan Monastery and to drive out to where the curious Xuanggong Si, the Hanging Monastery, clings to the wall of the Jinlong canyon. Finally, I would make a second autumn pilgrimage to Qufu, home of Confucius. It must be autumn for I want the town bathed again in dusty, golden sunshine and the squat mud houses garlanded in orange-gold corncobs.

Beyond that personal and selective list, drawn up in the knowledge of the important places I never saw at all, I want the streets of China: the raucous streets of Canton, the springtime streets of Kunming, the more sombre streets of Chengdu, the sulphurous, steep sloping alleys of Chongqin, the windswept avenues of Datong, the shoddy pilgrims' path leading up Taishan and even the dreary shopping streets of suburban Beijing. It was walking those streets, day after day, that I gained a more intimate view of China and learned most about this teeming, overwhelming country.

I have attempted to recreate the experience of travelling as an individual in modern China. I have tried not to romanticise anything or to exaggerate the problems and discomforts of travelling alone. When I first went to China in 1983 I found a few recent and useful guide-books but none of them gave me a real sense of what it was like to travel in the world's largest country among the world's largest population. Other travel guides published since then, though rather more practical, mostly limit themselves to dealing with individual works of art and architecture or other places of interest without creating a coherent picture of the whole country that faces the traveller. I hope this book will give the reader a vivid picture of what it is like to travel as an individual throughout modern China. The impressions and opinions that I have written are more those of a traveller than a professional sinologist or even what is now commonly called a China-watcher. I do have a deeper experience of other oriental countries which certainly helped me to understand both old and modern China.

My first conscious association with China years later reached an unexpected half-fulfilment. Since an early age I was strongly drawn to the East. My Buddhist friends put it down to reincarnation. I put it down to the precocious discovery of Joseph Conrad's novels around the age of ten. But before that, when I was only eight, I had an absurd brush with things Chinese. I was an avid film fan. Each time I managed to amass sixpence I would retire to a local 'flea-pit' to sit through three continuous performances. In the two years that the craze lasted I must have seen dozens of films but I can remember only one. It was a detective story and the sleuth and hero was not only a great detective but also an internationally famous expert on rare Chinese porcelain. With the bloodstained clue in one hand he would caress an exquisite piece of Qing *famille noire* with the other.

I was intoxicated, saw the film three times running and staggered out of the cinema with a blinding headache and a determination to grow up to be an international expert on Chinese art. The ambition faded quickly but the memory of the incident has remained vivid for fifty years. The irony is, that, while I did not become any kind of international expert, twenty years later I found myself working in the Ceramics Department of the Victoria and Albert Museum helping to curate *famille noire* of a quality that would have brought tears to the eyes of my detective hero. My humble dealings with Chinese ceramics were confined to sorting out a great deal of late blue and white porcelain which the public brought in for an opinion.

I did not have the intellect for ceramics study but during my five years in the department I learned to admire Chinese pottery and porcelain and acquired a basic understanding of Chinese art. The Chinese collections at the Victoria and Albert Museum are not the finest in London but there were enough good objects to teach me to recognise quality. This experience came alive again while I was travelling in China, reinforced by years of visiting nearly every great museum collection of Chinese art throughout the world, including several visits to the incomparable collection in Taipei. If my judgement of art and architecture in China often seems severe, reflecting a disappointment I often felt, it is because I judged everything by the highest standards based on great Chinese works of art of all kinds I have seen all over the world. The reader has to remember that vandalism in China was not an invention of the Cultural Revolution. The great monuments of China have been ravaged by war, natural disasters, dynastic rebuilding and plain neglect for centuries. Then came the iconoclasm of this century's revolution culminating in Chiang Kai-shek's removal of the greater part of the Imperial Collections to Taiwan. What is left is mostly Ming and later buildings heavily and clumsily restored and the splendid treasures unearthed in post-revolution archaeology. There are wonderful things to see but it is unwise to expect too much.

I pursued my fascination with the oriental world in a variety of ways all of which were to provide useful background for a study of

China. I travelled widely and before I ever set foot in China had visited every country in the East, most several times. I knew Taiwan, Hong Kong and Singapore. I had travelled all over South-East Asia and been twice to South Korea. My deepest experience of the oriental world has been in Japan which I have visited regularly for twenty years and where I have lived for the last six. Japan borrowed Buddhism and much of its culture from China during the Tang dynasty. Although the Japanese rapidly digested this massive borrowing, creating from it their own unique culture, there remain revealing echoes of China in every part of Japanese life, ancient and modern.

The fact that I have lived for several years in a Far Eastern country made me feel at ease in China. The similarities between China and Japan, like the common use of the Chinese characters on which the Japanese have based their writing system and the elements of Confucianism which remain the roots of modern Japanese society, helped me to understand China. The great differences between the two peoples were equally revealing since they alerted me to everything that was uniquely Chinese. But while Japan helped me to understand China, my experience of China has added to my understanding of Japan.

This is not a political book but it is impossible to ignore politics when writing about modern China. China is a political situation, a billion people locked into a desperate and dramatic political experiment to drag a medieval, largely illiterate society into the modern world. At one extreme China has the ability and capacity to produce nuclear weapons, to launch satellites and to harness the most advanced technology, even though it involves using their best brains and limited resources so desperately needed to solve more basic problems. At the other extreme there are millions of peasants still living in primitive conditions which have hardly changed in hundreds of years. How far communism – even China's new pragmatic communism – will succeed in solving the country's overwhelming problems remains to be seen. All I saw in China, the economic figures of the last two years and the basic spirit of the people encourage a cautious optimism.

The industrial nations of the world are learning to live and cooperate with communism, slowly accepting that it may be the necessary political system for certain countries. Chinese communism seems more palatable to the Western powers since it has become critical in the balance of power with the Soviet Union and because its vast population offers a new consumer market of irresistible potential. The Americans, the Japanese and the European powers are using every means to woo the Chinese to ensure their share of this market while the Chinese are exploiting this commercial promise to the full, accepting aid and technical advice in a splendidly patronising spirit of mutual cooperation.

As an individual traveller it is most fascinating to compare the communism of the Soviet Union and China as it appears in everyday life. I found walking the streets of Russia a grey and gloomy experience, walking amongst a people who mostly looked dispirited and badly fed to a point near to national ill-health and depression. China must not be glamorised. Chinese communism has exterminated millions, imprisoned and persecuted millions. Its political system has been sustained by a ubiquitous secret police and a network of informers.* More serious in the long term for the survivors of all this is the ever-growing system of bureaucracy which strangles growth and development by its greed, corruption and inefficiency. Despite all this there is a certain heroic element in Chinese communism which is evident at the highest levels of the government and in the extraordinary spirit and vitality still to be found among the ordinary Chinese which reminds the visitor that they have been an exceptional people, and resilient survivors, for 3000 years and more.

Whatever his eventual position in the Chinese pantheon Chairman Mao will remain one of the giants of human history, and the survival of Chinese communism in the Long March one of its great epics. The courage and resilience of Deng Xiaoping is reflected in his ability in his eighties to manipulate China's vast machine of government and with such power and skill that in 1985 he not only placed his own younger supporters at every level of the government but achieved the impossible by forcing the army to make considerable cuts in manpower. Chinese politics are seldom dull and are the substance of modern Chinese life though one is left with the ultimate feeling that the average Chinese wishes to be left in peace to enjoy

---

* Persecution reached a climax in the Cultural Revolution of 1966–76 when Chairman Mao unleashed a terrible anarchy on the country, theoretically to root out returning bourgeois influences but, in fact, to destroy all opposition to his own power. The youthful Red Guards were given licence to destroy or re-educate whomever they disliked, often simply their elders.

the slowly rising standard of living that Deng's pragmatic policies are now producing.

This book will leave the reader who is considering a visit to China with a more immediate problem. Should he or she travel to China with an organised group or go as an individual traveller? I hope that the description I give of my journey through China as an individual will help people to make up their own minds for it is something that no one can decide for them. The problem is easy to summarise. If you go to China in a group you will see a lot in basic comfort and convenience but you will be tied to a rigid and overcrowded programme which will give you no opportunity to explore anywhere on your own at a more personal level. For many people that will provide the view of China they require.

The individual traveller enjoys a freedom denied to the group, a freedom that is increasing all the time, but he or she will work hard for this freedom. The price is spelt out in the following pages, as are the benefits. It will be obvious that I prefer individual travel but I would not recommend it to everyone and I would urge anyone considering going to China by themselves to weigh the pros and cons carefully. It will be exhausting, it will be frustrating and there will be moments when the language barrier creates problems. But if you are in good health and have some experience of travelling in less 'sophisticated' countries, there is the bonus that China is in every way unusually safe and, if you have enough time, you will see more than the group traveller and you will see sides of China that they hardly see at all.

At the end of all my travels I was sitting in Hong Kong's airport waiting for a flight to London. Sitting next to me were an Australian couple and their look of deep exhaustion prompted me to ask them if they had just been to China. They had, travelling with a group for three weeks on a sweeping circuit up to Beijing and back. I asked them if they had enjoyed the tour. There was a long pause before the wife said, 'I'll need time to think about that, to absorb the whole experience.' She was right. China is not like other holidays. It is not primarily about enjoyment but it is an extraordinary experience that offers different rewards.

At present people are flocking there mainly because it has been closed to the world for so long and it has temporarily become the fashionable country to visit. Mostly these travellers are carefully insulated from the realities of Chinese life and the fascination of the

Chinese people who remain in the memory long after the temples and palaces have blurred. Despite the language problem the Chinese people will come closer to the individual traveller and they will form the heart of the individual traveller's experience. Through the Chinese people, with their generous, aggressive, maddening, extrovert yet withdrawn character, the greatness of their civilisation and history lives on reminding one all the time that the present, poor, struggling nation remains one of the great peoples of the world who may rise from the ashes of their poverty to write new chapters in the history of the oldest continuous civilisation.

The Chinese Language and Romanisation

Mandarin, originally the dialect of Beijing, became the official spoken language of China during the Manchu dynasty. Today it is spoken by about 70 per cent of the population. But China still has nine major dialect groups, quite apart from more local dialects and the languages of the minority people. This diversity of language combined with widespread illiteracy creates enormous problems for the government. The Chinese do share one written language composed of some 50,000 characters, many of them infernally complicated. Spoken Chinese of all dialects is marked by the use of four tones which help to distinguish between the many sounds that have more than one meaning. For all these reasons Chinese is not the kind of language that even the most gifted linguist is going to 'pick up' during a three-week holiday.

The exact origins of written Chinese are uncertain. It is one of the oldest writing systems in the world and the oldest in continuous use. Originally the characters developed from simple pictograms, possibly some 6000 years ago. The earliest surviving characters have been found on the oracle bones of the later Shang dynasty and 4500 have now been identified. There is a fascinating display of these bones and inscriptions in the National Museum in Taipei, Taiwan.

The Chinese government has taken a number of steps to simplify the written language to help overcome illiteracy. Classical Chinese has about 50,000 characters of which some 5000 are in common use and 1500 are needed to read a newspaper. A large number of common characters have been drastically simplified. For example the old character for 'cloud' was composed of fourteen strokes while the new character has only four. You must remember that a Chinese child not only has to memorise the whole character but must also remember the correct order in which the strokes must be written. There is a possibility that at some time in the distant future the Chinese might give up the characters and adopt a romanised system of writing but such a step is unlikely until a far higher rate of literacy has been achieved.

In 1958, as a first step in that direction, the 'pinyin' system of romanisation was introduced by the government, replacing the Wade-Giles system, the commonest form of romanisation up to then. For those used to such spellings as Peking, Canton or Mao Tse-tung, the new forms, Beijing, Guangzhou and Mao Zedong are at first sight confusing. In fact the 'pinyin' system brings the romanisation closer to the correct Chinese pronunciation and with a few important exceptions most sounds are the same as in English. The five most important exceptions are:

c is pronounced 'ts' as in *its*.

q is pronounced 'ch' as in *chair*.

x is pronounced 'sh' as in *shout*.

z is pronounced 'ds' as in *kids*.

zh is pronounced as the letter j.

In this book I have followed the precedent of other recent books on China and for the most part used the 'pinyin' system of spelling since that is the spelling the traveller will find in modern China. Like other writers I have not been entirely consistent and have used the Wade-Giles romanisation where I thought it might avoid confusion. Everyone is now used to Beijing but there may be readers who would not recognise Guangzhou for Canton or Sun Zhongshan for Sun Yatsen. In the index I have listed the names of people and places first in the modern spelling, with the Wade-Giles spelling in brackets. In the few cases where the order is reversed this is made clear.

Prologue

A FALSE START

I picked up a taxi opposite Ladbroke Grove tube station.

'Where to, Guv?'

'Victoria Station, the Gatwick train please.'

'Going abroad then. Mind if I ask where?'

'I'm flying to Hong Kong, then going to China.'

'China, eh? I was in Shanghai at the end of the last one. First Royal Navy boat in, Guvnor.'

I leant forward in my seat. I had not expected to start gathering first-hand experiences in Ladbroke Grove.

'Must have been pretty rough then. What sort of state were the Chinese in?'

'Well, didn't see much of them. Didn't want to get involved, you see. Usually a few tied to the buoys each morning but the tide soon swept them off.'

'But what was Shanghai like?'

'Well, preferred Japan meself. Know a little place called Nikko? Sort of brightly coloured temples and things. Had a good job up there. Well, not hard work really. We used to bring the lads up for a bit of a rest. Had a sort of, well, kind of brothel up there. They used to work in two shifts, you see. I was a Petty Officer and I had to see the place was cleared at the end of each shift. Nice job that.'

'But surely you have some memories of Shanghai?'

'Oh good gracious yes. Very vivid. I remember the first time I came off the boat an Australian officer came up and kissed me. Blimey! Thought I was back in Chelsea. Nothing like that really. Had dinner at his home in Sydney later. Nice wife and two daughters. Marvellous thing, travel.'

1

Gateway to China

HONG KONG TO CANTON

There ought to be something momentous about entering China for the first time. My imagination smouldered with exotic images: drum towers, moon gates, dragon screens and the alluring Silk Road. Such fantasising was instantly ended by the functional façade of Hong Kong's main railway station, point of departure for many latter-day Marco Polos. This concrete box provides a suburban entrance to the Middle Kingdom. Should any of your romantic illusions have survived this far, the long ticket queue will give you a corrective experience of life in modern China. Noisy, undisciplined and continually infiltrated by those who insist that they are cousins or friends of the people in front, the queue writhes like a distorted dragon-dance towards the ticket-window. The traveller is *blooded* and the battle of Chinese travel has begun.

The modern train that runs to the border is all steel and orange plastic. The lack of seating was designed presumably for the passengers' luggage rather than their comfort. This is a new Silk Road, a caravan of Hong Kong Chinese bringing gifts to deprived relations across the border: food, consumer goods, clothes, electronic gadgets, bundled into capacious red, white and blue striped plastic bags. Others on the train are small-traders exploiting the shortages on the mainland. In the last few years, stimulating their economy, the Chinese government has turned a blind eye to such trafficking. It is the first phase in the eventual marriage between Hong Kong and the mainland now agreed by the Chinese and the British for 1997.

I failed to get a seat on the train and was squeezed between a cornucopia of vegetables and a sharp-cornered package containing an outsize television set. Crouching between these obstacles I had glimpses of the passing landscape. On one side, stark highrise apartment blocks were packed together on the precious flat land of the New Territories, the nuclei of new and bleak dormitory towns. On the other side, rising hills were littered with shanties half-submerged in wild undergrowth. Briefly, a wide bay revealed the sea but immediately the industrial sprawl obscured the view of the South China landscape. The train slowed and we drew into Lo Wu station. We were at the border.

After only a few minutes at this overcrowded border station I realised that the hullabaloo of Kowloon had been a mere dress rehearsal. Within seconds of stepping off the Hong Kong train we were standing in the longest queue I had ever seen, snaking up and around the long platforms and disappearing into the distance. Since we were heading for the customs inspection and every Chinese had at least three huge bundles, it seemed unlikely that we should cross the border that day. But after only a few minutes of despair, all the foreigners were plucked out of the queue by policemen and led into a separate hall where we cleared the Hong Kong customs and immigration without delay.

The moment had come to pass through the 'bamboo curtain' and to enter mainland China. Our progress was not inspiring but characteristic of much that lay ahead. The larger railway stations of China always seem to be in the chaos of reconstruction. Carrying our bags, we struggled with the swelling crowd along a shabby corridor of scaffolding and rough screening. Behind this we caught glimpses of new buildings and a new bridge under construction. In such places it is always 'jam tomorrow'. Across the old bridge and we were in Shenzhen station. We shuffled under a tawdry arch of welcome into China and immediately into the Health Department, all white antimacassars and synthetic smiles. An official corrected our forms, the main activity of all such officials around the world, and we moved on to immigration and customs. Both processed us without fuss or smiles but I thought that I preferred their ill-fitting uniforms to the neo-fascist black patent leather of the Hong Kong police.

Finally to the bank where a pretty girl relieved us of our foreign currency in exchange for wads of the tourist money known as FEC, Foreign Exchange Certificates. The normal Chinese currency, RMB or 'People's Money', can be obtained from touts everywhere who will offer as much as an 80 per cent bonus on the exchange since with FEC Chinese can buy goods reserved for foreigners in Friendship Stores and hotel shops. Until recently, in all tourist centres bills could be paid only in FEC so that RMB had only a limited use for tourists when shopping in a local market or eating in a local restaurant. But the distinction between the two currencies is beginning to break down and even government agencies such as the

China International Travel Service (CITS) are both accepting and giving change in RMB. Foreign Exchange Certificates will no doubt continue as one of the government's devices for milking the tourist, a convenient disguise for the extortionate official rate of exchange.

The trains from Hong Kong connect with fast trains from Shenzhen to Canton, the journey taking from two to three hours. After another tussle in another ticket queue and the struggle through the crowds in the main hall and along the platform, we sank exhausted into the spacious 'soft seats', that comradely euphemism for First Class. The realities of Third Class are accurately named 'hard seat'. The train was comfortable in a dowdy, old-fashioned way, typical of China's idea of luxury. Lace curtains obscured the windows with blue velure draperies at the sides and drab cotton covers on all the seats. The train also offered two of China's necessities of life: tea and noise. Large-lidded cups of tea were regularly refilled by a woman attendant armed with a tall thermos of boiling water. Tea can be purchased in small paper bags and the tea leaves are poured straight into the cup which also acts as the teapot. After the infusion there follows a frustrating period while one waits for the coarse leaves to settle, unless one wants a bitter mouthful of tea leaves with every sip. Tea is available nearly everywhere. Even in the height of summer one develops a Johnsonian addiction for these mugs of scalding tea. The Chinese never travel without an enamel mug since these are often not provided. It is the mark of serious foreign travellers in China that they carry their own tea mug and chopsticks.

The train to Canton will introduce you to a less agreeable feature of Chinese life: the ever-present, ever-echoing loudspeaker. Big Brother may not be watching you but rest assured that Little Sister will be speaking to you, advising you, exhorting you. On our way to Canton we were regaled with a repertoire of sentimental songs, opera and two identical selections from *The Sound of Music*, punctuated with station announcements and admirable urgings to give up spitting in public places and to keep China tidy. The one thing we never got was silence. Should you travel by a night train, be warned. The difference between a soft and a hard sleeper is not just a matter of the bedding. The loudspeaker blares on much of the night. In a soft sleeper you can turn it off. In the hard sleeper you cannot. I have known silence to become far more desirable than a soft pillow.

The first sight of the Chinese landscape is attractive. This is another world, despite the increasing influence of Hong Kong's

INTO CHINA

U. S. S. R.

MONG

Urumqi

XINJIANG

G A

PAKISTAN

N

INDIA

QINGHAI

Lanzho

Yangzi R.

TIBET

SICH

Chengdu

•Lhasa

NEPAL

BHUTAN

0   100   200   300   400 Miles

0   200   400   600 Kilometres

China's international
boundaries

Other international
boundaries

Provincial boundaries

Railways

Grand Canal

Great Wall

BANGLA-
DESH

BURMA

Kunming
YUNNAN

VI
N

LAOS

prosperity in the neighbouring Guangdong province. Everywhere gangs of human labour move earth, rock, building materials and long lengths of metal pipe, no burden too heavy to be manhandled into position. China is short of most things but rich in unskilled man-power and, one must add, as one watches them shoulder to shoulder with the workmen, womanpower. The land is mostly flat with mountains in the distance. The rice fields stretch away, fringed here and there by lines of eucalyptus and other trees, the water catching a glint from the fading afternoon sun. Villages of mud bricks stand above large ponds and the threat of rain in the sullen sky makes this a watery world. At times the view is more enclosed: green pond waters surrounded by buildings of warm red brick, a fat sow rootling among the weeds and a line of white ducks waddling along the muddy path between the rice fields. These idyllic views belie the wretched life of many villagers whose only ambition is to escape to the higher living standards of the industrial cities. Not for nothing were the victims of the Cultural Revolution sent for punishment down on the farm. For the traveller there is often an uneasy contradiction between the picturesque and poverty.

The first time I came to Canton in 1983 I made the common mistake of dismissing it as an uninteresting commercial centre, famous only for its trade fairs. I stayed long enough for a good dinner and caught the night train to Guilin. On my second visit in 1985 I had more time and I determined to find out why some people recom-mended Canton and the distinctive character of the Cantonese. I now recommend others to do the same and to spare at least two days for this fascinating city. But beware of the official tours offered in Hong Kong. After three enthralling days in Canton I saw an official three-day tour brochure. The programme included only one of the places I had enjoyed and was taken up mostly with visits to craft markets and silk and porcelain factories, all of which reached an original climax with 'a shopping tour'. An intriguing evening was offered at 'a Cultural Show (if available)'. I puzzled over the kind of cultural show that could become suddenly *unavailable*, with visions of runaway pandas and absconding acrobats. One fact is that there are few certainties in China.

In the great square in front of Canton station the visitor is immediately made aware of the vastness of China's population. From there on one moves through China in an overwhelming crowd, heaving, pushing, shouting and spitting its way through life. As we edged our way towards the taxi-cab rank, I had the feeling that a large proportion of Canton's population of five million were pushing in the opposite direction. There is little that is obviously attractive about Canton. Across the square were large, garish hotels and along the wide avenues hoardings with crude posters advertising the latest Japanese consumer goods. It was another reminder that Canton is now linked to the booming economy of Hong Kong. It is now the main city and port of the surrounding Special Economic Zones set up by the Chinese government in 1980 to increase foreign trade immediately and to forge the necessary links with Hong Kong for its absorption at the end of the century. There is already an existing social link since a large proportion of Hong Kong Chinese fled from this area and still have many relations living here, in many cases helped by a share of the Hong Kong wages.

Canton is an old city, founded during the Qin dynasty in the third century BC and later becoming China's main point of contact and trade with the outside world. Canton has a long tradition of independence and its relationship with the rest of China is similar to Barcelona's relationship to Spain. Canton's remoteness, particularly from Beijing and the government, its long contact with foreigners, its distinctive language and culture and its fondness for new ideas, often revolutionary ones, created a sense of separation which has been reinforced by its recent prosperity and a new way of life leaning towards the capitalism of Hong Kong. It is now the only city in China where taxis cruise the streets and it is the only city outside Beijing where there are hotels of international standard that can be booked easily in advance. Although little of old Canton is now left, its few monuments do illustrate some part of its colourful and frequently turbulent history.

It was the Canton Orchid Park that led to Canton's oldest and most curious relic. The park has a great variety of orchids, mostly attractively cultivated in row upon row of green-glazed pots set in the shade of tropical trees and tall clumps of bamboo. It is a pleasant, rather secret place, a welcome respite from the crowds who are deterred by a high entrance fee. This includes a cup of orchid tea, served at the back of the gardens in a tasteless new pavilion of glittering coloured glass set into latticed wall panels. Outside plump birds sang in elegant bamboo cages. While savouring the dry, slightly dusty flavour of orchid tea, across the boundary fence I noticed an unusual wall decorated with what appeared to be an Arabic inscription. Referring to my guide-book I found a brief reference to a Muhammadan tomb near the Orchid Park.

Finding our way around the back of the Orchid Park was not easy, particularly as workmen were digging up the lane alongside the park. Picking our way through muddy trenches and piles of drain-pipes, we found a narrow path to the right and not far along it we came to the wall I had seen from the tea-house. It was a high-walled enclosure and inscriptions in both Arabic and Chinese were incised over the narrow central doorway. We entered a large courtyard where an unkempt garden straggled in pleasant disorder around a central pond, everything touched by a slight Islamic air. Several Chinese families were living in the buildings around the courtyard, groups of small children pausing from their games to stare at us. A burly old man approached and seemed to be telling us to leave. I could see the burial ground through an archway to the right. It looked fascinating and I was terrified that the man, as a devout Muslim, would not allow us to enter. Then an elderly woman came over. She was more friendly and when I pointed to the archway, she nodded and led us through.

The faith of Islam has spread to many places in China but this graveyard in Canton is particularly notable. Arab traders, said to have been accompanied by missionaries sent to China by Muhammad, started to settle in Canton in the seventh century AD. Beyond the lines of ancient graves on either side of us was a small stone building. Through the door, lit by guttering candles, we could see a rough sarcophagus, draped in a threadbare orange and blue pall. For those who wished to remove their shoes and enter, there was a scrap of worn carpet for devotions. The air of reverence comes from the traditional belief that this is the tomb of the Prophet's maternal uncle. He is said to have been the first missionary and the builder of the Huaisheng Mosque in the centre of Canton. Whatever the truth, this tomb remains the most sacred place in China for Chinese Muslims and the burial ground moved me as much as any place in China. The rows of tombs in the silent shade of the great banyan trees and the rough, stone sepulchre produced a vivid sense of history with two such different cultures living side by side for so many centuries.

Shamian Island, south of the city centre and against the north bank of the Pearl River, is a reminder of a different episode in China's foreign relations, the incursion of British and other European merchants and the shameful events of the Opium Wars. The British East India Company started trading in tea, silk and porcelain through Canton in 1685. In 1757 the imperial government decreed that all trade must be conducted through their agency, the 'Co Hong', and that all foreign merchants and their warehouses must be confined to a short strip of the riverfront to the east of the modern Renmin Bridge. Nothing remains of the confined but colourful life of the eighteenth-century British merchants, the busy commerce of the godowns and the East Indiamen at the wharf laden to their waterlines with tea and thousands of pieces of blue and white porcelain to satisfy the 'Chinamania' then raging in Britain. A few museum objects still recall what must have been an extraordinary way of life by the edge of the Pearl River. A number of quaint wax figures of British and other European merchants, commissioned from a Cantonese craftsman, have survived. One is in the National Portrait Gallery in London. More revealing is a charming album of paintings at the Victoria and Albert Museum, also by a Chinese artist, which record in exquisite detail the merchants' business life. I recall one painting showing a florid, heavily waistcoated British merchant enthroned in a chair ample enough to support his generous frame, haggling with two skinny, shrewd-eyed Chinese tea-dealers. Somehow the artist contrived to show who had the upper hand.

The Chinese restrictions of 1757 reduced the already not very lucrative profits of the East India Company's China trade. In 1773 they took steps to improve the position by importing 1000 chests of Indian opium which they could sell without difficulty for silver. By 1816 they were importing 5000 chests of the drug each year into Canton. In 1839 the Chinese government was determined to stop the opium trade and after a brief siege managed to seize 20,000 chests of opium. The British were outraged by this interference with their profitable trade and successfully attacked Canton. A treaty was signed in 1841 which, among other concessions, gave Hong Kong to Britain. The opium trade was successfully defended by British naval power in three further wars. The treaty of 1859, which ended the fourth war, led to the complete opening of China to European and American merchants and to a flood of Christian missionaries.

At the same time the foreign merchants in Canton acquired Shamian Island as their enclave. Shamian means 'sand flat' which is

what it was when the merchants first took it over. With land rec-
lamation the size of the island was increased to about one kilometre
long by 300 metres wide. The island is now a graveyard of
fascinating but decrepit nineteenth-century colonial architecture
whose huge buildings seem held together more by their stucco than
their structure. These were the mansions and the offices of European merchants, imposing buildings decorated with classical columns, baroque detail and neo-classical friezes, now burstingly
over-occupied by dozens of Chinese families. The architectural
glories are blurred by moss and rot, and shrouded by long lines of
washing, brave as flags on their bamboo poles. The old Roman
Catholic church, designed in an assertive gingerbread gothic style,
thrusts its pinnacles up into the spreading branches of the banyan
trees which give the whole area a tropical atmosphere. It is a place of
gloomy splendour. Sadly, development is nibbling at the edges.

The steep bridges on the north side of the island are picturesque
but the canal waters they span are murky as a sewer. Nearby, in a
small park, the local song-bird fanciers, a bamboo cage in each hand,
the cotton covers drawn back, were giving their charges their evening
airing while across the street a group of youths played a noisy game in
the local billiard hall. To the south of this bizarre backwater the Pearl
River remains a great thoroughfare. Its muddy waters are churned
night and day by the passing large and small boats: crowded ferries,
cargo boats, groups of lashed-up barges and the occasional family
junk, the small sail assisted by a chugging engine. The south bank,
once colourful and notorious for low life and opium dens, is now
commercialised and boringly well-ordered, linked to the main city by
China's first suspension bridge, built in 1932.

Immediately south of the old merchants' settlement, on recently
reclaimed land, a new monument has risen on Shamian Island
marking the latest foreign invasion. This is the stark white, thirty-
six-storey White Swan Hotel, symbol of China's growing foreign
commerce and tourist industry. It offers facilities and a standard of
comfort to be found nowhere else in China except Beijing and in few
establishments there. Beyond the spacious lobby and rising through
three storeys is an opulent Chinese garden and cascading waterfall.
Around this centrepiece, at different levels, are elegant souvenir
shops, luxurious Chinese and Japanese restaurants and a coffee shop
whose Western delicacies linger in the traveller's memory as later
he wrestles with the realities of Chinese cooking and service. This

galaxy of foreign luxury is given a peculiar and uncomfortable slant by the 'comrades' who are allowed just so far into these exotic precincts to admire and photograph the garden but far more, to stare at the foreigners eating their club sandwiches or taking their afternoon tea. One lunch in that coffee shop gave me a new sympathy for animals in the zoo.

Luxury hotels are not yet typical of large Chinese cities but public parks certainly are. Apart from the usual pleasure of walking in attractive surroundings, in China they provide quiet corners for student study, a space where enthusiasts may practise the waltz or the tango, a stone table for a game of chess, a track for joggers, ground for the *t'ai chi* exponents and slight privacy for young lovers. One- or two-room family flats provide no space for such pastimes. In China there are many married couples who have little opportunity for making love and less encouragement from a government determined to lower the birth rate. Liuhua Park is pleasantly laid out around the largest artificial lake in the city and is cleaner and better maintained than most city parks. On our first evening in China I remember sitting on a bench in this park watching a nimble elderly woman teaching a young man the basic movements of *t'ai chi*, the Ming dynasty martial art of boxing which has evolved into a gracefully balletic and popular form of physical exercise controlled by mental discipline. We then wandered around the lake until we discovered the Stream of Flowers, a well-known restaurant where we had an excellent meal. That was a suitable introduction to the city for in describing a paradise on earth, an old Chinese saying recommends eating in Canton.

Yuexiu Park is the largest and most interesting in Canton, built over a series of small hills with attractive gardens, ponds and pavilions near the main entrance. The park is best known for a number of monuments, each of which recalls some important event in the city's history. One glance at the massive Sculpture of the Five Rams reminded me how many such monuments, while full of civic pride, are without any aesthetic appeal. This towering piece recalls the mythical origins of Canton. Five magicians came riding through the air on the backs of five rams, bearing a gift of rice seedlings that ensured that the people of the area would never suffer from famine. The legend is charming. The five rams, hewn from rugged blocks of granite, in no way suggest their legendary role as airborne transport. The monument was erected in 1959.

On the top of a neighbouring hill is a more genuine relic of Canton's past. This is the Zenhai Tower, in fact a long five-storey rectangular building, with balconies facing north and south which give a good view over the city. It was originally a watch-tower, linked to the old city walls and built in 1380 for sentries to keep a lookout for attacks from the river. The tower was severely damaged during the Manchu invasion of the south and was rebuilt in 1686. It is painted a dark vermilion and its heavy proportions are broken by the narrow projecting roofs between each storey and the thin columns that support the balconies. The building now houses the Canton Museum, a collection of objects ranging from neolithic artefacts to late Ming and Qing porcelain. On a nearby terrace are a line of old cannons, some of European make, a reminder that the British and French occupied this strategic position during the Opium Wars.

The last famous monument in the park, the tall obelisk commemorating Sun Yatsen, is the first of several in the city which recall the political fortunes of Canton since the first revolutionary movements against the Qing dynasty during the second half of the nineteenth century. Canton has a tradition of being a radical city and a breeding-ground of revolution. Sun Yatsen was born near Canton in 1866 and led the movement to overthrow the emperor and establish a republican government. With the help of others he eventually succeeded and became the first president of the Republic of China in 1911. Almost immediately he gave up the leadership to Yuan Shikai who had a more powerful following in the north. Sun Yatsen spent the rest of his life until his death in 1925 struggling to hold the Republican Party together. But the factions composing it were too diverse and the original revolutionary movement slowly divided into the military republicanism led by General Chiang Kai-shek and the emerging Communist Party already under the leadership of Mao Zedong and Zhou Enlai, with the incessant conflict between them turning finally into open war. Many regard Sun Yatsen as the founder of modern China and he is one of the few modern leaders to be revered in both China and Taiwan. He and Chiang Kai-shek both married daughters of the vastly rich Shanghai Song family. Sun Yatsen's wife, Qingling, remained in China until her death in 1981 and although she never joined the Communist Party, she was active in many fields and was so respected that she was made honorary president of the Republic. Her house in Beijing has been turned into a museum-cum-shrine. The obelisk in Yuexiu Park

1 Wooden houses in the old quarter

KUNMING

2 Lake Dian from the West Hill

3 A guardian figure by the Dragon Gate

4 Holiday-makers in the Stone Forest

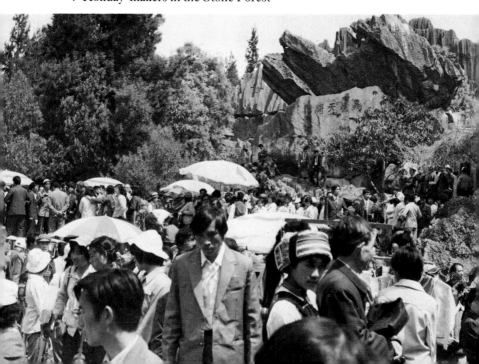

commemorating Sun Yatsen is peculiarly ugly though there is a fine view from the top. A more moving memorial is his last message to the people of China, inscribed on the south face of the obelisk, words which remain particularly apposite to China's present problems:

For forty years I have devoted myself to the cause of national revolution, the object of which is to raise China to a position of independence and equality among nations . . . to attain this goal, the people must be aroused, and we must associate ourselves in a common struggle with all the people of the world who treat us as equals.

Not far from Yuexiu Park are other memorials to Canton's part in China's modern political struggles. But like so many political monuments, their real significance is often obscured by an overlay of propaganda. However, for anyone interested in the development of China's radicalism and eventual communism, Canton played an important part and these places illustrate its contribution. The Monument of the Seventy-Two Martyrs marks Sun Yatsen's last and unsuccessful uprising against the imperial government when seventy-two of his followers were killed in April 1911. Stronger forces in the north established the Republic only six months later. Chinese from all over the world subscribed to this monument which celebrated China's new if somewhat illusory democracy. It was erected in 1918 and its design is an extraordinary democratic mélange of appropriate symbols of political freedom, such as the Liberty Bell executed in stone, borrowed from the monuments of older democracies around the world.

The communists were established in Canton by the early 1920s and in 1924 they founded a school to train peasant leaders, now known as the Peace Movement Institute. Mao Zedong was director for a brief period and Zhou Enlai lectured to the students. The school typified the ideology and the idealism of early Chinese communism. It was forcibly closed by Chiang Kai-shek's troops in 1927. The school was restored and opened as a museum in 1953 with a reconstruction of Mao's simple room and photographs of the institute's activities. The closure of the school took place during a communist uprising in Canton in which 5700 people are said to have been killed. They are commemorated in the Memorial Garden to the Martyrs, laid out on Red Flower Hill, one of the execution grounds where many of them died. Today it is an attractive garden with two incongruous monuments to China's friendship with the peoples of the Soviet Union and North Korea.

After this heavy dose of political history and bad sculpture, we went to the zoo, said to be one of the best in China. I wanted to see a panda, to that moment a gap in my education. I confess that we came away from the Canton Zoo having succeeded in seeing only the backsides of two giant pandas. During our visit the front halves were immersed in bundles of succulent bamboo, with no time to spare for admirers. To compensate for this rearguard action, a young keeper took visitors' cameras inside the cage to snap whatever was available of the front end. The zoo was scruffy and littered with rubbish, particularly peanut shells. These, I must emphasise, were for the visitors, not the monkeys. The collection of animals and birds was large but many of the cages were so heavily barred or wired that it was difficult to see the occupants. The whole visit was made worthwhile by the magnificent Manchurian tigers shown in a dramatic natural habitat setting. These great streamlined animals stretched themselves on the warm rocks or moved with silent power and grace, superb and awesome, through the dense clumps of bamboo.

The true character of a great city like Canton and the pulse of its daily life is not to be found among monuments, or in zoos and museums. They are little more than trinkets around the wrist of a fascinating woman. Her heartbeat is on the streets, among the millions of people thronging the avenues and alleys of Canton. Each large Chinese city has a character of its own. Canton and the Cantonese are distinctive in everything; their penetrating dialect, their piquant cooking, their independence and their cockney-like abrasive vitality that gives both humour and noise to life on the streets.

There is little elegance in Canton but even in its basic poverty there is a vibrant style and energy rooted in the people's ability to rise above their mean, crowded conditions and the austerity of their lives. I watched an old woman stall-holder eating her lunch. In the metal container was nothing but plain boiled rice flavoured with a few stalks of green vegetable, but with what zest and obvious enjoyment she consumed the vegetables. Everywhere in central Canton the streets are shut in by high tenement buildings with dreary façades of peeling plaster, broken windows and balconies draped with washing which never looks clean. Clumsy blue and white buses trundle up and down the main streets, each bus stop a battleground. Bicycles run like torrents, forcing pedestrians into a game of hopscotch at each street crossing where cyclists give way to no one, flooding relentlessly forward to the tinkling of innumerable bells. Only the spreading trees soften the harsh scene, the raw and raucous town-scape of large Chinese cities.

Unique to Canton and typical of its lifestyle is Qinping Market. There is a high stone bridge crossing the canal on the north side of Shamian Island and opposite, its name written in gold characters over the mouth of the alley, is the entrance to the market and a variety of gruesome sights and pungent smells. My guide-book accurately described it as 'a takeaway zoo'. It certainly confirmed all my darkest suspicions about Cantonese cooking. But no doubt centuries of hunger and near-starvation give people an appreciation of anything which is a source of flavour or protein. Since childhood I have been haunted by the scene in the film of Pearl S. Buck's *The Good Earth*, where the Chinese neighbours, driven to despair by famine, accuse a farmer of hoarding food. They crowd angrily around the steaming pot in his kitchen. He lifts the lid to reveal a cauldron of mud which Chinese fed their children to lessen their hunger pangs. I can still recall the impassive features of Paul Muni looking down into that awful stew.

Once inside the dark alley, the crowd runs like a strong current making it difficult to pause and examine the baskets and sacks of herbs, spices and local specialities, some for cooking, some for medicine and many for virility. We picked our way between clumps of mushrooms, neatly coiled dried snakes, petrified starfish, turtle shells, furred antlers, crinkled lizards, the limbs and skulls of monkeys and other exotica and aphrodisiacs. The alley is a curtain-raiser to the main food market, a wide street which runs across the top of the alley offering a fascinating picture of Cantonese life for those with a strong stomach.

This is the meat and vegetable market, a place of infinite variety. An old man with a bucolic face under a shapeless felt hat hacked away at a bloody carcass, scraping the last scraps off the huge rib-cage. Nearby were turtles, salamanders, squirming fish in buck-ets and basins, cages of cats, monkeys and other fauna, heaving baskets of snakes and sacks with frogs and giant snails spilling out. Some stalls presented a macramé of suspended innards, lights, offal and limp coils of intestines. On one stall were the carcasses of two flayed dogs. But most of the delicacies were sold alive, from indignant fowls to gasping carp; the poultry trussed up and tucked under the arm, the fish dangled precariously on a length of straw. Housewives selected their frogs with care, stuffing the frenzied legs into their string bags.

A light rain was falling and the crowds pressed through the muddy street, babies swaddled on their mothers' backs in crimson quilted shawls, a tame monkey picking the pocket of a boy who was absorbed in frying paper-thin pancakes. We moved on, dodging between overloaded bicycles and stepping between the wide puddles of rain and filth. It was horrifying and fascinating but it gave a truer picture of Cantonese life than any number of museums or monuments. It almost confirmed my suspicion about the basic principle of Cantonese cooking: if it moves, eat it.

2

The Painters' Landscape

GUILIN

I have travelled twice from Canton to Guilin. The second time I flew, which was cheap and convenient. The first time I went by train which was cheaper and more eventful. I was with my son and my daughter. On arrival in Canton we managed to book 'soft sleepers' for that night. It was a perfect example of the absurdity of Chinese bureaucracy. At that time tourists were not supposed to buy the normal price tickets at the station but had to obtain them through the local CITS office where they paid a hefty surcharge. At the CITS office the surly officer barely looked up from his newspaper to wave us in the direction of the railway station across the square. After two hours of bedlam in queues which several policemen were unable to keep in any semblance of order, we bought tickets at the ordinary fare. The train left at 9.30 p.m. We returned to the station early and one of those stern-faced women officials, who seem to control railway stations in China, led us to the 'soft' waiting room: cool, silent and, if one ignored the enamel spittoons, utterly without character. It was like a foretaste of limbo.

Our wardress returned in due course and led us to our train. We were delighted with its old-fashioned comfort and the comparative coolness of the four-berth sleeper. We shared it with a thin-faced Chinese official who, with a nervous smile, retired for the night to the corridor where he smoked and chatted with his colleagues. We were soon asleep but woke about 6.30 to enjoy hot tea and the dawn creeping up on the green and brown patterns of the rural view drifting past our window. In China I sat for hours by train windows enthralled like some television addict. We thought that the journey to Guilin took about twenty hours and had estimated that we should arrive there that evening. To our dismay, shortly after breakfast we stopped at some unknown station where the sleeping-car attendant insisted that we get off. Utterly convinced that the train would take us directly to Guilin, it was unnerving suddenly to find ourselves standing on the platform of a station whose name we did not know and could not read, without the slightest idea of our whereabouts. Add to that a morning temperature of about 34°C and a milling crowd jostling us about and the fact that in such a small town there was not likely to be anyone who spoke English and you may understand our dismay. I have seldom felt so lost in my life. We were swept along in the direction of the main hall where we found a corner to put down our baggage and review the situation. Across the crowded benches near the exit I saw a counter where women were serving tea. Standing by them was a boyish-looking policeman in a white, rather crumpled uniform. I struggled across to him and without real hope asked him if he spoke English. He not only spoke it, but helped out by a kind heart, he was adequately fluent and our saviour. He explained that we were at Hengyang, the junction where one must change for Guilin. He then told us, to our horror, that the next train for Guilin left in seven hours. We paled and he pressed us to free bowls of scalding tea, a gratuity which was to help us throughout that long day. He also assured us that we were free to walk about the town to help pass the time.

Once we had got over the first shock, we settled to the enjoyment of this small provincial town, at that time not the kind of place normally on the tourists' round. There was the usual crowded square in front of the station which led straight into a street-market which stretched away both left and right. The market showed the austerity of local life. Men and women squatted at the roadside selling a limited range of food, mostly small piles of tired vegetables and a selection of spices and herbs. There was more flavour in the housewives' bargaining and backchat than in their meagre purchases. Dominic found a man selling bamboo flutes, one of his interests at that time. He bought a flute for less than a penny and, hardly thinking, started playing scales and fumbling for a tune. The Pied Piper did not exercise a greater power. Within seconds we were surrounded by a staring crowd, probably more drawn by curiosity than the quality of the music. Embarrassed, we moved off down the street only to be followed by twenty or thirty locals endangering the goods spread out by the roadside.

By now it was unbearably hot and we went into a small restaurant opposite the station. We ordered beer which arrived wet but warm. Refrigeration still hardly exists in China outside the tourist hotels, not even blocks of ice. A few locals were eating but we were too cowardly to order any of the dishes we could see. I have heard since that the food served in the restaurant upstairs is good but the heat was so intense we had little appetite. We returned to the notional shade of the station where the young policeman cleared a space on one of the wooden benches and insisted on bringing us more bowls of brown, leathery tea. Five long, sticky hours still remained before our train left. The waiting room was as raucous and restless as an overcrowded rookery. People constantly pushed past us and children scrambled around our feet, suddenly squatting to pee in the dust. One old peasant, frail as a twig, his parchment face fringed with a straggling beard, hobbled over to examine our luggage and to peer searchingly into our barbarian faces. As the hours wore on I could feel my skin glazed with sweat and dirt and I tried to ignore the continual background of hawking and spitting. Rising above these distractions we somehow passed through the furnace of the afternoon. It was a long day but eventually our policeman led us to the platform, said goodbye and put us on the train for Guilin.

Guilin and its fascinating surrounding landscape has for centuries been a mecca for Chinese poets and painters. Today young Chinese dream of honeymooning in Guilin, one of the most idyllic places in China. It has often been said that the neighbouring countryside where the river winds through endless craggy mountains was the original inspiration of Chinese landscape painting and it is certainly true that many Chinese paintings stir memories of Guilin. In the last few years the foreign tourists have also discovered Guilin. It is the first Chinese town to be blighted with the unpleasant sides of tourism with nagging touts and money-changers, inflated prices and petty dishonesty. The tourist facilities are as inadequate as anywhere in China, but elsewhere one does at least enjoy the unlikelihood of being cheated.

We arrived in Guilin long after dark and humping our bags down the long main street we found a hotel. The rooms were shabbily adequate but the restaurant was closed. Back in the street, we found a hole in the wall which contained a few reasonably clean-looking tables. The sensible serving girl – waitress would hardly be appropriate in this context – wasted no time with a menu and put down in front of us large bowls of delicious and comforting chicken and rice gruel. It cost almost nothing but I still remember it as one of the best dishes I have ever eaten in China.

We had hardly started our meal when a young Chinese sat himself at our table and offered to buy us cheap tickets for the famous river trip to Yangshuo. His price was reasonable. We accepted and agreed to meet him outside our hotel at noon the next day. He spoke good English, said he was a student and asked for no advance payment. I felt he was honest but I was worried that he had not mentioned any kind of reward for the saving he was making for us. We met the next day and retired to a tea-house. He had the tickets and I paid for them. I was about to offer him a reasonable percentage of the saving when he beat me to it by saying that he wanted to buy a transistor radio in the Friendship Store where only tourist money was accepted and would I reward him by giving him sufficient tourist yuan in exchange for the equivalent sum in Chinese currency. For us, since it was impossible to spend more than a fraction of that amount of ordinary currency, it would have meant making him a gift of some £50. He took great offence when I refused and was too indignant to accept a contribution towards his transistor. There was nothing fraudulent in his brand of touting. The fault was entirely mine in not finding out beforehand what he was expecting for his services.

Two years later a more professional type of tout was waiting for us at Guilin airport. He did not bother with any academic guise. He found us an equally shabby room in a similarly mismanaged hotel, offered to obtain river-trip tickets at about four times the former fare and asked if we would be interested in having dinner at one of Guilin's famous exotic restaurants. Since my mind was occupied at that moment with the problem of getting out of Guilin at the end of our stay, I agreed to all his suggestions. But I was aware that this time we were in the hands of a real tout, part of that new private enterprise that is being encouraged to stimulate the economy and as a remedy for some of the ill-effects of the Cultural Revolution, not least serious unemployment amongst urban youth. Who was I to kick against the pricks of this new entrepreneurship?

Our friend was back at our hotel at seven, accompanied by a bicycle-rickshaw, ready to conduct us to one of Guilin's places of shame. No, it was not some Chinese massage parlour or a 'girlie show'. Guilin is notorious throughout China for its *haute cuisine* of rare fauna; so rare that most of the items on the menu are officially preserved species, some in danger of extinction. In France they have that helpful custom of standing a menu on the pavement. The specialist restaurants of Guilin go one step further. Outside are plaited bamboo baskets very much alive with the *plat du jour.*

writhing snakes, scaled Chinese pangolin (a Chinese armadillo) or a crouching monkey. It's all so much more alive than a menu card.

This is the most exotic end of Cantonese cooking and on my second visit to Guilin I was unable to curb my curiosity. The restaurant was in a dark street near the river, little more than an open-fronted shanty with ten circular tables. These were unappetisingly covered in cracked, once-white oil cloth and surrounded by small wooden stools. One look at the manager and I knew that the bill would be outrageous. Like many people who hang around restaurant kitchens, his face was puffy and damp, like a sagging Chinese dumpling. His manner had also acquired a touch of greasiness and he hovered over the menu with that authoritarian obsequiousness common to head waiters high and low. Rejecting the snake soup and the civet, we chanced our arm on the pangolin stew and a less ambitious pigeon dish. While we waited for the moment of truth we watched our fellow diners in the packed restaurant dextrously fishing in their stewpots with nimble chopsticks. The pangolin stew did have an interesting flavour but with each thrust into the other pot, white-eyed pigeon heads rose out of the gravy in an unnerving way. Beaver, monkey, racoon or muntjak might have proved even more disturbing. The meal was an eye-opener and, when it came, so was the bill.

It was not the gastronomic delights that drew Tang poets to Guilin but the unique landscape formed by hundreds of beautiful, irregular limestone hills, some rising steeply in the centre of the town, the majority scattered for many miles around. It is thought that some 300 million years ago this region lay under the sea. After it emerged, the thick layer of limestone was eroded by natural forces into a multitude of hills and caves creating a magical world both above and below ground.

There are other interesting facts about Guilin and its province, the Guangxi-Zhuang Autonomous Region. This region was established in 1958 and its ponderous name indicates that this is one of the areas of China densely populated by a minority people of different origin to the Han or Chinese race. Among the province's 37 million population there are at least eleven minority races, dominated by the Zhuang people, the largest minority in China. They number around 14 million people, of which 90 per cent live in this province occupying 60 per cent of the land.

There are several misconceptions about the minority races in

China, some of them cultivated by the Chinese government. Many people imagine China as a kind of colourful folk dance group, town and country brightened by the presence of small communities in traditional costume living a distinct way of life. No doubt part of this image is rooted in the dance groups that China circulates around the world and which also appear almost nightly on Chinese television. Life is all leather-booted Mongolian herdsmen and coy Tibetan girls living harmoniously bound together in common purpose by love of the Party. Reflecting this view of China, several people have said to me things like, 'Even in those long ticket queues, it must be so fascinating picking out all the different ethnic groups.' I must confess that most queues have looked much the same to me, too long and monotonously Chinese.

A few facts may be an antidote to these romantic or propagandist views. Although there are about fifty-five minority races living in China, they are only 6 per cent of China's one billion population. An unidentified minority was recently discovered but their numbers were in the hundreds. China is dominated by the Chinese – the Han people – and most of them not only look similar to the Japanese, Koreans and other Asians but they also look like many of the minority people – that is, if you get to see any minority people. Many of them live in sensitive border areas still closed to foreigners. Although several are still conducting exotic village festivals, you and I are unlikely to see them. But the new government policies of the 1980s are relaxing restrictions and, for example, in 1985 the mysteries of Tibet and the Tibetans were suddenly opened to the individual traveller. Many of the most colourful minority peoples live in Yunnan province on the borders of Vietnam, Laos and Burma. This remains a problem area for China, not least because the local people have their ethnic origins, and possibly their political loyalties across the border.

The Zhuang people who occupy much of Guangxi-Zhuang themselves belong to the Thai linguistic group which characterises their dialect. Apart from that they are indistinguishable from any of their Chinese neighbours. Although treated as a minority people, they were largely absorbed into Chinese society after their territory was captured by the Qin army in 214 BC. At first they were not wholly conquered and for a time were ruled through Zhuang chieftains. Later they absorbed Han culture and over the centuries lost most of their racial identity. Other tribes, such as the Yao and Miao, driven south from Hunan and Jiangxi, took to the hills and in this isolation took longer to be absorbed by their Han rulers. Today, few foreign visitors, unless they happened to be specialists in Asian linguistics, could tell the difference between a Zhuang, a Yao or a Miao, although they might pass any of them on the streets of Guilin. There are notable exceptions, but disappointingly the Chinese ticket queue is usually only notable for its uniformity, and its anarchy.

Guilin was founded as part of the Qin military expansion to the south. To improve transport for their armies in this region, in 214 BC they built a canal linking the waterways of the Yangzi and the Pearl River. The Ling Canal was 64 km north of Guilin and joined to it by the Li River. This system of waterways encouraged the growth of Guilin until in about 1370, in the early Ming period, the dynasty's founding emperor, Wong Hu, made Guilin capital of the province and sent one of his sons to rule the area. It remained the provincial capital until 1914 when it was replaced by Nanning. The town was severely damaged by the Japanese in 1944 and was one of the last cities to be taken by the communists. Today it has a population of some 300,000, a developing economy of mixed light industry and a tourist trade that is bursting at the seams. The town has a pleasant semi-tropical climate. The cassia trees, for example, which give the town its name, shade the hot streets in summer and flower in early autumn.

The romantic appearance of Guilin is created by the limestone peaks that spring out of the plain on every side, some in the heart of the town. None is of any great height but they rise so sheer and with such craggy faces that they apppear as mountains rather than hills. The town is dominated by these miniature peaks rising above the Li River on the eastern boundary and the smaller Peach Blossom River to the west. The main street runs north to south and is dominated by two phalanxes of cyclists who move at a stately pace in opposite directions, a few battered trucks and other vehicles squeezed in the central lane. It is an ideal town for cycling, if you can adjust the peculiarities of your Western skeleton to the frame of a Chinese bicycle. There is some kind of ergonomic cultural gap at work. You can pedal on your rented bike to mountains and grotesque caves, each one more romantically named than the last.

The two large lakes in the middle of the town are the remains of the Ming moat. To the north is the Peak of Solitary Beauty, at its foot a few remains of the Ming palace. Although only 152 metres high, the peak is exceptionally steep. If you want an easier elevated view of the town, you could continue a little further north to the beautiful Folded Brocade Hill, 223 metres high but an easier climb. Here you will find Tang and Song engravings in the rock face. In Guilin there are about 2000 cliff carvings though many were damaged during the Cultural Revolution.

The Seven Star Cave is large and has been a tourist attraction for at least 1700 years but I would recommend the smaller but most spectacular limestone formations of the Reed Pipe Cave, dramatically lit to produce weird, almost science fiction landscapes. This cave was only opened to the public in the 1960s and its colours have not been sooted over by centuries of sightseers' candles. I am usually bored by caves but I found this one most dramatic.

It is not for these local sights that people flock to Guilin. They come for the 80-km, seven-hour boat ride down the Li River to the small town of Yangshuo, passing through a mountainous landscape of exceptional beauty. The Tang poet, Han Yu, wrote of it:

> The river runs like a belt of green gauze;
> the mountains appear like blue jade hair ornaments.

I have a particular sympathy for a more legendary scholar-poet who wrote: 'I'd like to praise it but find it difficult to describe.' He spent so long considering the next line that he turned to stone. For fear of a similar petrification I shall move from poetry to the pandemonium of the early morning departure from Guilin's steamer jetty.

At seven in the morning the tourists are a bleary-eyed crowd and shattered by the noise on the quayside. The Chinese are the noisiest people in the world. It seems to stimulate them like alcohol. Sorting out a crowd of tourists of at least nineteen different nationalities gave full play for total cacophony. As we were herded into the crowded steamers, negotiating sagging gangplanks and picking our way among the vegetables already being prepared for lunch, the boatmen shouted, the boatwomen shouted louder and the cooks screamed. Chinese music from loudspeakers on the shore competed with the disco beat of loudspeakers on the boats. In a quiet counterpoint to this discordance four Hong Kong Chinese at the next table slapped down their cards in a gambling game that was to distract the players from all the beauties of the next seven hours. With a final grinding, shuddering vibration we were away on one of the most beautiful river journeys in the world and, equally wonderful, to the quietness of the countryside.

The steamer had a long, enclosed dining room and, above, an open deck running the length of the boat which provided an ideal place to enjoy the scenery. The first two hours of the journey are less interesting for the land is flat and in the early morning often hidden by a river mist. We sat at our table and talked to a honeymoon couple from Hong Kong who pressed us to a late breakfast of oranges, dried apricots and Smarties. The man was a lorry driver and unusually burly for a Chinese but he was charmingly tender to his pretty bride. After an hour it got warmer and I went up to the deck to watch the life of the river banks. All the way, except where the gorges leap straight up from the water, there are villages and small settlements. It was spring now. The trees were breaking everywhere alongside acres of white flowers contrasting with the red earth of ploughed fields and the patchwork of vegetable plots. On small buffs above the river houses clustered, graceful with their curving roofs. Women scrubbed clothes on flat rocks by the river while mud-caked buffaloes stood in the shallows. Lively brown and naked children shouted and dived off the high banks and silent fishermen squatted precariously on bamboo rafts, large woven baskets ready for their catch. One was so large that it comfortably accommodated the two grinning children of a fisherman.

About 10.30 a.m. the mountains appeared and the water ran faster through the first gorge. We were surrounded by the beauty and variety of the limestone crags and the cliffs that enclosed the dark green waters of the river. The landscape changes all the time as the river twists and turns. There is a variety of colour, of height, of surface and shape. The limestone changes from harsh white to orange and grey and black. Some faces of the rock are bare, stark and deeply crazed. Some mountains are shrouded in the bosky green of trees and vegetation. The limestone has split into huge slabs almost suggesting some kind of primitive human structure, megalithic and impressive. By the river bulging faces of rock, pocked with holes, clefts and caves, hang out over the water or tower above it like massive walls. Suddenly, the gorge gives way to a receding landscape. Small mountains of every shape and size rise sheer from the plain. Some are mere shoulders of rock 20–30 metres high, others steep-sided pinnacles rising to over 200 metres.

Some stand alone, the classic sugar-loaf mountain, others stretch out in clusters to form a range of peaks. The mountains are humped, turreted, pepper-pots, ragged rock towers, perfect cones, giving an infinite variety to this miniature yet grandiose landscape. At moments the mountains vanish and the land flattens into a vista of rice fields and rough meadow with buffaloes heavily ploughing and lean-shanked cows grazing. Around another bend in the river and a new panorama of mountains is revealed, the steamer gliding again between the limestone walls that drop into the fast water. The variety of colour, deepened by the falling shadows, is bright in the sharp sunlight of midday. The stillness and remoteness is broken only by the howling sirens of passing steamers. The spring softens the landscape, the full light of summer hardens it, but both seasons create a scene that is unforgettable.

Yangshuo, where the river journey ends, has completely changed in the last three years. It used to be a quiet country town. It is now a bedlam of tourism, dozens of buses congesting the centre of the town and rows of souvenir stalls touting for business all along the quay overlooking the river. Worse, new building is under way everywhere relentlessly demolishing the old town. The worst effects of tourism that have already infected Guilin are now spreading to Yangshuo. Every few minutes another steamer arrives and another tourist bus departs. I know of few places in Asia that have so quickly acquired the tourist trinketry of Capri or Benidorm but it is a relentless and irreversible process.

I met some people in China who thought that Guilin and its landscape were overrated. Others insisted that one could enjoy the landscape more on a rented bicycle from Yangshuo and that the steamer trip was not worth the fare. While the bus ride back to Guilin suggests the pleasures of exploring these mountains by bicycle, for me the river trip from Guilin to Yangshuo is uniquely beautiful and even on the second occasion it remained one of my most enjoyable experiences in China.

3

A Southern Climate

KUNMING AND YUNNAN PROVINCE

We wanted to fly to Kunming. The CAAC office in Guilin was shabby with an air of inertia.

'I would like two seats for Kunming next Friday.'

The clerk didn't look up. He was rolling his pen with his finger across his papers.

'There is only one flight that day.'

'I know. That is the one we want to take.'

'The flight is fully booked.' The clerk looked at me with small, bureaucratic eyes. 'All flights are booked until next week.' He raised his bored gaze to the middle distance.

I knew the form. In Japan it's apologies, in China persistence. I held my ground and gave him a determined look. 'We must get to Kunming on Friday. Our itinerary depends on it.' As if he cared. I leant casually against the counter trying to catch a glimpse of the passenger schedule. I saw nothing but the finger methodically rolling the pen.

The clerk now gazed at the opposite wall and yawned. 'There is one seat on the Friday flight.'

'But we need two seats. What about cancellations? Is there a waiting list?'

The clerk ignored my questions, pushed back his chair and walked to a cabinet at the back of the room which appeared to contain nothing but tea mugs. I bore the long silence until he returned to his seat.

'When did you want to go to Kunming?'

'On Friday, but we need two seats.'

The clerk looked at me as if he had never seen me before.

'The flight leaves at 07.55 hours. I will make out your tickets.' From the pile of papers in front of him he pulled out Friday's passenger schedule. Only nine seats were taken.

At moments like these I half believe that the refinements of Chinese torture are part of a hideous curriculum used in training schools for petty officials. But such crude methods as the 'water drip' have been replaced by various agonising forms of indifference. Such encounters are the daily experience of the individual traveller, leaving one's itinerary one big loose end.

Kunming has a kind of magic which, although hard to define, casts a spell over most visitors. It is one of my favourite Chinese cities and most people seem to share that view. Several ingredients contribute to its character. The sights are attractive and interesting, the people markedly open and friendly and even the duller parts of the city are brightened by Kunming's warm, spring-like climate and clear air, the result of its altitude of nearly 1900 metres. Beyond that, it has a mellow character, almost Mediterranean, still touched perhaps by a lingering French influence and borrowing some fragile charm from South-East Asia which encloses the province of Yunnan on two sides, Kunming being the provincial capital.

One day in Kunming I met a New Zealand agricultural adviser to the province of Yunnan and his stories of his travels in the region together with the glimpses we had of the surroundings of Kunming left me with a frustrated longing to travel freely all over the mountains and forests of Yunnan from the lush, tropical border with Vietnam, up through the volcanic region around Baoshan along the Burmese border to the great mountains of the north where the province meets Tibet. The beginnings of great rivers, the Mekong and the Yangzi for example, cut deep through the mountains and the area has a number of large and beautiful lakes. China has long prized Yunnan's exotic tropical timber and its minerals. The high plateau of Yunnan produces a wide variety of crops, rice, wheat, maize, tobacco, cotton and sugar cane and, since the Second World War, the government has done much to stimulate local industry. But much of Yunnan remains remote and the New Zealander told me of the difficulties of travelling in the mountainous areas.

He was also cynical about his own advisory role. He had, with foreign loans, been encouraged to establish a modern, computerised laboratory. In theory this was fine, in practice the endless power failures made much of the sophisticated equipment almost useless, and with the smallest breakdown he had to take the faulty part by air to Hong Kong to get it repaired. He thought that in such a Third World context less money would have produced more significant results spent on simpler and more suitable remedies.

Yunnan, 3179 km from Beijing, has always seemed remote to the

5 Home from school

CHENGDU

6 Rice-fields in the outskirts

7 The bird market

CHENGDU

8 A tobacco-seller

Chinese. The name means 'south of the clouds'. It remained a partly independent kingdom until the eighteenth century, despite various attempts to absorb it into the empire. At the time of the Han dynasty it was known as the state of Dian. By the eighth century a people of Thai extraction, the Nanchao, ruled over a wide area down into South-East Asia and had their capital at Dali. In AD 751 the Nanchao defeated an invading Chinese army. The Mongols were more successful in the thirteenth century and established rule over much of the area bringing in their own administrators who succeeded in converting some of the local people to the Muslim faith. Today the Hui people are still a Muslim minority. But it was the Manchus in the eighteenth century who finally subdued the whole of Yunnan and made it a part of China. In 1876, as part of the Opium Wars, the British gained trading rights in Yunnan, followed by the French in 1896. A series of Muslim uprisings, the skirmishings of warlords and the opium trade made the nineteenth century a restless time for the province, but early in the twentieth century the French unofficially began to colonise the area, completing the railway from Haiphong to Kunming and establishing administrative buildings and hospitals in the provincial capital. Today, French influence in Kunming is charmingly reduced to an unexpected coffee shop and, down the road, producing delectable European aromas, a bakery. There might be worse monuments to colonialism.

In such a remote province, with its towering mountains and hidden valleys, and with Vietnam, Laos, Burma, and Tibet and Thailand only a sneeze away, it is not surprising that Yunnan has more minority people than any other part of China. There are some twenty-one minorities, about one-third of the province's total population of 31.5 million. The best known of these include the Bai from around Dali, the Yi, the Dai of Thai extraction, the Miao, the Naxi and the recently discovered Jino people. One may occasionally see a few of these people in the markets of Kunming and there are now local areas which can be visited with special permits. Many people recommend a visit to Dali both for its lakeside beauty and a closer look at the Bai people.

The Chinese government's attitude to its minorities varies with the circumstances. They are well aware that their colourful lifestyle is a tourist attraction and a potential moneyspinner. Hence the touring folk dance groups. Many of these picturesque tribes are so few in number that they offer no threat, particularly if they live away from the sensitive southern borders. Faced with larger minorities, however colourful their way of life, the Chinese have been less benevolent. We shall see how ruthlessly a large minority has been treated when we reach Tibet.

Marco Polo noted a number of interesting facts about the commerce and life of Kunming: 'The natives do not consider it an injury done to them when others have connexion with their wives, provided the act is voluntary on the woman's part. Here there is a lake almost a hundred miles in circuit, in which great quantities of fish are caught. The people are accustomed to eat the raw flesh of fowls, sheep, oxen and buffalo, the poorer sorts only dip it in a sauce of garlic.' That was in the thirteenth century. The lake and the sauce of garlic are still much in evidence but Deng Xiaoping is doing his best to ensure that Chinese wives are less free with their favours.

Modern Kunming is a large city with a population of about two million. Warmth and dust and diesel fumes mingle in the streets where trees and flowers break everywhere into spring growth. The first evening Yuki-san and I wandered down the main avenue to a large open square which at night was taken over by a variety of tented restaurants, fringed with other activities. At one end of the square clothes and cheap jewellery, including crucifixes, were for sale. Under a variety of awnings the night-restaurants flourished, muscular cooks tossing cascades of vegetables and fried rice in huge woks over glowing stoves of pressed coal dust whose sulphurous fumes imparted an unusual flavour to the dishes. One old man, who specialised in pigeons, invited us with the wave of a scrawny cooked carcass into his tent. People sat on rough stools or squatted on the ground shovelling food into their mouths with characteristic Chinese gusto.

At the far end of the square there was loud music. Outside a large wooden building crude posters appeared to advertise a circus. Inside, however, a packed crowd of young couples were doing their best to swing to the wailing tones of Chinese music. This must have been some kind of post-Cultural Revolution compromise disco, a bureaucratic blend of old and new. The dancers were giving it all they'd got.

Outside, along a nearby wall, was the best entertainment of all. Small groups of men crouched on the ground absorbed in various pursuits. The first group were admiring a Chinese pangolin complete with a pup, if that is the right term. The next and larger group were gambling. The proprietor had introduced high-technology into the gaming which clearly impressed his simple customers. Across a large board, segmented and marked with numbers, a small and battered electric toy car had been programmed to move in a circle, if erratically, and where it finally came to rest marked the winning number. Feelings, if not the stakes, ran high. Science was generally well represented. Surrounded by gawping admirers, the local quack doctor was applying an evil-looking unguent to the severely bruised knee of a young man who sat in silent agony on a stool. Next door a wild-eyed youth, with a religious fervour, harangued his crowd about a mysterious electrical experiment he was conducting for their benefit. He appeared to be extracting enough electricity from a few pebbles in a tumbler of water to illuminate a small light bulb. Perhaps he was a salesman, or even conjuror? The streets of Kunming are full of bizarre entertainment and unusual views of Chinese life.

Even the Kunming Hotel offers a warmer welcome than one usually receives in China. In general there is an abysmal standard of hotel service; at the front desk, in the restaurant and in the bedrooms which leaves one with the suspicion that every capable clerk, chef, waiter and chambermaid, intellectuals to a man and woman, were disposed of during the Cultural Revolution. They have now been replaced across the nation by a catering team whose lack of recognisable skills can only be matched by their absolute indifference to the job. Being realistic, a lack of management and any incentives is not likely to produce enthusiasm for any job. The Kunming Hotel is a pleasant change where staff smile, the food encourages appetite, the bath water is scalding and everything works, which in China is not far short of miraculous. I made a few notes on the restaurant. The local beer was weak with a dusty flavour. But to compensate there was a strong-flavoured fried goat's cheese, a pungent cold salami and crunchy spring rolls in a subtle sweet sauce. But the gastronomic crescendo lay elsewhere.

Kunming has a reputation for noodle dishes and who could resist a speciality called 'noodles over the bridge'. The dish derives its name from a charming legend. Once, long ago, a scholar was preparing for his exams. He retired to a cottage on an island in a lake south of Kunming. He grumbled at his wife that her food was always cold by the time she had carried it over the bridge to his retreat. One day she nodded off while cooking noodles with chicken. When she woke the fire had gone out but the stew was still hot. She realised that the layer of fat from the chicken had held in the heat and in future she had no problem in carrying hot noodles over the bridge to her delighted husband. The specialist restaurant we went to was supposedly more elegant upstairs than downstairs. I was unable to detect the difference. We sat at a large circular table, having bought our meal tickets at the desk, and before long a huge bowl of chicken soup was put before each of us accompanied by individual dishes containing a variety of meats, mostly I suspect from the innards of various animals. This abundance was tipped into the noodle soup producing a dish of gargantuan proportions. For anyone requiring additional flavouring, there was a large bowl of red sauce, gory and flaming hot. I suspect it was 93 per cent chili with a spot of water to prevent the customers catching fire. At neighbouring tables the sauce was generously ladelled into the noodles turning the whole dish dark red.

We had just got our noodles suitably spiced when a youngish man slid into the chair next to me.

'Want to change money,' he murmured.

I wanted to eat my noodles, so I took no notice. For a Chinese the man was obviously a sharp dresser. The spiv has long been an international character, recognisable in London, New York, a Mexican cantina or even a Kunming noodle-shop. He was not to be shaken off. Clearly I looked a promising victim. Between frequent murmurings of his basic line, to prove that he was serious, he produced huge wads of tourist money which he riffled at me under the table. I was impressed as I could not imagine how he had acquired such a large sum of money. I was further intrigued when he was joined by a sleazy and also unusually well-dressed girl. He had obviously struck it rich somewhere but even with China's new permitted private enterprise I was surprised that whatever he was up to was allowed since clearly he was up to nobody's good except his own. When we finally left, satiated with delicious noodles and the persistence of the tout, he made it clear that I had been a great disappointment to him.

The centre of Kunming is large but ideal for cycling and bicycles can be rented from the hotel. I most enjoyed the old area of the town which spreads out to the east of Green Lake Park. Suddenly, as you leave the wide and dull modern avenues, you plunge into an older China of crowded narrow streets lined with dark vermilion and green wooden buildings, a busy world of trade and tea-houses. It is picturesque and genuine, but like a sudden leap back to the nineteenth century. At first the streets were lined with two-storeyed green houses. At street level most were open-fronted cavernous stores, varying in size and closed by heavy wooden shutters. Above were the domestic quarters or storage, the windows closely barred with various lattice patterns. Suspended from the eaves of the brown-tiled roofs was a motley array of ragged laundry, singing birds in elaborate bamboo cages and hanging shelves crowded with plants and small trees potted out in bulbous brown and black jars. Some wispy weeds, like greying beards, hung in a dry fringe from the tiles themselves. The lintels and upper beams were carved with running patterns of leaves and flowers, elaborate if crude. A few timbers and rafters had been picked out in garish pinks, yellows and blues. Further along the houses were painted in a sombre dark vermilion with smaller brick houses tucked in here and there.

The busy life of these streets had as much period character as the architecture. Bicycles, trucks, pony carts, handcarts and heavy barrows fought for progress along the streets. Street vendors occupied half the pavements, while the merchandise of the shops spilled over onto the other half. Ironmongery, basic hardware, dry goods, huge sacks of beans, baskets of rice, cheap clothing racked overhead, carpenters putting the finishing touches to furniture of abject crudity, and here and there a notice painted with a gruesome set of false teeth advertising the local dentist and sawbones. No less alarming was the grubby interior of the barber's shop, not to mention the itinerant ear-cleaner, a wizened old fellow with an alarming selection of probes. Shoe-menders squatted by sewing machines which anywhere else would be found only in an industrial museum. In one dark interior a group of women crouched over ancient sewing machines producing what appeared to be political banners. The restaurants and tea-houses rattled with life and chatter. Women in cotton mob-caps ladled this and that into customers' bowls who slurped down the food at steel-topped tables, while old men nodded over chess boards drawing occasionally on fat bamboo pipes. In the heat of midday there was an air of contentment. Life here was basic, obvious enough from the contents of the shops, but people had enough, and wished only to be left to themselves and a way of life that did not seem to have changed for a century or more.

In and around Kunming are a number of pagodas, temples and mosques in varying degrees of repair after the vandalism of the Cultural Revolution. The most pleasant excursion can be made by taxi. We drove south of the city to where paths climbed the face of the Western Hills with beautiful views over Lake Dian, the sixth largest in China. Our taxi wound its way up a forested road past various ornate temple gateways until the road ended at a cluster of souvenir stalls, parked taxis and buses and a throng of Chinese tourists. A path leads up from here to the highest viewing point, Dragon Gate. On the long and steep ascent we passed a number of small temples, some caves in the rock face with decorative medallions and lively lions and turtles carved out of the stone; other small, elaborate buildings housing brightly coloured gods with staring eyes and threatening eyebrows. When the pressing crowd allowed, it was pleasant to stop and admire the view from the stone steps and narrow platforms. At times the ascent disappeared into low rock tunnels, the cause of much shouting and laughter as the youths going up jostled those coming down. It was all good humoured and we were drawn into their holiday mood with occasional banter in broken English.

Amongst the crowd were a few genuine pilgrims. On the way down I saw a group of elderly peasant women together with a granddaughter kneel in turn to pray at one of the altars. Surprisingly, kneeling pads of woven straw were provided and the child with the old women was clearly familiar with the ritual. A temple building nearby was in the process of being restored. I also noticed a number of young Chinese going through the ritual of prayer as a kind of half-embarrassed joke.

The Huatingsi Temple, one of those intriguing gateways on the road up to the Western Hills, was a star attraction for me and one of the most picturesque temples I have seen in southern China. One marvels that places like these survived the Cultural Revolution as they are so vulnerable to fire. The temple has a long history dating from the fourteenth century, with rebuilding on a number of occasions. It has been both a country villa and a temple and that mixture is happily reflected in the informal relationship between the gardens and the buildings. The temple buildings are laid out against a steep mountainside densely covered with trees and tall bamboos, a background of soft greens and deep shadows.

The temple buildings are terraced and between each is a wide courtyard garden. In front of the first temple hall is a large pond guarded by stone lions. In the upper garden, unkempt and the more charming for that, trees, flowerbeds and potted trees and shrubs made a colourful chaos. The cherry blossom was out, shaking gently over beds of snapdragons, camellias, roses, blood-red poppies, a profusion of milky daisies and towering pink double hollyhocks. The garden admitted no season and little sense of nationality. It could all have been nodding over the fence of Anne Hathaway's cottage. This profusion of colour made a pleasing contrast against the temple's plain walls and the elaborate patterns of the roof tiles, the eaves curving delicately to the blue sky.

We visited another well-known temple on that excursion, the Zen Bamboo Temple, slightly nearer the town and up a different hilly road. The exterior is severe, in keeping with its Zen character. Inside, it is stark and neglected, the main courtyard filled with trees and stone tables and seats. In two separate buildings were one of those collections of grotesque, near life-size figures of Buddhist saints which are the main attraction of a number of Chinese temples. Modelled in great detail out of clay and vividly painted, some of these 500 *arhats*, or Buddhist saints, ride the waves on blue dogs, giant crabs and other marine vehicles, while others remain land bound. Their bizarre iconography is depicted with grotesque realism more suggestive of a waxwork museum than a Zen temple. They were modelled by a famous Sichuan sculptor, Li Guangxiu, and his disciples around 1890. They have the fascination of artless but intriguing science-fiction cartoons. It must have been this late style of Chinese sculpture that spawned the famous Hong Kong and Singapore Tiger Balm Gardens. The growing decadence of Chinese nineteenth-century life, a result of the dying imperial system of government, is reflected in much of the art of that period.

There are two good reasons for making the one-day excursion from Kunming to the Stone Forest, 126 km south-east and three and a half hours each way by bus. First, the dramatic limestone formations of the 'forest' and the swarming crowds of holidaymakers are both worth seeing. But more than that, the long bus ride provides one of those rare opportunities to see the Chinese countryside. When I look back on my travels in China it is surprising how much time is inevitably spent in towns despite the fact that more than 75 per cent of Chinese still live on the land. It is common knowledge that the villages included in official tours are less than typical of Chinese rural life. Even glimpses from a bus window have more to tell than the model communes made available to foreigners.

The elderly bus vibrated its way out of Kunming, along the wide avenues with lines of cyclists on their way to work and past a massive sculpture of stark white but well-clad cavorting maidens which seemed to me nothing more than a symbol of totalitarian lack of artistry. Out through the grey suburbs, the balconies of the apartment houses cluttered with potted plants and neatly packaged collections of urban flotsam and jetsam, often in such quantities that it projected far beyond the balustrade. With a shortage of everything in China, little is rubbish. Wang Keping, the celebrated dissident sculptor, had to beg his first material from a neighbourhood workshop supplying kindling wood. This is the 'scrap and ingenuity culture' and probably on those balconies are stored the means to future dreams, a home-made sofa or a new toy for the child.

On this side of Kunming you are quickly out into the countryside. At one moment an incongruous water buffalo is grazing on the urban verges, the next moment you can be looking over a spreading plain of small rice fields, across acres of vegetables, beans and golden heads of wheat, the crops at noticeably different stages, no doubt because of the mild climate. Everywhere are large and small villages, red brick and grey-black tiles, terraced above large muddy ponds. The soil is red and heavy and I marvelled at the seeming ease with which the women swung the heavy, long-handled hoes, breaking the clay into huge clods. The older women picked beans or, with buckets on long poles, ladled out night soil onto the growing plants.

Most foreigners who catch these charming glimpses of rural China from buses and trains, form an idealised and unrealistic picture of life in the farming villages which in reality might better be described as, 'nasty, brutish and short', an opinion which has been bitterly expressed by hundreds of thousands of people sent to be re-educated among the peasantry during the Cultural Revolution, vast numbers of whom never returned to express any opinion. Nothing is more significant than the basic fact that most of China's 800 million peasants still working the land regard the other part of the population living in the towns as highly privileged, however grim their conditions may seem to Western observers. It is true that the worst starvation has been alleviated by the communists but with Mao's obsession with heavy industry, agriculture was neglected and still is not receiving the subsidies it requires to achieve modernisation.

Those farmers who live within 30 km of a large city, such as the farms around Kunming, have fared better with a nearby market and some share of the town's growing prosperity. This has enabled them to introduce small factories into the area to produce necessary extra income. But like the townspeople they derive benefit from, they are more easily controlled by the Party machinery in proximity to the main centres of bureaucracy and have not been allowed to follow the old ways, particularly in choosing the size of their family.

There are still an enormous number of farming communities scattered all over China living in extreme isolation. Their inaccessibility makes it difficult for bureaucracy to control them and they continue to live in much the same way and according to the old beliefs of their ancestors. They raise large families and, it is said, occasionally still practise infanticide with unwanted daughters. They seek the advice of the local shaman or the village witch and they live out their mean lives in poverty and wretchedness, however picturesque their village.

My own view of Chinese rural life was darkened forever after I read a highly realistic short story called 'The Child Bride', the fifth chapter in *Tales of Hulan River* by Hsiao Hung, her autobiographical novel published in 1940. The book is a searing attack on traditional society but there is a frightening reality in the writing that confirms that much of the material was drawn from the writer's experiences in Heilongjiang Province in the extreme north-east of China. She was herself the daughter of a wealthy landlord but no doubt had ample opportunity to observe the cruelties going on around her.

There was excitement in her neighbourhood. The Hu family's child-bride had arrived. From the start nothing was right with the girl. The Hu family sensed it, the neighbours voiced it. For a twelve-year-old she was too tall, for a child-bride she was too independent and she ate too much. The beatings started. Her screams filled the village compound daily, but the more the elderly neighbours suggested leniency, the harder her mother-in-law thrashed her. In late autumn the Hu family became convinced that the child-bride was possessed by an evil spirit and each night that winter a sorceress was employed to perform dances and incantations by the child's window. Nothing happened except that the child-bride fell ill, losing her healthy colour. Further witches were employed but the child grew worse. The various cruelties she had been subjected to had driven her into a state of nervous hysteria and the slightest touch from her mother-in-law set her writhing in a fit.

Everyone for miles around offered advice, professional sooth-sayers and old aunts with quack remedies. Eventually, in full view of a crowd of neighbours, under the supervision of a sorceress, the child was forcibly stripped naked and to the enthrallment of the crowd was pushed down into a vat brimming with scalding water, those around ladling the water over her head while the sorceress beat her drum. The neighbourhood crowd hooted with brutish laughter. The girl's face turned brighter and brighter red until she stopped struggling and collapsed inside the vat. Thinking her dead, the crowd rushed forward to help. A moment before, while she was alive, not one person had offered her any assistance. But when the child eventually came to and the sorceress announced that two more baths were necessary, the enthusiasm of the crowd was immediately restored. The child-bride was immersed twice again, each time eventually losing consciousness, and each time the brutish ignorance of the villagers was as terrible as the ghastly act itself. Not long after the child-bride died.

Although that story was written in the days of the landlords and the warlords, the awful mixture of brutality and ignorance, common enough ingredients in Chinese rural life, still seems real enough in modern China and the story has much in common with what so many suffered during the Cultural Revolution and at other times in Red China. With little doubt there are still many remote rural areas where ignorance and superstition are dominant. Nor can I say that I found anything romantic or enviable in the lives of those girls wielding the heavy hoes along the roadside. There is little that is romantic in the Chinese countryside except for the view.

Along the road from Kunming the increasing industrialisation of the small towns was evident. At one moment the view was idyllic with large lakes and rising hills in the distance. But suddenly, across the green countryside a dark cloud appeared and a few minutes later we came down the hill into a small, smoky industrial town and a traffic jam. Ancient, ramshackle lorries, overloaded with poor brown coal, were interlocked across the town's main crossing. The town centred on what seemed to be a large coke-burning works. Wretched coolies, weighed down by baskets across their shoulders, climbed up and down the great mounds of black grit creating a gloomy scene worthy of Gustave Doré. It seemed extraordinary that this grim world could exist in the middle of the countryside, isolated from any other industrial activity. However, it is probable that those benighted coal workers were better paid and better fed than the peasants working the nearby fields.

After about the second hour the land became more barren with large outcrops of rock as we started to climb into the mountains. Apart from weedy firs there were few trees, but here and there sparse plantings of wheat grew on precipitous terraces and everywhere there were beautiful pink and white wild flowers. From time to time, where the land levelled, there was another small village, then back to the bare mountainside with an increasing outcrop of limestone karst forming small pinnacles. We were nearing the famous Stone Forest – one of several in this area. Quite suddenly the road flung around a sharp corner and down the dusty road our mountain isolation was ended. Ahead of us lay a crowded bus park, several buildings and swarms of Chinese holiday-makers kicking up a din and the dust.

In China there is little entertainment for the masses and Kunming's two million people make good use of those few sightseeing centres outside their city which are served by regular buses. Around the entrance to the Stone Forest, by the side of a lake reflecting the stone pinnacles beyond, were lines of stalls selling a variety of cheap foods, sinister-looking soft drinks and, mainly for young couples, cameras for hire with one roll of black and white film. The films are quickly developed in a bucket at the back of the stall and eagerly examined by the proud amateur photographers.

One reason for visiting the Stone Forest is that you can see the minority people who live in this area, Lunan County, the Sani branch of the Yi tribespeople, complete with colourful embroidered folk costumes. I was easily deceived. Ignoring the crowds I walked up the road alongside the Stone Forest to stretch my legs after the long bus ride and to seek a few moments of peace before braving the crowds. I turned a corner and there was a handsome woman with a small boy mounted on a horse, both dressed in richly embroidered hats and robes. Detecting a distinctly individual, presumably Sani cast of features, I raised my camera to capture a shot of my first minority people. Through my viewfinder I saw not only the equestrian group, which had now turned its back on me, but, beyond, a professional photographer complete with black cloth and tripod. Something I had read in my guide-book came back to me. These were no Sani tribespeople but Chinese tourists in borrowed fancy dress posed for the deathless snapshot. Within the Stone Forest itself the fancy dress and the photographers attract such crowds that it is difficult to reach the most popular places where the locals in their finery wish to be snapped against such rocky silhouettes as 'The Moon-Gazing Rhino' or 'Lotus Peak'.

By the rough tables that held the fancy dress country youths stripped off their khaki and blue drab and assumed their new identity with silken cloaks and swashbuckling velvet hats, posing bravely with a decorated wooden sword clutched manfully across their stomachs. For the girls even hairdressing services were provided, pigtails quickly manipulated into crowning tresses falling elegantly from the elaborate headdresses of gauze and twinkling spangles; every farm girl or factory hand a Sani princess. Behind the table was a select exhibition of the photographer's past masterpieces, leering, ferocious Sani warriors, the line of the moustache melting here and there, and fair Sani maidens still flushed from the long bus ride. It was all more exciting than sticking your head through a cardboard cutout, and if nothing else it proved that the Chinese still retain a few dreams, if only for a little colour in their colourless lives.

The karst formations of the Stone Forest cover some 80 hectares, a maze of paths and steps between the hundreds of limestone peaks which rise as high as 30 metres. In the quieter areas where the paths climb steeply between the grey pinnacles and down again into caves and grottoes, this miniature mountain landscape planted out like a garden is rather beautiful. Back among the crowds and the stalls it turns to bedlam. The limestone formations soon become monotonous and I really enjoyed the pleasure of the crowds more than anything else. There are indeed genuine Sani stallholders selling their embroidery and crafts and if you choose to stay the night there is a Sani village within easy walking distance. Others recommend staying the night because they say that the Stone Forest reveals its beauty only by moonlight. It is one of those rare areas of countryside which is easily accessible.

4

Spice of Life

CHENGDU AND SICHUAN PROVINCE

I lay between waking and sleeping dazed by a medley of uneasy dreams. Somewhere there was a pale light and, below, a steady, metallic rhythm which punctuated our movement. I surfaced just enough to wonder whether it was two or three in the morning. At that moment the door of our sleeping car was hurled open by a burly woman in a blue cap and overtight uniform. She slammed a thermos of hot water on the small table and bawled in strident Mandarin, 'Seven o'clock. It is time to wash. Breakfast is ready.' Comrade-tourists, like other comrades, do what they are told. Apart from anything else, lie-abeds may find that when the desire to urinate overtakes them, the lavatories have been locked. I washed and dressed. But venturing along to the dining car, I found Big Sister's last statement not wholly accurate. It was totally deserted except for the overpowering smell of last night's garlic. Half-relieved, I retreated to the compartment for a furtive cup of bourgeois instant coffee.

We were travelling along the famous railway line, almost impossibly constructed through the mountains between Kunming and Chengdu, one of the worst sections of the Long March in 1935. The line was constructed between 1958 and 1970 with a delay in 1962, probably when Soviet engineers left China. The direct distance between Kunming and Chengdu is 650 km. The railway line is about 1100 km long, with 653 bridges and 427 tunnels which enclose 40 per cent of the total length. At its highest point the railway reaches 2240 metres and it has been calculated that the materials excavated would build a wall one metre high and one metre wide 2½ times around the earth. The project was pioneered and carried out by the army and is thought to have claimed at least a thousand lives. The line at last opened up the remote south-eastern corner of China making industrialisation and economic development possible.

We had come to Kunming hoping to go on to Chengdu by this celebrated line, renowned for its mountain views. We had been warned that the train was often full and we had to wait for three days to obtain soft sleepers for the twenty-four-hour journey. Bookings can take longer than that. When we arrived at Kunming station at 6.30 p.m., one hour before departure, we saw the reason why. It was chaotic. We struggled through the crowds trying to find the platform only to discover that we had to queue in the street in front of the station, by then a line of about a thousand disgruntled and restless people. One man, in an unusually smart suit and that unmistakable look of the barrack-room lawyer, was haranguing every official in sight, mostly hard-faced uniformed women who remained indifferent to his insults, or whatever he was shouting. When the queue was allowed to move into the station, nothing daunted, this character launched a further attack on three policemen who, to my surprise, took it calmly, merely urging him towards the train. For all I shall ever know, he may have been the Governor of Yunnan province.

When we were settled in our sleeper and the train had started, it was time for supper. The dining car was open and there was considerable activity in the kitchen. However, the only people actually being fed were the dining car staff. Equality is a wonderful thing. Suitably humbled, we crept back to our sleeper and made do with a couple of Chinese pastries. I then read three chapters of *Pickwick Papers*, largely devoted to a detailed description of a lavish picnic. What the train lacked in evening refreshment it made up in nocturnal noises. As the train passed through the first of the tunnels and over the first of the bridges, we enjoyed an ever-changing background of metallic music, rattling, chunking, clanking and chonking all in a vibrating counterpoint to various hootings, howlings, whistlings, the odd bird and the unending bedtime story vibrant on the loudspeakers.

From seven in the morning the train constantly passed through tunnels leaving only glimpses of sunlight, steep-sided valleys, towering mountains, waterfalls, turbulent rivers, sharp, rocky gorges and, occasionally, a small plateau holding a farming village enclosed by terraced fields. Often the river valley was so tight there seemed hardly room for the railway line. Most of this landscape was rocky, bleak and barren, high red cliffs hanging over the line until it was swallowed up again by another long tunnel. Even travelling the line, it was hard to imagine how anyone ever conceived putting a railway through this terrain, let alone actually doing it. The Peruvian railways that cling to the face of the Andes are the only rival. The scenery was superb and the frequent tunnel blackouts became as irritating as breaks in a fine movie. The panorama in the compartment window was exchanged every few mintues for darkness and the sour smell of soot.

Lunch was an unappealing sight. A large bowl of dirty rice was accompanied by bony knuckles of chicken steeped in a chili sauce, a dish of scrappy pork fat lurking under chopped vegetable stalks and slices of pungent garlic sausage, curling at the edges. The Chinese sitting next to me consumed his meal with amazing speed, not least because half of each mouthful was rapidly spat onto the floor between his legs. I ate what I could and hurried back to enjoy more of the view.

Now the scale of the landscape was enormous. The mountains and the cliffs towered into the sky and the valleys were wider. The river was brown and fast flowing. The scattered trees were breaking into a fresh green that contrasted softly with the dark rock, the grey soil and the old grass of winter. Each time I saw houses tucked in among the mountain folds I wondered how these isolated farmers made a living. But there were occasional small stations along the line and, according to a Chinese I had talked to the previous evening, with the new free market some farmers were now earning good money. 'You'd be surprised,' he said. 'Some of them may well be travelling soft class on this train, going to Chengdu to sell produce or buy farm machinery.'

The soil and the rocks varied in colour, orange-red, grey-white or yellow, in places beautiful, elsewhere drab. By the river were wide pebble shores, the water surging down, churning white foam against the rocky narrows. Suddenly we came out of the mountains into a vast plain, fertile with trees, fields of brilliant yellow rape and terrace upon terrace of rice fields stretching away into the distance. The mountains continued far away to the east. The train stopped at Emeishan and the two Hong Kong teenagers who had shared the compartment with us got off. They had cuddled and snoozed their way through the entire visual feast oblivious to everything except for the frequent snacks that appeared from their huge rucksacks. By now the sleeping compartment had been stripped and turned back to daytime use and we were joined by three Chinese men for the last three hours to Chengdu. A morose young man remained silent throughout the journey. We were more fortunate with the two elderly men, one of whom spoke good English, and Russian, having studied in the Soviet Union for three years.

'I am a professor of mechanical engineering at Emei University. The university is very famous.'

More used to the self-denigrations of the Japanese who ramble on for sentences telling you about the poor, humble, unknown, third-rate institute they work for before finally disclosing that they are employed by Sony or doing advanced research at Tokyo University, this direct, almost challenging approach took me by surprise. The other man was benign and friendly though we could communicate with him only through a small number of simple English words and by writing some Chinese characters which had the same meaning in Japanese. He was also of a mechanical bent and quietly humming to himself he set about mending the broken lid of the thermos. Having adjusted that to his satisfaction, with further soft humming he produced a package from his bag and generously served everyone with slices of cake made of rice flour dusted with sugar, a speciality of Emei he said. He had been born in Dali, a beautiful place north-west of Kunming. Now he had to work in Chengdu but he remained homesick for his lakeside home town. He made the remainder of our journey such a pleasure with his good humour, his generosity and his humming that we nicknamed him 'Mr Pickwick'.

We arrived at Chengdu after dark. It was a nightmare. Crowds poured off the train to converge with crowds thronging off another train. The station was under reconstruction and the platform was like a battlefield, half excavated, half littered with steel girders and scattered piles of paving stone, all obstacles to the flow of people. We were diverted across the railway lines and came out of the station through a temporary back exit into a frenetic and almost unlit bottleneck in a narrow street shut in by apartment houses. Our Chinese friend, Mr Pickwick, had herded us so far and now looked anxiously about for taxis, since he knew that our hotel was the other side of Chengdu. The moment his back was turned a ragged bicycle-rickshaw driver snatched at our cases and urged us to get into his vehicle. When Mr Pickwick returned he advised us to take the rickshaw as there was no other transport to be found. After a short argument Mr Pickwick told us that the man would pedal us to the hotel for 4 yuan. He helped squeeze us and our baggage into the passenger seat and waved us on our way. I hate riding in rickshaws of any kind. I find them not only degrading to the wretched operator but at one remove degrading to the passenger. But with the hotel some 4 km away this did not seem the moment for high sentiments.

9 The Potala Palace

TIBET: LHASA

10 The old market

11 The devout prostrate themselves

LHASA: JOKHANG TEMPLE

12 The mystery of faith

13 The mystery of magic

We gathered speed and I sat back with a certain relief. It was premature. We had hardly swung round the corner into the first dark street when the driver dismounted, and started to demand double the agreed price before he would go further. I think he tried to look threatening but apart from a certain unpleasantness I could not help finding his situation rather comical. He was a very small man and I am a very tall one. But quite apart from the unlikely event of a personal trial of strength, with two of us and our baggage wedged so tightly in his narrow vehicle I couldn't see any way he could get us out unless we gave him maximum co-operation. So while he shouted and hopped about in the road, I remained silent and, literally, sat tight. Eventually he realised that his bluster was not going to work and with a certain amount of muttering mounted and rode on. We seemed to be going in a large circle, as indeed we were. We emerged from a narrow sidestreet into a brightly lit square which proved to be the front of the railway station. Again the driver stopped and tried to renegotiate the fare but at that moment I saw the bus which I knew went past our hotel. Ejecting ourselves from the narrow seat we ran for the bus and a few seconds later, hardly less compressed, but this time standing up, we were on our way to the Jin Jiang Hotel. At last we were in Chengdu and in the heart of the famous province of Sichuan.

Sichuan is the largest province in China, a little bigger than France and with a population of at least 100 million, although it boasts the best birth-control record in the country, reducing the rate of increase from 3.1 per cent in 1970 to 0.44 per cent in 1980. Despite its many claims to fame the present province was constituted only in 1955 when the mountainous plateau of Sikang and the Red Basin area were incorporated into it. The name of Sichuan means 'four streams', probably referring to its four main rivers. It is surrounded by high mountains rising to 7000 metres to the west and 3000 metres to the east, the westerly Gongga Shan, the highest mountain at 7556 metres. The central Red Basin, fed by the Yangzi and its tributaries and named for its rich, red soil, is the most densely populated and intensively cultivated area in the world. In some parts of the region they can grow three crops of rice a year, while wheat, maize, sweet potatoes, soya beans, cotton, rapeseed, sugar, tea, herbs, spices and oranges are also grown. The province also has coal, oil and gas and, where there is the necessary bamboo, the panda.

There is a danger of searching too assiduously for distinct regional types or characteristics in China. Of course, if you can find them, Tibetans, Mongolians and some other minority people are distinctive, both in looks and culture. But the great mass of Han people, as the Chinese call themselves after the Han dynasty (206 BC to AD 220) – the period in which the basic patterns of Chinese society were formed – are not so easily distinguished by distinct regional groups. Since the establishment of the People's Republic in 1949, the regime has discouraged all kinds of difference, seen as various forms of reactionary individualism. In more practical terms, since that time vast numbers of Chinese have been moved from their home areas, either to 'colonise' the border regions or, as during the Cultural Revolution, for re-education or simply punishment. Those sentenced to long terms of imprisonment in remote corrective labour camps, even at the end of their sentences, have often been forced to settle in the same area outside the prison boundaries. There are no statistics for these thirty-five years of enforced migration but there can be no doubt that the figures run into millions. Besides all that, both in the more distant past and in recent times, the Mongolian invasion of the thirteenth century, the Manchurian incursion of the seventeenth century and the communist mass migrations must have led to a great deal of mixed blood which today is reflected in the variety of facial types of the Han people. Like the Japanese, the Chinese tend to think of themselves as an exceptionally homogeneous people, but in reality a vast number of them must have mixed ancestry.

Sichuan, if only by reputation, does occupy a special place in the world's imagination, a reputation that has partly been propagated by its distinctive and famous cooking. That is by no means irrelevant. It is easy to argue for a valid link between culture and cooking. Sichuan is synonymous with spice, particularly those palate-numbing small, red chili peppers that suggest a parallel between their assertive flavour and the strong independence which seems the main feature of the Sichuanese character. China's present leader, the diminutive but explosively down-to-earth Deng Xiaoping was born in Sichuan in 1904. He typifies the pragmatic and independent spirit of his province. He has made many earthy statements to illustrate his policies, all with the strong flavour of his province's cooking, such as his famous exhortation 'If you're sitting on the bog and can't shit, move over and make room for someone who can.' He would probably be the first to admit that while it is easy to make such headline-catching statements, it is a great deal more difficult to get the entrenched bureaucrat to budge.

Deng Xiaoping has surrounded himself with old provincial allies, what is called 'the Sichuan *bang* (group)', with Hu Yaobang as Party Chairman since 1981, and Zhao Ziyang as Prime Minister, having been the First Party Secretary in Sichuan from 1975. No doubt, with the unending jostling within the Chinese politburo, it is wise to surround oneself with tested friends. But Sichuan put colourful characters in Chinese national life long before this century. Sichuan first became part of China in the fourth century and, as the state of Shu, was led by the famous Emperor Liu Bei and his minister, Zhuge Liang. Two famous poets, the Tang Li Bai and the Song dynasty Su Dongpo came from Sichuan. In modern times, Sichuan produced the historian, Guo Moruo, Marshal Zhu De and the Belgian-Chinese writer, Han Suyin, best-known for her novel *A Many-Splendoured Thing.* The province suffered from the Mongols during the Yuan dynasty, and even worse in their strong opposition to the Manchus who destroyed many people in the province though eventually the opposition of the Sichuanese made a major contribution to their downfall. But during that period there was a large migration to the province of people from elsewhere, yet another factor making it difficult to identify the true Sichuan character.

I cannot say that, out on the streets, it was possible to make a definite identification. I walked about for several days, asking myself two questions. First, how did Chengdu differ from Kunming, and second, from my observations of street life, could I really sense a distinct Sichuan character? Chengdu was different from Kunming, but how much of that was due to the fact that we enjoyed warm, caressing spring weather in Kunming and a good deal of grey, steely rain in Chengdu? It is difficult to be objective.

Without question, I enjoyed Chengdu as much as I had enjoyed Kunming but, even allowing for the rain and the greyer skies, it seemed a darker, more sombre city, though equally alive. It had none of that suggestion, if a faint one, of Kunming's lightheartedness, but on the other hand the vitality of the streets and the markets was more robust, its human colours richer, more complex and at the same time more earthy. Wandering, through the markets or along the river, into the semi-rural outskirts, I was never bored. The surroundings were mostly dreary but the people were full of life, creating new scenes at every step.

On our first morning we met an enterprising Japanese student, Shinobu-san, who seemed to have travelled all over the remotest parts of China in the backs of lorries with unending diarrhoea. He introduced us to Sichuan cooking. All of us spent an exhausting morning fighting for air tickets in the crowded, backstreet office of CAAS. Exactly at the moment that we got to the counter, lunchtime was declared and without a word the clerks retired for their two-hour break. Shinobu-san, his charming face a symbol of undefeatable good humour, self-deprecating yet determined, suggested that we go for lunch at a well-known 'ravioli' restaurant nearby. We slithered through the skim of mud and sleeting rain, Shinobu-san typically insisting on lending us his umbrella while he got resolutely soaked until we found the restaurant which specialised in these small Chinese dumplings.

Much has been written about the grander end of the Sichuan cuisine and I am sure you may enjoy breathtaking and throat-burning menus if you are lucky enough to be cooked for by one of the six master chefs said to be entitled to that rank in Chengdu. The cuisine in our hotel might have been prepared in any third-rate Chinese restaurant between Pasadena and Portsmouth and did not even have the virtue of a pinch of spice to disguise its mediocrity. At a humble level, this little restaurant gave us one of the two excellent meals we ate in Chengdu. It was so crowded that even when you acquired a stool, you were still left slightly more standing than sitting, clamped between the shoulders on either side of you. I noticed that Shinobu-san took great care in wiping the restaurant's chopsticks. He said that they were a frequent cause of infection, particularly hepatitis, and that one should carry one's own if one was going to eat regularly in local restaurants. At last the food came, dumplings in soup with a hot, spicy sauce. It was delicious and as the sauce was served separately, you could regulate the degree to which you wished to go native. Glancing at Shinobu-san's darkly spiced soup I presumed he had taken out naturalisation papers.

All around this restaurant there was a market area, or more precisely, many market areas for here there was a distinct specialisa-tion. Grinning women, indifferent to the rain, sat amidst an array of plastic buckets and wide enamel bowls, exchanging expertise with the collectors of what we vulgarly call 'goldfish'. These exotic creatures were every colour of the rainbow from sheer black to blinding golds and reds, their transparent, wavering fins and tails as extravagant as the plumage of rare pheasant. Other aficionados gazed longingly at the lines of caged singing birds, the plump choristers as decorative as their ornate bamboo cages, complete with charming blue and white feeding and water bowls. Square cages were humped on the ground, the more elegant circular cages suspended on strings under the eaves of the old brick houses behind the stalls.

Further along we moved into the gardening section, gnarled bonsai trees in flat bowls spread along shelves while across the street were lines and piles of crude red earthenware flower pots of every traditional Chinese shape and size. In another place were plants and young trees, their roots carefully bound and wrapped ready for instant takeaway. It was all fascinating, but beyond that it seemed extraordinary that there were still Chinese with either the money or the enthusiasm left for black frilled-gubby and miniaturised wistaria. But it is true that the endless potted plants that live precariously on the apartment balconies are a reminder that despite everything, the Chinese have retained their traditional love of nature and gardening. Also these remain one of the few pleasures available to all and less expensive than manufactured goods.

I have never been convinced that travel broadens the mind. All too often it merely confirms people's awful opinions they already had of how 'the other half' lives. There are, however, along the way occasional little perks, human diversions, and Barbara was one of these. We met Barbara in the hotel. She was German, friendly, worked in Bonn as an interpreter, spoke five languages fluently and, better still, lisped in all of them. Barbara was not so much worried about her health as fascinated by it. It was her hobby. She was a robust fraulein, well able to travel around China and face its rigours alone, but she enjoyed an unceasing obsession with her health and why should anyone wish to deprive her of that pleasure since there was clearly absolutely nothing wrong with her. Barbara's hobby was quite expensive. One department of our enormous hotel was a medical section where, at a price, they offered instant courses in Chinese massage, acupuncture and herbal medicine. By the second day Barbara had had them all. Her three medical advisers, with one voice, expressed the opinion that she should remain under treatment for at least three weeks, but fortunately Barbara's wanderlust was slightly stronger than her hypochondria.

Is it necessary to add that Barbara was a vegetarian? It was not a matter of principle, more a point of further interest. Partly because of this we agreed to go with her to Baoguangsi, Temple of Divine Light, about 20 km north of Chengdu. We all wanted to see the temple and Barbara was particularly keen to try its famous vegetarian restaurant. The bus dropped us off in a suburban street and we soon found the road leading to the temple, lined with another market which had stalls selling brightly coloured fireworks and bundles of incense. A large wall concealed the entrance to the temple. On the other side of this wall, overlooking an open space, carved into the centre of the inner wall was a huge Chinese character meaning 'happiness'. The space was crowded with people, including a large number of children who were enjoying a school outing. All attention was focused on the great character for 'happiness' as in turn Chinese faced the wall, closed their eyes and raising their arm walked towards the red character and reached with their hand as high as possible. No doubt the place where one's hand came to rest had some auspicious meaning. I stood watching, enjoying the fun until suddenly I realised that the crowd had fallen back and I was the centre of attention. I knew what was expected of me, not least as I am close to two metres in height. I closed my eyes and marched towards the wall. As my hand made contact, way above the greaseband on the character marking the normal lowly target, a great cheer went up. I was mostly a figure of fun but I fooled myself that I had reached a particularly auspicious height. Anyway, the crew-cut, blue-drab dressed children with shouts and grins jumped up and down with genuine amusement and it was reassuring to know that fooling about is an international language still understood in China.

The Temple of Divine Light is large with five main halls set back one behind each other. To the right of this main complex are more buildings and a garden and to the left the vegetarian restaurant. There were a number of monks about, mostly small and old, wizened and bent in their shabby brown cotton robes with knitted skull-caps. I did also see two or three younger monks. The whole temple was crowded and alive with both sightseeing and devotions. Visitors were making small donations, in one courtyard throwing paper money into a pond while an ancient monk fished it out with a bamboo pole, drying the notes on the central rock. The main buildings were painted in deep red and black, with graceful black-tiled roofs with corners that turned up like delicate horns making spiked patterns against the sky. Near the entrance was a tall, lopsided stucco pagoda.

The temple had an architectural dignity if no great quality. The insides of the temple halls were garish with red and gold banners and well-paunched gilt Buddhas seated on the altars. But it is a miracle that so much survived the iconoclasm of the Cultural Revolution and that again the place is used, for prayer and pleasure. Everywhere the air was sweet with incense.

Barbara was hungry so we walked towards the restaurant. By the entrance to the restaurant garden courtyard, the menu for the day was on the wall, eighteen small slabs of wood hanging from two wires, each naming a dish and a price. Yuki-san was able to decipher most of the menu and we proceeded to the kitchen, on the other side of the restaurant, and ordered a spiced tofu dish, a dish of eggplants and some rice. The kitchen was clean and sparsely equipped but the food proved to be excellent. The tofu was certainly rather hot and the eggplants had been cooked so that they had a meaty flavour. Yuki-san and I tucked in but though Barbara had chosen the dishes, she ate practically nothing, pushing the lumps of tofu round her bowl in a disconsolate way. As we left the restaurant, I asked Barbara had she enjoyed her meal?

'No', she lisped, 'it was too spithy.'

After lunch we continued looking round the temple, puzzled that we could not find the large hall holding the temple's famous collection of *arhat* figures. We were standing in a courtyard to the north-east of the temple when suddenly a small door opened and a smiling woman with an official manner beckoned us to follow her. It turned out that she was guiding a small party of foreigners and luckily had mistaken us for members of her group. She led us into a beautiful courtyard garden, potted flowers and plants forming a pyramid of green and brilliant reds around a central tree and a huge rock from which water trickled away into the shade. She sat us at one side of the garden and served tea. It was cool, quiet and the bosky garden contrasted with the regular patterns of the lattice balustrades and panels which enclosed it. It was like stepping into one of those over-coloured but charming nineteenth-century paintings, missing only some Qing dynasty princess or a robed mandarin taking the afternoon air. It was also a welcome respite from the hustle and noise on the other side of the door.

We were soon back in modern China, struggling to admire the grotesque *arhats* crowded together like the spectators, and walking past a pond and a busy tea-house from which noise emerged like a raging wind, all excellent training for the struggle at the bus stop where we fought our way onto the bus taking us back into Chengdu. Our last glimpse of the temple was of a huge school party and it was good to see that while the clothes of all the little girls were of poorish quality, they were made of attractive fabrics giving the children an air of individuality. This small sign of independence was matched by the children's noisy vitality.

The large tourist hotels of China tend to conform to a pattern, though the service is an unknown quantity varying from friendly and excellent to what I can describe only as indifferent-awful. Each time I stay in one I remember an American friend telling me of a hotel he had once stayed at somewhere, it could have been China, where above his bed, signed by the management, were instructions to the guests to maintain a high standard of *self-service*. I do remember one breakfast in Chengdu's Jin Jiang Hotel. After twenty minutes of frantic tick-tacking, I managed to engage the attention of one of the many waitresses chatting in groups around the walls of the monumental dining room. She took my order and hurried back to her colleagues. After another twenty minutes I noted that she had not been to deliver my order to the kitchen. I walked over and asked her if I could have my breakfast. Five minutes later she proudly placed a lordly dish of jam on my table and returned to her group. It was a prolonged and losing battle. Each time I made the long walk across the room to jog her memory, after five minutes there appeared a token offering; after the jam came a pat of butter, then egg and bacon, next the orange juice, rather late in the day the untoasted toast and, just as I was about to leave, the only thing I really wanted, the coffee. It was not the order I had looked forward to nor had I wanted to spend ninety minutes over breakfast.

In such situations across China I have tried every reaction, politeness, shouting, wheedling, humour, pleading and, in extremis, mad laughter. All were met with the same great wall of Chinese indifference, impenetrable. Those who work in China's service industries are poorly paid but provided they turn up for work, whatever their actual performance on the job, they are certain of lifetime security. With no incentives of any kind why should the waitress or the room maid make the slightest effort to do more than the absolute minimum? The situation is made worse as there seldom seems to be any form of management or anyone in charge to whom one might complain. On the occasions when one does receive good service, be grateful for a bonus. You have simply had the good fortune to fall into the hands of a Chinese with a warm heart.

As Sichuan's provincial capital, Chengdu has a number of interesting places and attractions, temples, parks, literary pilgrimages, theatres and, always, the life of the streets and the markets. One can also make the excursion to climb Emeishan, one of China's five sacred Buddhist mountains, or visit the 2000-year-old Dujiangyan irrigation system, built in the Qin dynasty by Li Bing and still today irrigating some 7 million hectares of land, a notable piece of early engineering. I enjoyed the ancient Wenshu Monastery, in the northeastern sector of the city. It was built during the Tang dynasty but has been rebuilt several times. The present largely Qing dynasty buildings are dignified and restrained with pleasant gardens of rocks, water and bamboo between the temple halls. It was packed and many older people knelt devoutly before the decorated altars offering incense and prayers.

A day or two later, when the rain had given way to hot sunshine and suddenly Chengdu shared the springtime feeling of Kunming, I set out on a long walk to explore the southern part of the town with the aim of finding one or two parks in the outskirts of Chengdu. It was long walks like these that made me realise that there have been real changes in China in the last six or seven years. I had read some of the best-known Western accounts of China written between 1973 and 1981 by leading American and European journalists posted to Beijing. Already much of what they wrote reads like a description of another country and a different regime. I am aware of the danger of making judgements about the state of China from superficial impressions, and I am saying no more than that in the last three years or so there have been some widespread *superficial* changes. Only time will reveal their true depth, significance and permanence. As I walked around the back streets of Chengdu, many people smiled welcomingly when I stopped to look or to photograph. Two or three ordinary Chinese did their best to help when I got lost and twice, in an unselfconscious way, students in the parks came up to me to practise their English and tell me about their student lives. This is a far cry from the cold isolation from the Chinese described by Simon Leys in his haunting *Chinese Shadows*, written after his stays in China in 1972 and 1973, long before the individual traveller was allowed to roam about. Later, when Fox Butterfield was describing his life as a journalist in 1979 so vividly, he was always conscious of the secret police within his shadow and the risk of making contacts with Chinese people.

I don't doubt for a moment that under the seeming liberalisation of Deng Xiaoping, the apparatus of the police state, down to the junior informer at the factory and the spying neighbour at home are still at work and that the ordinary Chinese is still circumspect in keeping his thoughts to himself. But things have changed. Now foreign experts from all over the world, many of them fluent in Chinese, are allowed some glimpse of the workings of China while many Chinese-speaking students from Taiwan, Hong Kong and other countries are free to roam over most of China and to talk with anyone. Equally, the government now allows the masses to be exposed to a certain amount of Western television – contemporary comedies and thrillers as well as costume dramas – for the growing number of people able to afford a television set. The Chinese are being exposed to the outside world as never before, each year making it harder, if not impossible, for government to turn the clock back.

So I walked that long afternoon, first along the river past lines of houses built in the Chengdu half-timbered style, past crowded tea-houses rattling with chess pieces and tea-cups, by a high bridge where four boys were diving into the scummy waters of the river, and stopping to watch groups of old men, whisps of hair on their chins, their advisers at their shoulders, hurling the elongated playing cards onto the small stone tables that were placed along the river embankment. Further out the road narrowed, the houses grew smaller and meaner, and thatched cottages mingled with dilapidated small factories. People sat out before their doors, young women scrubbing in enamelled bowls on the kerbside, older women minding the children and old men smoking cigarettes or black stumpy cheroots. Out in the suburbs the streets widened and came to life again, lined with shops and restaurants often gruesomely advertised by racks of fly-blown entrails. Ancient buses moved majestically down the centre of the street hooting the bikes, barrows and small trucks out of the way. I visited the Wuhou Temple and park but ignored one of those so-called Cultural Parks which are usually less than cultural with their kitsch murals, concrete Chinese pavilions, shrubberies dense with rubbish and cavorting animals sculpted in cement.

Finally, on the edge of the city, where fields of vegetables were taking over, I found the entrance to the park containing the thatched cottage of the celebrated Tang poet, Du Fu (712–70). He lived in

Chengdu for four years where he wrote many poems. His rural retreat has now expanded to 20 hectares of well-planted parkland, the original cottage overshadowed by additional buildings and the memorials to Chairman Mao's visit in 1958. Chairman Mao had adopted Du Fu as an honorary poet of the Revolution which, if it did nothing else, protected this pleasant place during the Cultural Revolution. I saw two amusing sights which were splendidly contrary to the spirit of the Red Guards. The Cultural Revolution produced a variety of tragedies for the individual and for China as a whole. Perhaps nothing was more disastrous than the almost total closure of China's educational system. Now, in the quiet of this park, several students were studying at the small stone tables, books and pens spread out, muttering their lessons over to themselves. As much as anything it was an encouraging sign that China was returning to sanity and progress.

All work and no play; in a large neighbouring pavilion a group of university students were studying the tango and the old-fashioned waltz with admirable diligence. The old tunes blared out from an enormous tape-deck and the dancers plunged and pranced, a bizarre cultural mix among the nodding bamboo groves. It is still difficult to sort out what is and what is not culturally respectable in China. To a Westerner, few things in the world could be more wholly bourgeois than old-time dancing.

I made the long walk back to the hotel via the bleak and scruffy Renmin Park. It was uneventful except for a street alchemist who had spread out on the pavement an alarming display of fragmented dead animals. Pangolin lay alongside turtle shells while the dried limbs and antlers of deer pathetically enclosed particularly nasty furry lengths of monkeys' limbs and gaping skulls. When I need an aphrodisiac, I shall stick to oysters.

5

Splendours and Miseries

LHASA AND TIBET

I never dreamed that we should go to Tibet. I did glance enviously at a leaflet in the travel agents in Hong Kong which offered a five-day tour at US$2600 per person. I could not have afforded the $5000 or so needed for Yuki-san and myself and, although it was probably sour grapes, I did not want to share my first glimpse of the Potala Palace with a lot of blue-rinsed ladies from California or Munich. For us Lhasa looked like remaining the 'Forbidden City' as it was available only to group travellers.

In Kunming we heard differently. I cannot remember who told us but in China rumours pass along a kind of backpackers' grapevine. We were told that at certain Public Security Bureaux individual travellers were being issued with passes for Lhasa on condition that they flew from Chengdu. The PSB in Kunming had the reputation for being particularly liberal. The other advice was to go at once as the new regulation could easily be rescinded. In a state of nerves, with that 'so near, so far' feeling, we found the large and gloomy PSB building, headquarters of both uniformed and plain-clothes police. Outside the main gate was a display of grim photographs of criminals and dissidents, trussed like turkeys, being paraded and humiliated before jeering crowds. The techniques of the Cultural Revolution are still in use, the photographs capturing so vividly all the implications of that sinister phrase, 'struggle session'.

Inside the courtyard we saw an office labelled 'Aliens' Travel Permits'. The welcome we received could hardly have been more different to what I had expected. A diminutive uniformed police-woman sat helmeted in plastic curlers while her colleague gave her a home perm. The policewoman in the chair gave us a charming smile and asked in excellent English if we would wait three minutes while her friend finished. Painlessly, ten minutes later we were holding our neat, pink Aliens' Travel Permit marked up and officially stamped for Tibet, valid for four months. The permit would allow us to purchase air tickets when we reached Chengdu, which we did our first morning there.

We got up at 4.30 a.m. to a coldish start. The taxi for the airport was waiting for us. The streets were almost empty with a few cyclists and the occasional elderly jogger. We had a quick journey to Chengdu airport and arrived an hour and a half early. The place was already packed, the restaurant serving tasteless coffee and buns. We had just lined up to board the plane when it was announced that the ground mist was too dense and departure would be delayed for ninety minutes. I was feeling sick with anticipation. I still could not quite believe that I might be on my way to Tibet. At 8.15 we were called and we squeezed ourselves into the packed plane. The engines picked up, we taxied forward and three minutes later we were on our way.

The Chinese have developed their own style of air travel. The seats seem about one-third narrower than on any other airline, every available spare space is jammed with the bundles and wicker baskets usually associated with country buses. The cabin crew pay scant respect to the passengers but do make two appearances, first to hand out cardboard lunch-boxes and a little later to distribute bizarre souvenirs such as a badly moulded and coloured plastic yacht with silver sails. This flight's gift appeared more practical, a mirror and comb set, except that the teeth of the comb would have been more suitable as a back-scratcher. The Chinese passengers were enthralled by their gifts.

There were soon magnificent views of snow-covered mountains on both sides of the plane seeming to stretch away forever. From the west of Sichuan we started to fly over that great chain that begins with the Daxue Mountains, spreading west to the Himalayas with the huge Tibetan plateau to the north, itself enclosed on all sides by great mountain ranges. The world below the plane was utterly remote, pristine, awesome and vast beyond imagination. The whites of floating clouds blurred over the harder whites of the steep slopes and sharp pinnacles, the contours of the mountains making intricate swerving patterns running endlessly to the horizon with occasional walls of dark shadow and the utterly blue sky putting colour into this silent and beautiful world.

The mountains eventually gave way to a wide plain, our first sight of the Tibetan plateau and we landed on a large dusty patch with a few modest buildings in a distant corner. The airport is some 90 km from Lhasa and we still had a bus ride which can take anything from four to ten hours, depending on what breakdowns and other disasters overtake you on any particular day. Some people were grumbling about this long bus ride but it seemed to me an added bonus, a chance to see a good stretch of Tibetan countryside. But considering we were just about to undertake a cross-country ride which many would have hesitated to make in a sturdy jeep, the rusty and dusty old buses seemed hardly suitable. The moment we were under way it became obvious that these old buses were stronger than they looked and the experienced drivers treated them exactly like jeeps, plunging into river fords, hurtling over bone-shaking ruts, skidding across thick mud slides, accelerating fiercely on steeply banked corners of loose rock and largely ignoring the crater-like pot holes. There is a rough, shale-surfaced road, but much of the way this was out of action as it was being turned into the foundations of a new road, so frequently the bus was forced into appalling diversions, the faintest tracks across open country. The track was often so faint that the driver had to turn back until he picked up the correct route.

Mostly the day was clear and beautiful but every now and then a wind swept across the plain raising a wall of dust which came straight through the loose windows of the bus and into the nose and throat, a quick introduction to the greatest trial of the Tibetan plateau. The wide plain was surrounded by tawny mountains, on their flanks great sandfalls and scabrous rocky surfaces. It was a landscape of subdued colours, browns, greys and blacks. The farming land was arid and there had clearly been much erosion, but bullocks and shaggy yaks, their yokes decorated with red flags, ploughed the light soil. Much of the way we followed a wide, sparkling, brown-green river. The shapes of the mountains kept changing; humped shoulders of rock, broken crenellations, tumbled boulders, sharp single peaks. In this brown landscape the leaves of spring made each tree precious, a green promise of life in a dying landscape. At one place we turned into a new valley which was greener, the fields more fertile, the mountainsides touched with scrubby grass. All along the way were small walled settlements, mud buildings painted white and brightly topped by festoons of prayer flags. In other places gangs worked on the new roads, forced to live in grim tented camps which must have been particularly vulnerable to the dust.

It was a long journey but never boring. There was a special and subtle beauty in the semi-arid, mutely coloured landscape which emphasised the enormous sense of space. The Tibetans at work in the fields, small roadside temples, the movement of the river and the local leather boats, rather like large Welsh coracles, touched in the fascinating detail of this world spread out here at just over 12,000 ft. The magic and mysticism of Tibetan tantric Buddhism seemed to fall into place here. One could feel how men's minds were opened to myths and legends by this land. As we neared Lhasa the landscape grew dustier and more arid and suddenly, in the brown distance, rose the white walls of the Potala Palace, an unmistakable silhouette, a glint of gold among its roofs. We were approaching Lhasa, the dream of travellers for centuries and my own one remaining major travel ambition. My immediate reaction was absurdly contradictory. While I could hardly believe I had arrived, yet everything looked exactly as I had expected.

The bus drew into the airline office compound immediately beneath the walls of the Potala. In the street outside everything and everybody was of potential fascination. But before we could explore we had to solve practical problems, mainly of somewhere to stay. I had been recommended a place called the Snowlands Hotel but the small group of English and American backpackers we had met in the bus favoured another place. Nervous that the Snowlands might be beyond their budget, we deferred to their choice. The only thing we all knew was that beds were scarce in Lhasa, though I believe there is a modern hotel for the groups somewhere outside the town. Our luggage was coming in a separate truck, so we struck out down the main street unencumbered. Along the way, down a narrow street to the right, I saw the Snowlands Hotel but kept quiet. After a longish walk into the heart of the old town we found a long, low traditional building which seemed to be the hostel for which we were looking. We needed only one glance at the pitch black cells offered as rooms and one sniff at the dark, smelly corridors to be certain that if possible we should all like to stay somewhere else.

I volunteered that I thought I had seen the Snowlands some way back. I suggested that Peter, a young Englishman, and I went to find out what it was like while the girls rested and guarded what might turn out to be better than nothing. It was further back to the Snowlands than I had estimated and by the time we got there I was beginning to feel the effects of the altitude. The word 'hotel' applied to the Snowlands was somewhat flattering but it was better than the other place and they had a dormitory with six iron bedsteads which would take our small party. I left Peter to guard the room, since back-packers were now pouring in off the bus, and made the long walk back to fetch Yuki-san and the other girls. After their two hours' waiting in the cells, I could thrill them with the simple amenities of Snowlands; light, fresh air, a water pump in the yard and those basic facilities that come to mean so much in remote places.

By the time I had installed them in this Tibetan palace, which it could have been when the Tibetan nobility occupied such large houses in Lhasa, it was time to return to the bus station to collect our luggage. Another long walk, but miraculously Peter had acquired an old man with a handcart. Despite his help I was exhausted by the time we got back. I had a blinding headache and an emerging cold which the Tibetan dust was busily thrusting to the back of my raw throat. I found poor Yuki-san hiding from the altitude and general cultural shock under a rough quilt and after a bowl of instant noddles we went to bed too busy nursing our various ailments to notice much else.

The Snowlands Hotel was a largish but simple three-storey building, the two wings enclosing a large and muddy courtyard centring on an old iron water pump and piles of roughly split firewood. The architecture was typical of Lhasa: the outer façade with lines of large, closely placed windows, above each a strip of decorative painting, flowers in pink and blue, and above each frieze a wooden bracket painted bright orange. The older houses were not so highly finished and had less and larger windows, often shaded by a brightly coloured cotton pelmet. Prayer flags on bamboo poles fluttered above all the buildings. Around the Snowlands' inner courtyard were open balconies supported on vermilion columns. All the dormitory rooms opened onto these balconies which were also the corridors. The general layout and the total lack of comfort and privacy was like a Western prison. The place was packed with a fascinating assortment of travellers, backpacking hippies and drop-outs from at least fifteen different countries. Between them they must have had a remarkable experience of the world's dust and dirt. In one matter they were in accord. The single men's lavatory of the Snowlands Hotel was voted the most gruesome in the world. I will not labour the detail except to say that I used to lie in bed in the morning fighting a battle of mind over bladder to delay the awful moment, but when it came I realised that there are smells so strong that they can almost lift a man off his feet at five metres.

14 Along the river

LHASA: OUTSKIRTS

15 A bridge and prayer flags

16 Guardian of the Summer Palace

17 The splendour of the Renmin Hotel

CHONGQIN

18 The poverty of tenements by the Yangzi

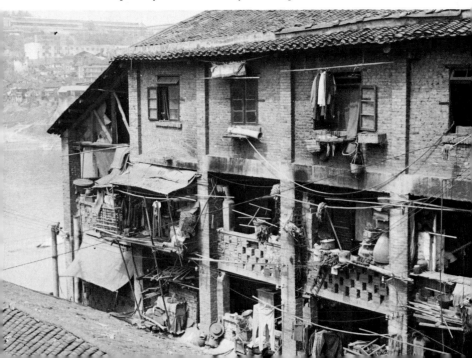

The next morning, we spent over two hours queuing for our return air tickets to Chengdu the following week. We were told that tickets were sold only two days in advance but I did not believe that. By simply hanging around, looking miserable, eventually we got our tickets just as the office was closing for lunch. In fact the young clerk stayed on to issue them and we had a short talk with him. He was keen to improve his English and asked me how he could make progress. It was not easy to make practical suggestions for a man living in Lhasa. Everywhere in China young people ask about learning English and it was said that the English girl giving the BBC English lessons was the best-known foreigner in China.

That afternoon and all the following morning we devoted to the old town of Lhasa and particularly the central Jokhang Temple and the markets that surround it. Lhasa is an extraordinary mixture of colour, fascination and exotic sights mixed with abject poverty and primitive dirt and squalor which combine to produce an unforgettable world. Even the complexion on the flat cheeks of the Tibetans is a compound of hot sun, mountain air and a patina of grime. That rich dark red of the lamas' robes could not be achieved by dye alone, but given that deeper hue by dust and dirt. The people who endlessly throng the streets, many heading for the temple, are wonderful with huge, good-humoured grins, dark, ruddy cheeks, and flowing black hair elaborately bound in skeins of scarlet wool. The men's swagger is confident but not aggressive and there is great style in the way they adjust their heavy sheepskin coats for comfort and temperature; one bare arm out, two arms out, or a bare chest and the coat dropped to form a skirt. They must develop considerable resistance to cold and the nomads living at high altitudes need to take great care. A young boy was too lazy to remove his felt boots one night and overnight one foot was so severely damaged that it led to amputation of the leg a week or two later. Extremes of temperature dictate the way of life.

Everyone smiles, huge toothy grins glistening with ill-shaped lumps of gold. Lamas move among the crowd, some old, some young, folded in their red robes, rosaries in hand, mysterious bulging bags over their shoulders. In several places old buildings were being demolished amid additional dust. Everyone looks healthy and the women and girls work like beasts of burden. The young girls stoop down and large lumps of rock are strapped to their backs with crude ropes. Drudgery, but at least it is a job with a small wage. It is all colour, bright or sombre, movement, flashes of old jewellery and ornamental daggers, laughing family groups, the occasional girl of great beauty, always the lively crowds flowing through the paved and filthy streets.

The markets are a strange mixture of tradition and modern incursions. Dominating everything, not least the senses, are the stalls mountainous and pungent with huge hunks of yak butter, wrapped in old yak skins. The smell of yak butter is seldom far away in Lhasa, all over the market, along the streets and at its sickliest in the temples. It is the staple of the Tibetan diet. The yak-butter tea mixed in tall wooden churns is vital in keeping out the cold, while yak hair provides a coarse wool and the fabric of the nomads' tents and yak dung is dried for fuel. I learned to live with the smell but I funked the tea.

Elsewhere there were stalls selling bundles of incense, rolls of brilliant brocades bright with gold thread, the accoutrements of male and female Tibetan dress, heavy silver necklaces enriched with semi-precious stones, brooches, rings, jewelled belts and purses, a range of handsome felt hats, white scarves for temple offerings, sutras, and the occasional primitive street dentist. Here and there, alien and tawdry, were widespread displays of Chinese plastic goods of the poorest possible quality, sandals, combs, plastic sheeting, pink and pierced bracelets and similar trinkets, a variety of bowls and containers and, alongside, piles of the cheapest Western clothing. I moved on to the food market where even the hunks of darkening meat seemed preferable to plastic psychedelic colours. I examined evil-looking tobacco, mounds of rice, beans, spices and herbs and grinned at friendly shoe- and bike-menders. Although the Tibetans have a reputation for excluding foreigners from their country, they are a friendly people, perhaps partly as all foreigners are a kind of ally against the unwelcome Chinese invasion. In reality, it seems more likely that for centuries they kept foreigners at bay, not least the British in India, since they sensed the predatory intentions of foreign interest in Tibet. How right they were, but sadly in 1959 they were unable to resist the ultimate predator.

It is very difficult to observe exactly what the Chinese are trying to do in Tibet. With Tibet's enormous Indian and near-Russian borders, China's original occupation made sense. Since then the threat of India has evaporated and the threat from the Soviet Union lessened but China's overstretched resources must, one way or another, continue the 'colonisation' of this vast, physically and

culturally intractable country. All forms of propaganda and indoc-
trination are at their most ineffective faced with deep-rooted, simple
faith combined with widespread illiteracy. The Tibetans' faith is as
much part of their lives as herding yaks, and how do you bring about
a proletarian conversion when the proletariat speak another language which most of them neither read nor write? It is impossible to
control a nation of nomads who wander the highest pastures in the
world.

The professional 'China watchers' can be rather didactic and
much of what they write goes out of date almost overnight. The
Chinese have done drastic things since they invaded Tibet: many
monasteries have been destroyed, communities of Tibetan monks
were killed, abused and scattered and the Panchen Lama, second
only to the Dalai Lami, was imprisoned for years in Beijing's
notorious Qin Cheng gaol. More serious than any of this, the
Chinese have failed to improve agriculture in Tibet and many
Tibetans live on the edge of hunger. Without doubt, in Lhasa and
other larger Tibetan centres, huge numbers of Chinese immigrants
were *drafted* to Tibet with the ultimate aim of swamping Tibetan
culture out of existence and by Chinese-oriented schooling to
produce a new generation ignorant of old traditions.

In the last year or two there has been a change of heart, or at least
the development of a more pragmatic and realistic attitude. The
Dalai Lama has been invited to return. He fears that if he did, he
would be used as a political puppet. I can say only that his people
hunger for him. Wherever you go, walking along the streets of Lhasa,
in the temple precincts, in the Potala Palace, ordinary Tibetan
people and, more particularly, the lamas, badger foreigners for
photographs of their exiled leader. In their isolation they associate all
foreignness with the world in which the Dalai Lama now lives. Their
persistence was heartbreaking. In a chapel in the depths of the Potala
Palace I found an elderly lama who spoke reasonable English. After
showing us some portrait-sculptures of previous Dalai Lamas, he
asked me if I could tell him anything about the present Dalai Lama. I
said that some years ago, just as I was entering the Temple of the
Golden Buddha in Bangkok, we were suddenly held back while the
Dalai Lama arrived to pray in this famous temple. He passed within a
metre of me as he entered. The old lama was overwhelmed. For him
I represented a closeness to his holy ruler that he had not felt for
years. I was both upset and moved, upset by my helplessness. Such

experiences left me with the probably naïve feeling that the Dalai Lama should return to his people, even at the risk of becoming a puppet. Whatever the Chinese did, the Dalai Lama could never be a puppet to his own people. And if the Chinese intend further destruction of Tibetan culture, it is strange that they are now allowing anyone to wander freely in the streets of Lhasa and, if you have the energy, beyond the capital.

Chinese pragmatism does lead to some strange decisions, particularly where foreign tourists are concerned. Like official encouragement of tourism anywhere in the world, the motive is foreign currency. I do not believe that the British government benevolently wants Germans or Japanese to enjoy the beauties of West Sussex any more than Deng Xiaoping wants backpackers in Lhasa except for the fact that they pay a hefty airfare to get there. One can see such monetary thinking at work. Up to the moment we arrived in Lhasa, it had been allowed, if unbearably exhausting, to travel east and north by bus back into China proper. A number of people in our hostel had intended taking this route, particularly as they did not have sufficient money to pay the return airfare to Chengdu. Quite suddenly, no reasons given, all roads out of Lhasa, except the route south to Nepal, were closed. Police were out on the road, lorries were being searched for hitchhikers and even the known rendezvous with lorry drivers were being watched. The reason was obvious enough. No territory east of Lhasa had suddenly become a sensitive area. It was simply that since Lhasa had been opened to individual travellers, too many 'customers' were leaving Lhasa the cheap way. The new regulations simply forced them to travel by plane, east or west. Aeroplane tickets to the east remained expensively available to all.

The various travellers at the Snowlands Hotel were a study in themselves. I particularly remember a rather emaciated hippie from Limerick, his dirty beard so thick that it seemed to drag him forward into a perpetual stoop.

'Where do you come from?' I asked, meaning to pinpoint him to a particular town.

'Ah begorrah!' The voice emerged richly from the entangled beard. 'O'im from Oirland.'

And people say that Irish jokes are exaggerated.

We shared the dormitory with Peter, an Englishman working in Alaska, and his American girlfriend, and two warm-hearted English girls who had grown up together in Leeds. Their attitude to travel typified most of the backpackers I talked to in China. From the moment our group dumped their packs on their beds they were obsessed with how they were going to achieve the next place on their itinerary which unfortunately for them was in the now forbidden surrounding area. They walked energetically around Lhasa, but arrived totally ignorant of Tibet and I doubt if they understood much of what they saw. They were consumed by the business of travelling and the main purpose of arrival was that it gave a pause to wrangle about the next destination. The process of travel was the adventure, the boast the number of countries one had passed through. To be fair they were prepared to put up with a great deal of discomfort and they paid their own way without the hippie-type scrounging. But the exercise made them fiercely competitive with a meanness to others contrary to all traditions of the road. If you found any kind of short cut, in terms of distance, convenience or money, you kept it strictly to yourself as it might enable you to chalk up another destination before the others got there. And chalking up another destination was not only the name of the game, it was psychologically a form of identity.

The Jokhang Temple is the most holy place in Tibet and a great centre of pilgrimage. Set right in the middle of the old town, it was built around AD 640 by King Songtsang Kampo who unified Tibet and married the Tang princess, Wen Cheng, who is supposed traditionally to have brought Buddhism to Tibet. Although rebuilt many times and under further restoration now, it is an impressive building, particularly the extraordinary interior which together with the pilgrims was for me the most memorable experience in Lhasa. It was thronged with Tibetan pilgrims making fervent devotions, muttering their prayers and endlessly turning the great bronze prayer wheels with exotic Tibetan script cast into the surface.

In the open forecourt before the temple doors, elbow to elbow, many pilgrims prostrated themselves, hurling their bodies to the ground, falling on some slight padding and sliding their hands above their heads with bits of cloth or cardboard. The most devout simply stretched out on the dirty stone. This is the Tibetans' traditional form of pilgrimage and some make their way to Lhasa by endless prostrations over hundreds of kilometres of road and track. Here, at the doors of the holy shrine, the act was stationary but hardly the less exhausting. Everywhere the dirt was indescribable and within the temple, the sweet pungency of rancid yak butter thickened the air. In place of votive candles small lighted wicks float in great trays of melted butter and the pilgrims replenish the yak butter from the containers they bring as their offering. On a plain altar stretching across the antechapel, pilgrims had placed piles of cheap sweets, small mounds with smoking sticks of incense sprouting out of them. I was overwhelmed by the sense of devotion. I had been here before, but then it had been called Fatima or Lourdes.

Inside Jokhang every surface is covered with crude panels of flower painting against vivid blue backgrounds, crimson columns and multicoloured statues with remote golden smiles draped in white votive scarves, surrounded by brilliant banners, stars of light floating at their feet. The side chapels were mysteriously dark with esoteric figures of the Buddha or threatening gods who looked more Hindu than Buddhist. From somewhere deep within the building drums throbbed to the chanting of priests. Lamas stood in the dark corners, folding scarves, cleaning altars, trimming the floating wicks, conducting mumbled services for groups of the devout in shadowy side-chapels. Everywhere the groups of pilgrims circulated, pausing before each statue, feeding the great trays of yellowing yak butter; bonneted old women, dark, squat men and wide, white-eyed boys. They shuffled before the altars and behind the temple they passed down the rows of cylindrical prayer-wheels, their fingertips brushing the bronze invocations in silent prayer.

Buddhism, like Christianity, has fragmented and developed into many forms. Few are stranger than the Buddhism of Tibet with its tantric branches and its absorption of the early folk beliefs of *Bon*, a simple nature worship, together with shamanism, astrology, geomancy and thinly disguised magic. The Tibetans make no real separation between documented history, revered legend and primitive myth; all are part of their reality. After the introduction of Buddhism into Tibet in the seventh century there followed a long period of dissension, part religious, part political. The indigenous faith of *Bon* continued, while simpler forms of Buddhism and the esoteric practices of tantric Buddhism wrestled for supremacy, both drawing inspiration from Indian sources. Because of certain erotic elements, and also as tantric Buddhism was frequently misused and misunderstood, it has been misrepresented in the West as a form of religious sexual licence. In fact, true tantric practices demand the severest ascetic disciplines and control which would have no appeal to those Westerners who think they detect a source of sexual titillation in this strange branch of Buddhism. Out of political dissension and theological debate the idea of a reincarnated leader, the Gyalwa Rinpoche or Dalai Lama, emerged and this divine dynasty is incarnated in the fourteenth Dalai Lama, now in exile. One wonders what will happen on the death of the present Dalai Lama, now in his sixties. Normally, his successor would be discovered within a few months, often, like the present incarnation, in some humble and remote family. They say that the signs are unmistakable. The Chinese must also have been speculating on this problem and, who knows, perhaps they have already made arrangements to 'plant' a comradely new Dalai Lama. Reincarnation is an unusually vital part of Tibetan Buddhism and various other Tibetan religious figures are regularly reincarnated, discovered, and trained to become abbots of important monasteries.

Whatever misinterpretations have been spread about tantric practices in Tibet, without question primitive forms of magic and shamanism are commonly woven into Tibetan Buddhist belief. After I had wandered around the interior of the Jokhang Temple I returned to the antechapel just inside the main doors. I saw an oldish, dark-faced priest squatting near one end of the long offertory altar, surrounded by bundles, brass vessels and, before him, a low square table on which he was modelling small, pinnacled mountains in a kind of dough. He wore a dark red robe with a rough fur collar. His head was shaven and as his hands worked busily at his material a self-satisfied smile played over his face. His robed acolyte was so dark-skinned as to be slightly negroid in appearance, his own grin given a slightly sinister shade by a number of scars between one eye and his mouth. The two busied about, the older lama concentrating on his sculpture, the assistant rummaging in bags to produce small drums, brass vessels and a sutra book. While the preparations were still going forward a group of Tibetans appeared and squatted around the lama. They looked like one family. When the tiny mountain landscape was complete, the lama settled himself and to rhythmic tapping on the drums he and his assistant chanted in a low tone from the sutra text, the lama occasionally passing a hand over his little mountains. Then, without warning, he lifted the wooden board supporting his magic sculpture and placed it carefully on the offertory bench among the other mountains of sweets and the smouldering sticks of incense. He then returned to his chanting.

I shall never know exactly what he was practising but I cannot believe it was a conventional Buddhist ritual and I feel certain that the family were seeking the help of additional powers. It was fascinating but in no way sinister, and from early on, when the old lama spotted me, he made it clear that he had no objection to me or my camera. I am left only with the memory of that small group locked in their own spiritual world. The crowd surged around them, other devotees hurled themselves to the floor and this extraordinary world of faith and filth went on its way as it had been doing for centuries, involving young and old in a religion of many strands.

That afternoon we walked south of the town, along the river, to find the Summer Palace of the Dalai Lama a few kilometres to the west. Across the wide river was a gentle view to the mountains. The afternoon was warm and there was no snow anywhere. A few people were standing on the islets in the middle of the shallow river which further ahead was crossed by a narrow suspension bridge fluttering with hundreds of prayer flags. We had come along the river in the hope of avoiding the dust of the main road. But this end of Lhasa is being developed as a Chinese town and the building sites stretched to the river road with clouds of dust from excavations and passing lorries. After we had walked a long way we found the small side road which led to the Summer Palace. Two grotesque, white lion-dogs guarded the entrance, their stone lips turned back in perpetual growls. The outer precincts of the Palace were now a neglected public park but when we reached the main inner gate it was shut.

We continued walking around the large walled enclosure, hoping that somewhere we might catch a glimpse of the gardens. As we came to the end of the southern wall we noticed an open wooden door. We peered in but there was nothing but a courtyard with piles of building materials lying everywhere. At the far end a group of workmen were resting and it was obvious that they were restoring the wooden building along the wall. We could see nothing else. We walked on and just around the corner, still within the sound of the workmen's voices, we found another open door, probably for the delivery of materials. Here there was a direct entry into the main gardens. The workmen were hidden around the corner and the next moment we had crept past them and were inside the Summer Palace.

The buildings and the gardens had been neglected though it looked as if the small pavilions were being restored. The remains of the garden were charming, brightened at that moment by a mass of pink and white cherry blossom. The skeleton of the garden was a system of ponds and canals crossed by small bridges, all surrounded by stone balustrades. The small, elaborately roofed garden pavilions were covered in brightly coloured paintings, the timbers painted with the usual floral patterns, the walls with complicated legendary scenes. Over a far wall, in an inner part of the garden, was a more Tibetan-looking building, crowned with gold ornaments, which may have been the Dalai Lama's residence. There was nobody about and I suffered only one fright when three aggressive dogs shot out of a hole under one of the pavilions. Otherwise, the place was deserted and bedraggled, its ponds and waterways drained dry. But there was enough left to suggest what an enchanting place it must have been when kept in good order, a secret garden suggesting both the influences of India and China with its twisted rocks and formal waterways.

By good luck we managed to hitch a lift back into town in a filthy trailer. The ride left us coated with mud on the outside and a coating of dust on the inside, but at that altitude no hitch is to be despised. That evening we went out with the other members of our dormitory to what seems to be Lhasa's number-one devil's kitchen. It was an annexe of the hostel we had rejected. The restaurant was one gloomy cavernous room, the tables and stools fitting in amongst the cooking. By our table, red and raw, lay two metal bowls of scraped carcasses and bones while alongside a man chopped vegetables on a huge slab of tree trunk. Mean-eyed and mangey dogs snuffled amongst the accumulating filth on the floor and inevitably an odour of yak butter provided the background to this vivid world. There were no problems of deciphering a Tibetan menu. In one corner a large table was covered with enamel bowls. The cook stood surrounded by his ingredients and flavourings. As you made your choice he took them up by the handful and tossed them into a sizzling wok. His hands looked like those of a motor mechanic who had just completed an oil and grease on a large lorry. The flames leapt, and those black fingers sprinkled pinches of salt, garlic, generous quantities of cardamom and ground chili and, with a dextrous tossing and stirring, another infernal omelette was ready. It was delicious. The whole room was black with smoke, nearby was a cauldron of awful-looking tea and in the middle of the room a boy was carving up a huge carcass of dark meat with an axe. Women carried in more vegetables and children humped in bundles of firewood. I walked home wondering if I should make it through the night, but the food lay lightly on my stomach.

Other things did keep me awake. I was still suffering from a severe headache and it was much colder. During the afternoon a patch of black cloud had appeared between the mountains in the far west. By nightfall the higher mountains around Lhasa were dusted with snow and a sharp wind blew straight down onto my bed through the broken window frame. The fragment of curtain fluttered with each gust. In the earlier hours of the night I lay watching the mountains and the cold sky, half a moon and few stars appearing now and then. For a time the old town remained lively, people meandering home, maybe a few drunks, shouting and bickering across the streets. Slowly the lights went out and for a short while a total silence gave me a strange feeling of remoteness. It did not last long. The small hours of Lhasa belong to its dogs. They take over their kingdom in the pre-dawn, barking, howling, mating, fighting, whining from every corner of the old city. There was no cock to break the dawn. Merely the pneumatic drills on the surrounding building sites, rousing us to a new, dusty day.

We got up to be met by the grumblings of a small group who had risen early to walk 6 km north-east of Lhasa to the Sera Monastery in the hope of seeing the gruesome dawn ritual of corpses being dissected and fed to the birds of prey, a necessity in some parts of Tibet where burial is difficult and there is no wood for cremation. That morning the group had been chased by the relatives who had thrown stones at them. These people found it incomprehensible that families might wish to bury their dead without the intrusion of foreigners and cameras. There is nothing to prevent a visit to the other monastery in the vicinity of Lhasa, the great Drepung Monastery which spreads like a white city across the western hillside, said before the Chinese invasion to house some 10,000 monks. Now only a handful remain in this vast shell of monastic life. The Chinese forced most of the monks to return to working the land and nobody knows what became of many of them. A lama can always return to secular life, marrying and raising a family.

The great Potala Palace, built on the rocky foundations of the Red Hill, like a mountain itself, dominates Lhasa and the surrounding countryside. It was built by the fifth Dalai Lama, Ngawong Gyatso (1617-82), so outstanding both as a priest and a statesman that he is known as 'the Great Fifth'. He not only built this huge palace which became to every Tibetan the symbol of their theocracy but he also completed the work of previous great reformers. He unified the different elements and sects of Tibetan society and established the principles of theocratic rule which continued until the Chinese invasion. In theory, under Ngawong Gyatso's constitution, the lamahood, led by the Dalai Lama, ruled Tibet jointly with a large group of secular noblemen who undertook the important administrative work. In theory the nobility were not supposed to be hereditary but to earn their positions of power and wealth, by personal virtue and ability. Every Tibetan paid taxes to the monastic rulers but in turn the monasteries were supposed to protect the people and to provide for them in time of need. Since the Tibetans base their whole life and society on their religious faith, for them a theocracy is the natural form of government and the system as drawn up by 'the Great Fifth' was a benevolent one, if not entirely democratic as it placed enormous power and wealth in the hands of the leading lamas. No doubt, human nature being what it is, abuses crept into the system. Just as many lamas have perverted tantric Buddhism, proving that not all lamas were holy men, so many others must have taken advantage of a political system so easily abused. Certain highly placed Tibetans have written of Tibet as a land where lamas, farmers and nomads lived in Utopian harmony under the guidance of an almost wholly benevolent clergy. Other, Western, accounts have told of the abject condition of many of the lay-monks living in virtual slavery and of such facts that some 80 per cent of Tibetans suffered from some kind of skin-disease. I find the latter particularly easy to believe.

The white walls of the Potala Palace rise sheer from its rocky base, its decorated roofs some 125 metres above the floor of the valley. All round the foot of the Red Hill is a crumbling town with decrepit but originally grand buildings with carved entranceways. These were once occupied by the administrative nobility. Passing through this now dusty slum, long, wide flights of stone stairways lead to the main entrance on the east side. Above are a further four-storeys of vermilion balconies and higher still, a crowning central block with yellow-orange walls, the roof corners glinting with gilt finials.

Inside all is exactly what the foreigner has imagined of this ancient and secret place. Only the Dalai Lama and his retinue are missing. The palace rises through many levels, an extraordinary mixture of royal palace, monastery and temple. It is confusing and cavernous like an impenetrable oriental-Byzantine labyrinth. The gloom, the steep stairways, the glittering chapels, the sweet smell of the yak butter lamps, the occasional lama squatting in a dark corner, muttering his devotions or tending the floating lamps, the towering, threatening statues and the images of previous Dalai Lamas, the silver altars and the reliquaries encrusted with pearls, all help to conjure up the former life of the palace. Tibetan pilgrims throng through every room and chapel, the women offering liquid butter, the families half-curious, half-devout. In theory the Dalai Lama is a mere human vessel for the reincarnation of Chenresig, protective deity of Tibet, but in practice the simple Tibetan reveres the Dalai Lama as a divine person. They ask you to pray for his return; they implore you to give them his photograph. Whatever else, they are a tolerant people and in these sacred places one is made welcome.

The devotional objects, the textiles, the sculpture are all fascinating if not of any great quality. From the roofs to the subterranean chapels the palace is crowded with images, draperies, bizarre devotional objects and wall-paintings depicting the legends and history of Tibet. The Chinese have now even opened up the Dalai Lama's private apartments and chapels, incongruously equipped with light fittings in the cheapest and worst taste of the 1940s. There was the throne room, the withdrawing room, the private chapel and a quaint bedroom, all of them oppressively gloomy, an over-draped and over-furnished claustrophobia which no doubt to the Dalai Lama seemed normal enough and even luxurious.

In contrast to all this is the bright, wide view of Lhasa and the southern surroundings from the roof of the palace. One can follow the narrow streets of old Lhasa to the east from this near-aerial view, the old houses clustering around the golden pinnacles of the Jokhang Temple. Below and to the west the newer Chinese town, drab from any angle, spreads and keeps on spreading, workers' apartments and soldiers' barracks. Beyond in every direction the rugged mountains enclose this part of the plateau, a rough, rising wall, the mere foothills of the great mountains that lie beyond around the old 'Forbidden City'. Having seen so much, I cannot help wishing that I had seen it all fifty years ago. That is a kind of traveller's greed. On the other hand at present so much is left which may be gone in another fifty years that my greed is balanced with gratitude.

6

The Long River

THE YANGZI: CHONGQING TO WUHAN

The flight in the small Russian plane from Chengdu to Chongqing was packed. So was the bus from the airport into the city. The ride was fascinating and at first beautiful as we lumbered up and down steep hills where the terraced vegetables fell away sharply to the glistening wet rice fields on the floors of the small valleys. A morning mist hung over this green landscape which for a few kilometres was idyllic enough. The road grew steeper until, almost like tumbling downstairs, we rumbled headlong into a sulphurous smog and the dark outskirts of industrial Chongqing.

The town is built on a steep hill above the confluence of the Yangzi and the Jialing Rivers. In the 1930s, during the Sino-Japanese war, it became the capital of the Nationalists who brought with them institutions and industry which led to the growth of the city. It was severely bombed by the Japanese and one still sees the old air raid shelters all over the city, but in recent years the population has increased to over 6 million with large-scale production of iron and steel, machine tools, vehicles, chemicals and textiles. Chongqing is burning hot in summer, covered in mist and fog in winter and with an industrial smog at all seasons whose sour smell and taste even follow you into your hotel bedroom.

But the town has a distinctive if sombre character, some of the old, jettied houses left among the newer ones built of brick. It is a city of curious, lopsided alleys, many running up and down the hillsides in long, steep flights of stone steps. Every lane and every narrow alley was crowded and alive with activity: buying, selling, laundry, crafts-men, garbage, mud and little children going about their business in the gutters. One afternoon I walked out towards the oldest part of the town on a dramatic promontory raised above the river. I might have been walking in London's Limehouse of the nineteenth century. The flights of steps ran up and down from the main street, leading into gloomy alleys where decrepit tenements and dark-stained stucco houses clung precariously to the urban cliffside, a clutter of disintegrating habitations blackened by grime, smoke and decay. Factory chimneys darkened the sky along the river and men and women on several building sites manhandled rough blocks of stone and humped overloaded baskets of gravel. I passed a few markets in the side streets and on the main street, small restaurants, women with baskets of oranges and a street lending library where small boys, perched on tiny stools, devoured what seemed to be cheap comic books.

The hazy view down to the river and the docks opened up like a dark chasm. The ramshackle houses were scattered across the hillsides, their balconies crowded with rubbish. The steps snaked everywhere with small railway lines running up from the shore to the factories. The river water was as muddily polluted as the dirty atmosphere. One tenement building looked particularly filthy and disordered, each balcony an individual rubbish dump of rags, old baskets, cracked pots, dead plants, matting, broken boxes and other bric à brac. Then I happened to catch a glimpse through one of the windows into a poor but spotless room where a man was finishing washing at an enamel basin, drying his hands with a clean white towel. I marvel at how the Chinese maintain such a high standard of cleanliness amidst such total poverty. No doubt part of their pride, it is worthy of admiration.

The Renmin Hotel is certainly the most memorable sight in Chongqing and probably the most lavish piece of hotel architecture in China. I remember struggling down a main avenue with our baggage and suddenly the sky above us was filled by a vast and richly decorated circular tower, obviously inspired by the Temple of Heaven in Beijing. Around the next corner the whole tower was revealed with two massive wings spreading out on either side, the whole building raised on the crest of a long hill with a huge flight of steps leading to the main entrance. The central drum tower with a green-tiled roof in three layers is below supported by ranks of small vermilion pillars. The tower houses a large concert hall with a capacity of 4000 seats. At the end of each wing is a pagoda-shaped turret, balanced by smaller turrets at the inner ends. The main façades of each wing are of four-storeys, supported by large single or smaller paired columns, with white Chinese railings between the columns acting as a balustrade. There the imperial splendour ends abruptly. The hotel is fronted by a bedraggled garden while on the opposite hill is an amphitheatre of gloomy apartments.

On arrival I must have made the same mistake made by most foreigners. I struggled to the top of the very steep flight of stone steps to check in at this most impressive hotel only to find a charming Chinese lady eager to sell me a couple of tickets for a concert of Chinese classical music. I expect she wondered why we were so late and why we brought such a large amount of luggage to a concert. It certainly never entered her head that we were looking for the hotel front desk as after five minutes of trying to explain I gave her up and sought help elsewhere. Eventually we discovered that the hotel was housed in the two wings and we had to retreat half-way down the steps to find the front desk obscurely hidden at the back. From then on it was all anticlimax. Behind that magnificent façade lurked a seedy, third-rate hotel run with the minimum of efficiency. The service in the surprisingly small restaurant was friendly but the food dull despite the fact that we were still in Sichuan. But we had come to Chongqing as the starting point for the famous boat ride down the Yangzi and fortunately our tickets came through in two days so we had only a short stay in this extraordinary mausoleum. I think that the residents on the hill opposite had the best of the Renmin Hotel – the view.

At 6.15 a.m. we arrived at the ferry terminal in the heart of the Yangzi docks. The area seethed with people, some crowding around street restaurants, others surging towards the entrances to the quays. Moving amongst them were dozens of porters, each eager to grab his share of the passengers' baggage. The group of foreign passengers were led down the vertical flight of steps to the landing stage. Most of the steps were occupied by a massive queue of would-be passengers, patiently seated from top to bottom, charmingly headed by a small girl in a bright red dress. I wondered if she had been here all night to achieve this leading position.

We had another forty minutes' wait before one boat pulled out and ours came alongside, already heavily laden on the lower decks with third- and fourth-class passengers. We scrambled aboard, edging our way through the packed gangways, the accommodation for the fourth-class who had already established themselves on woven mats, enclosed by their boxes and bundles. The noise was overwhelming. The spitting followed closely behind. Our second-class cabin was inside on the upper deck. There was no first class in this egalitarian society. How comforting the euphemistic 'second class' must have been to those prone on the steel decks for the next three days.

Our cabin was surprisingly large and in an austere way comfortable. Forward there was a pleasant saloon with a good view over the river and a long way aft, through the third-class section, a dingey dining saloon with reasonable food. All these river boats looked delapidated but despite the enormous number of passengers, once we had pulled out into mid-stream we moved forward at a good speed. We were due to reach Wuhan in three days, with a number of stops on the way, and that was a distance of about 1500 km. The second-class section was occupied mostly by a large group of Americans and Germans, who looked both bored and bewildered. There was one other solo traveller, an elderly, skinny Australian, a sparrow-like figure perpetually on the scrounge. He had hardly arrived on board before he was working out how he could get a free lift in the group's bus at Wuhan. Well equipped with stories of the outback, Wagga-Wagga, his experiences in the Second World War and contemporary life in Canberra, he proved our Ancient Mariner, skinny arm and all.

As we moved away from the dock and down the river, the sun struggled to break through the dark early morning cloud and mist. We were heading for the three great gorges of the Yangzi, some of the largest and most perilous in the world, but we should not reach them until the following day. For the moment it was exciting enough to be speeding down the world's third longest river after the Amazon and the Nile, with a total length of 6300 km and a drainage area of more than 1,800,000 sq km. The river's source is way to the west in the Tanggula Mountains dividing Qinghai from Tibet. It flows south through Sichuan and Yunnan where it turns eastwards and the main Yangzi flows across central China and into the East China Sea at Shanghai. For centuries it has been China's main line of communication, mother of life and culture. It was between the southern Yangzi and the northern Yellow River that the civilisation of the Middle Kingdom was born, at least 6000 years ago.

That first day the Yangzi was muddy brown, and turbulent with eddies and currents. The channel was clearly marked by frequent buoys but it must have been necessary to keep a sharp lookout for the narrow channels passing great humps of rock sticking out of the water with no doubt larger obstacles below the surface. There was not as much river traffic as I had expected though there was considerable variety. Long bamboo rafts drifted with the current with the aid of long oars fore and aft. Small junks, some with five

19 River traffic

YANGZI RIVER

20 Heading into the gorges

21 A lakeside view

HANGZHOU

22 General Yue Fei's assassin

23 Rock carving at Lingyin Si Temple

oarsmen, some with a small sail, kept a respectful distance from the tugs and steamers hauling groups of barges, mostly carrying coal, a few with bricks or timber. It was enough to give the feel of the ancient waterway, now servicing small black towns huddled around smoking factories, lime- or brick-works, scarring the rural banks of the river. Spring was everywhere, a freshness in the vegetable plots, a vividness among the crops, blossom on the fruit trees. At sunset, the boat followed the twisting river in a westerly direction. A huge white-gold sun hung among the clouds and across the dark water spread flashing scales of soft gold, like a sea-dragon glittering just below the surface.

The following morning we entered the Qutang Gorge in bright sun, but with mist still clinging to the mountains. The first of the three gorges is only 8 km long, the shortest, but with its towering cliffs enclosing the river, the most dramatic of the three. One enters through the Kuimen Gate, with the Red Armour Mountain on one side and the White Salt Mountain on the other. The waters are turbulent, the cliffs rising sheer out of the running currents, faces of rock mingling with clinging green vegetation. At the head of the cliffs morning mist lingered in smoking patches with higher rocky peaks behind. The passageway between the great walls is narrow and the boat is dwarfed in the depth of the gorge. In places the banks jut out into the water like floating gardens, softening the stark grandeur. But this is a gorge of towering rocks and cliff, the river squeezed into cross-running currents and lines of foam where the water is pressed against the cliff face.

The Wu Gorge is 44 km long, stretching from the Daning River to the Guandu ferry in Hubei province. It is famous for its depth and the beauty of the great cliffs rising on both sides with views of forested mountains stretching away into the distance. It is a landscape of strange rock formations and layer after layer of hills. The twelve beautiful peaks of Wu stand on either bank with trees breaking and softening the long views. In places the cliffs rise to about 900 metres.

Eighty kilometres long, the Xiling Gorge runs from the mouth of the Fragrant Stream through to the modern Gezhoura dam. It is full of large stone reefs and dangerous shoals, the mountainsides green with small pines. Again there are deep, receding vistas into the surrounding mountains and tremendous sandstone rockfaces, rising sheer from the river or shadowing it with long overhangs. There is a greater variety of colour here with black, red, brown and grey rock set off against the greens of spring, fresh leaves and new vegetation.

During the passage through the gorges I moved about the boat, pushing along the crowded decks to find the best viewing points. Despite the discomfort the Chinese were travelling in, they remained good-tempered and friendly though their quarters became more and more squalid. In these wanderings I found one woman with an exceptionally lively face who had taught herself good if stilted English. She was working on a water purification project and she not only took her work with deep seriousness but seemed likely to be an earnest member of the party. We were passing through the huge Gezhoura Dam when foolishly, but in all innocence, I asked her if it had been built with Russian help. She assured me with tight politeness that it was a completely Chinese project.

One goes through the gorges too quickly and as the boat turned a corner and some magnificent view disappeared I desperately wanted a replay. The boat moved so fast, despite the difficult navigation, and I had mere glimpses of historic caves, a pagoda high on the mountainside, small towns along the river and many historic places. I would like to do the journey again in a small boat in my own time, stopping to examine all the places of legend and history or simply to pause and give the views the time they deserve. There is nothing more frustrating than to be rushed through a vast scenic marvel of this kind that requires at least three weeks, not three days, to appreciate it. People often say, particularly those who have made the boat ride at Guilin, that after that the Yangzi trip is too long and a disappointment compared to the Guilin landscape. The truth is that both are magnificent and both are different. I am normally reticent in making emphatic recommendations to other travellers, but I recommend without reserve the three days on the Yangzi. It is not just the dramatic beauty of the three gorges, it is the whole experience of riding that historic river, the shabby river boat, the steady throb of the engines under your pillow through the night and your fellow passengers, tired tourists and the hoardes of ever-chattering Chinese, not to mention the hardest of hard-boiled eggs for breakfast. Each is part of a memorable experience.

Our cobber from Wagga-Wagga, or wherever it was, not only wheedled himself onto the group's bus, but had got places for Yuki-san and myself. Faced with the frenzy of the quayside and the total lack of taxis at the Wuhan port I was grateful. But a small voice inside me predicted that we should come to regret the free ride. I had already consulted my guide-book which listed three hotels and said of the last that it was among the worst in China and to be avoided at all costs, not least because it was a long way from everywhere.

We were hardly seated in the bus when the local guide from Wuhan started to address the group through the microphone. He welcomed them to Wuhan and went on to say that by the greatest good fortune, the group was going to stay at the Shengli Hotel, which he described in glowing terms in direct contradiction to the entry I had open on my knee. The guide-book was totally accurate but we were trapped. It was too late to think of moving. In case anyone should think of staying there I will ignore the general hopelessness of the front desk, of trying to get a taxi and the poor food and concentrate on the description of the bedroom. The main wall of the bathroom had grown a huge green, spongey fungus. The basin was cracked and plugless. The bath was interesting: the hot tap produced no hot water and the shower was firmly fixed so that it sprayed outwards towards the basin. The choice therefore was a cold bath or a hot shower followed by a sharp attack of 'slipped disc'. The bedroom was humid and smelt damp, and once you were in bed, ugly, brown, seeping blisters in the ceiling dropped flakes of soggy plaster onto your face with a fiendish irregularity. I will not linger on the rats who left a large hole in the bag where Yuki kept our emergency rations. But why should the Chinese waste their money doing up such a place? After all, you've nowhere else to stay. In a way the Wuhan guide was right. It is good fortune to stay at the Shengli Hotel if the alternative is the street.

It was raining heavily the next day and we had to go miles across town to find the airline office to buy tickets for Shanghai. We wasted half an hour at the front desk before we realised that our request for a taxi was absurd. Taxis simply didn't get as far as this suburban area. In the end we took a bus and at the other end with considerable help from a kind Chinese we found the office and bought tickets for the following morning. Everywhere we went in China people took great trouble to help us find our way, frequently walking with us consider- able distances out of their way. It is amazing to read books written less than ten years ago when Chinese turned away rather than become involved with a foreigner. It may not be enormously signifi- cant but it does show a marked change of attitude, some of which must have filtered from the top. On the way back to the hotel we passed the great bridge over the Yangzi where in 1966 Chairman Mao made his well-publicised swim across the river. We left Wuhan with a good memory of Chinese kindness and a feeling of satisfaction that we had cruised through the Yangzi gorges along one of the greatest rivers of the world.

7

Along the Grand Canal

SUZHOU, HANGZHOU AND SHANGHAI

The Grand Canal is one of the few remaining vast projects which demonstrate not only that China has possessed the longest continuous civilisation in the world, but arguably the greatest. When the whole canal was in working order, it stretched 1800 km from Beijing to Hangzhou, joining the four great east-west rivers – the Yangzi, Yellow River, Huai River and Qiantang – and providing China with an enormous grid of navigable waters. The Grand Canal (Da Yunhe) was constructed at three different periods. The first sections were dug in the north about 400 BC to help with troop movements. The main part of the canal was built during the Sui dynasty (AD 581–618) by the ruthless Emperor Yang Di who wished to link his new capital Luoyang with the old capital of Xi'an. This not only speeded up the movement of his armies but brought the grain taxes north to feed them. During the Tang dynasty it has been calculated that one million tonnes of grain went north each year. Later Yang Di extended the canal south to Hangzhou, while on the thirteenth century Kublai Khan brought the canal north to his new capital at Beijing.

It is now impossible to calculate the work and manpower involved in creating this long waterway, particularly as it was dug with only rough tools. At its narrowest points the canal is 9 metres wide and up to 3 metres deep. Remembering that the canal is crossed by countless small bridges, the boats that navigated it must have been flat-bottomed vessels of a maximum of about 600 tonnes. There is no doubt that the canal was heavily used for grain and other bulky freight and on occasions, Emperors in their state barges had other traffic cleared so that they might make their stately progress.

Much of the Grand Canal has fallen into disuse and been allowed to silt up. A great deal was lost through neglect between 1960 and 1980 and today, even at the best season for navigation, probably about 900 km are still in use. In the area between Suzhou and Hangzhou there is still heavy traffic adding great character to the area. The Grand Canal, which brought power to the Emperors of China, also brought great prosperity to the towns along its banks, cheap transport fostering their local crafts and industries. The silk industry flourished and the same towns were centres of the grain market. The tradition of 'light industry' has come through to the present day and southern Jiangsu province and northern Zhejiang have not been blighted either by the ugliness or the failure of Mao's beloved heavy industry. Neighbouring Shanghai also provides a huge and ready market for all light industrial products.

An old Chinese saying maintains that 'Heaven is above; on earth we have Suzhou and Hangzhou.' Certainly, those who seek an older and more picturesque China will find some of what they are hoping for in these two fascinating towns, even if the willow-pattern plate is rather chipped around the edges. I believe that there is now a tourist boat running on the Grand Canal between them but it has a poor reputation and both towns are easily accessible by train from Shanghai. That is how I went to Suzhou with my son and daughter and I remember the charming landscape from the train and, more vividly, our arrival at Suzhou station.

The Chinese have a habit of siting their railway stations at the opposite end of the town from all tourist facilities such as hotels, an admirable piece of town planning if there were adequate transport between the two areas. When we stepped out of the station at Suzhou, the place appeared totally deserted. I knew that the hotels were in the southern part of the town 4 km away and the thought of walking there with our luggage through the midday July heat was not appealing. Suddenly, at the edge of the area in front of the station, I saw a shadow move and walking over found three rickshaw men dozing in the shade. We gave them the name of the hotel and despite their considerable age they sprang into action, piling us into their equally frail vehicles, dumping the luggage in our laps and setting off at a good pace along the roads shaded by plane trees. We caught glimpses of small waterways, bridges, a pagoda and what were almost certainly entrances to some of Suzhou's famous gardens. At last we came to the compound of the hotel which included several buildings surrounded by pleasant gardens.

Although Suzhou is not large by Chinese standards, with a population of only about 600,000, it seems large when you are walking and there is a great deal scattered around the town which is worth seeing. Too many sites here are too good to miss and Suzhou is a place where it is a good investment to hire a car and driver for at least one day, as the driver will probably save you hours in finding the more obscure places. But the car is specifically for sightseeing. You will get the flavour of Suzhou only by walking. I think I would recommend the first day walking, taking in the few famous gardens near the hotel and having a car on the second day for the more distant sights. Apart from temples and pagodas, there are now at least seven fine classical gardens open to the public but unless you are a specialist, you may find seven monotonous and in a short time might get more pleasure from a limited choice. Whatever you decide to see, I think you will find Suzhou one of the most picturesque towns in China.

But few things in China are exactly as one expects. I went to Suzhou primarily to see the gardens and while I was not exactly disappointed, they were different from what I had expected. I had already spent many years enjoying the gardens of Japan in all their gentle subtlety and I had expected to find a familiar archetype in China which provided the origins and inspiration of so much in Japanese culture. Although it is a matter of fact that both Japanese gardening and branches of special horticulture such as bonsai derived from China, to my mind it is one of those cases where the pupil improved on the master. I make this judgement largely on the experience of the seven celebrated gardens of Suzhou. However, these gardens have obviously been seriously neglected for many years, although by a miracle they survived the Cultural Revolution. The expert books say that gardens of this kind tended towards a stark style in which the carefully chosen and often grotesque rocks could be fully appreciated but there is a difference between stark and bleak. I have a feeling that in the time of the mandarins who created these retreats they were more fully planted, more carefully tended and that in those days there was a gentle dimension to the view which neglect has turned into a slight harshness. The warmth of the personal creation has been eroded by time, leaving only a bare skeleton of the original design. Everywhere, garden design is a fleeting glory, often vanishing in a few years of neglect.

The Chinese have long made a distinction between imperial and private gardens and they also agree that the finest private gardens are to be found in Suzhou. Even before you have visited them, you may be enchanted by their romantic names suggesting the lacquered pavilions, the ponds and the drooping willows that await you. You may choose between the 'Humble Administrator's Garden', or meander through the 'Lingering Garden', going on to the 'Lion Grove Garden', or the 'Master of the Nets Garden'. Nature and landscape painting contribute to these private dreams where a few friends gathered to talk, to drink wine and to read poetry. In every way they fulfil the Western imagining of cultured Chinese life, each garden a private world beyond the main residence fronting the busy street, a place of retirement in every sense. But it would be misleading to emphasise a sense of privacy. Sadly, you will not enjoy these gardens in the company of their erudite owners. You are more likely to make a noisy circuit in the company of many Chinese holiday-makers. Whatever their contribution may be, it will not be serenity.

Like most Suzhou gardens that of the 'Humble Administrator' is hedged by legend. It was built early in the sixteenth century by Wang Xianchen, an official censor, who some say built the garden in retirement after being demoted, others that he built it with money he had extorted through his official position. In the north-east of the town, the garden consists of 5 hectares of water garden, its various pavilions separated by wide ponds, streams, stone bridges and islands with flanks of large stones rising from the water. This is a garden of water, the soft surfaces of the ponds, the myriad reflections and the lily pads and willow tails trailing in the rippled mirrors.

The 'Master of the Nets Garden' is the smallest in Suzhou, first created in the twelfth century and restored in the eighteenth century. One tale reports that it was founded by an official who, weary of his official duties, retired here to fish. The garden makes clever use of the limited space. There is a perfect harmony between the buildings and the parts of the garden, joined by covered winding walkways where red-lacquered pillars and delicate latticework contrast with the contortions of old trees and rocks. Across one stream is the 'Bridge-leading-to-quietness', the smallest in Suzhou, town of bridges where Marco Polo exaggeratedly estimated 'that there were fully 6000 stone bridges'. Today, there are certainly over 300.

Each garden has its special features. The 'Lion Grove Garden', built in 1350 by a monk in memory of his spiritual master, has fine rocks suggesting lions' heads and small grottoes among the rocks. The 'Surging Wave Pavilion' is a small garden dating originally from the eleventh century. To make the garden appear larger the design uses its surroundings, creating the illusion that they too are part of the garden. This technique of 'borrowed gardening' was widely and cleverly used in Japan. Nowhere is the harmony between garden and architecture better seen than in the 'Lingering Garden', a large garden built in the Ming period. In the buildings and along the covered walkways attractively shaped windows, some blank, some latticed, give sudden glimpses of the garden providing a further link between garden and architecture.

In all these gardens, trees, shrubs and flowers soften the designs and give different moods for each season. From the wistaria of late spring through to the cascading gold of the autumn ginkos the changing beauty of the seasons enlivens these artificial microcosms of nature and the admired and idealised mountain scenery of southern China. It is a wonder that so many Suzhou gardens have survived, and in such basically good condition. I hope that the Suzhou Garden Society, founded in 1979, will continue the restoration of these gardens and eventually bring them back to their original beauty and restore the subtlety that the men of taste originally imbued them with when they created these retreats from the busy world.

Even allowing for Marco Polo's tendency to exaggerate, I envy him his view of Suzhou in the late thirteenth century, this town of rich silk merchants and criss-crossing canals which must have made the Venetian feel at home. Marco Polo has a strange habit in his eulogising to switch from the obviously magnificent to the strangely obscure. 'In the nearby mountains they grow ginger and rhubarb in huge quantitites. The small Venetian coin would purchase forty pounds of the finest ginger.' His interest no doubt reflected the high prices that exotic spices fetched in medieval Europe where ginger would have been a precious commodity. Suzhou at that time was enclosed by rectangular walls surrounded by an outer moat, with six gates around the walls. The town was crossed by six canals running north to south and fourteen from east to west, the town's canal system linked to the Grand Canal. Even if Marco Polo's estimate was generous, there is evidence that around that time the town had 359 bridges, some fifty temples and twelve pagodas.

The physical glories of Suzhou have been diminished and the air of wealth has vanished, but it remains a fascinating town of waterways and water life where one can wander for hours along the canal paths or the streets where the low white houses back onto the canals. In the shade of the broad planes people sit at their front doors or scrub their washing by kerb or canal side. There are still many stone bridges of different designs, square, curved or steep and humpbacked like Wumen Bridge, the highest single arch in Suzhou. The sampans and the barges move slowly along the waterways laboriously rowed by pairs of men or girls. Children in bright coats hurry to school over the bridges, men shout and strain as they load barges on the narrow wharves, housewives gossip by the crouched, black-tiled houses while from a nearby window a woman tips a bucket of night-soil into the picturesque canal which a few yards away a local artist captures for a romanticised woodblock print. Every day and any day these scenes are yours in return for the effort of a walk. It is a romantic scene, despite the occasional intrusions of reality and it is unique in China.

And there is still more in and around Suzhou. You can climb the nine-storey pagoda of the North Temple, which not only gives you a fine view of the town and the neighbouring countryside but is an interesting opportunity to examine in detail the elaborate construction of a great pagoda. In the centre of Suzhou's main market is the Taoist Temple of Mystery, founded in the third century but frequently altered in later times. The founder of Suzhou in the sixth century BC, King He Lu, is buried to the north-west of the town on Tiger Hill where there is a leaning pagoda built in AD 961. Evidently in the present century it came near to toppling over but as the symbol of Suzhou that is unthinkable. It has now been elaborately underpinned. Having toured the gardens, motored around the temples and walked the canals and lively streets of Suzhou, good food awaits you. Food in Suzhou is particularly seasonal, crab caught in a local lake, squirrel fish or candied strawberries washed down with Snail Spring tea. The interiors of even the best restaurants are not elegant but who cares if you are hungry enough and the food is good. A yearning for elegance in China would be a short cut to starvation.

Following the Grand Canal, or the railway, south of Shanghai, one finds the second paradise on earth of the old saying: Hangzhou. It is a larger and wholly different city to Suzhou, each with its own beauty, character and special attractions. At the end of the twelfth century (1126), the Song court, defeated by the barbarian Jurchen, fled south and made their new capital at Hangzhou, founding the Southern Song dynasty (1127–1279). Although Hangzhou had prospered ever since it had been joined to the Grand Canal, now it enjoyed a great political and cultural flowering, the population increasing by over a million to 1¾ million by 1275. During this period

Hangzhou became not only a great commercial centre but enjoyed a great renaissance which made the city famous for calligraphy, painting and all the arts which were fostered by the court and the administrative classes. In the Chinese view of history it remains China's Florence. Much of its influence continued even after the Mongol invasion when they made Beijing their new capital. In the nineteenth century, first the Taipings in 1861 and the imperial armies after that virtually destroyed the city and it never recovered its former importance. Today the population is about one million.

We travelled to Hangzhou by train from Shanghai. By express it takes three hours and on that spring day it was a beautiful ride. It is always a relief to be free of the congestion of Shanghai, released into the countryside where the landscape is characterised by water; rivers, canals, streams and ponds, all feeding the irrigation ditches and the rice fields. This is a richly fertile area and the wheat and rice are soft and green around the low white farmhouses with their curving tiled roofs. Everywhere there were great sweeps of bright yellow rape adding brilliance to the land and in marvellous contrast to the clear blue sky. Vegetables grew in such profusion and variety that in the end we gave up trying to identify them.

We travelled with a Chinese who had been born in China but must have fled early in his life to Taiwan. He had taken his degree at London University and was now working for the United Nations, obviously with a good salary and a pleasant American life-style. He was scornful of everything and everybody in China and unsympathetic to the problems of the country. It seemed sadly typical that a senior bureaucrat of the United Nations should have such an unbalanced view of his own country. But his wealthy arrogance was typical of the Chinese families who fled from China and established the republican regime in Taiwan. Whatever one might feel about the record of the Chinese Communist Party, the Kuomintang under the leadership of Chiang Kai-shek behaved with appalling brutality and greed wherever they went, in China and later in Taiwan.

At Hangzhou station we knew we had to find the number seven bus for our hotel. In trying to find it we acquired a charming elderly Chinese man. He spoke only about ten words of English but bravely put them at our disposal. He took us to the correct bus stop and indicated that he was also catching our bus. It must have been the evening rush hour for there were at least seventy Chinese waiting for the bus. When the first bus came, already hopelessly overcrowded, a violent fight, complete with fists and kicking, took place as people struggled to get on board. I can understand that tired workers become frustrated by the inadequate bus services, tempers fray and fists fly. Our friend was charmingly solicitous, and unnecessarily apologetic, and kept holding Yuki-san back until with the sixth bus forty minutes later he decided that it was safe for her to get aboard. Once on board the crowded bus, however, we were shown the reverse side of Chinese public manners. An elderly woman got up and insisted that I take her seat. I suspect that she was twenty years older than me but there was no refusing her. It is hard to make judgements about the Chinese faced with such contradictions.

Hangzhou caught me completely by surprise. I had expected another rather cosy small town like Suzhou, compact and picturesque. In every way Hangzhou is on a grander scale. It is a large city with a population of about one million, its streets so packed with bicycles that our bus advanced in a zigzag fashion dodging its way forward at about 8 kph, meandering through shady streets before we eventually came to the edge of the beautiful West Lake. In a way there are two towns: the main teeming Hangzhou, and another more spacious tourist resort all around the edge of the lake. The main town has plenty of character, with lively market areas, pleasant tree-lined streets and, between the crouching backs of old houses, filthy, winding waterways. Everyone should break away from the obvious delights of the lakeside for at least one long walk through the main town.

The Hangzhou Hotel turned out to be an oasis of comfort and modern facilities. The hotel, composed of several buildings, stood in a large garden on the hillside by the lake. The main building was still old-fashioned but a neighbouring building had been renovated to the point of luxury with attractively decorated rooms enjoying marvellous views across the lake. Nor had I ever expected to lie comfortably in a Chinese hotel bed and watch *Singing in the Rain* on closed-circuit television. The hotel restaurant was memorable for the small and youthful orchestra which played each evening, rather than for its mediocre food. They played with great verve but somehow nine violins and cellos, an electric guitar and a frustrated jazz drummer do not make a good musical mixture. Their star piece was a special arrangement of *The Sting*, and they turned the Scott Joplin syncopations into the disciplined beat of a military march. They played every evening, always exactly the same tunes in exactly the same order. In its own way it was all very Chinese. I hurried back to my room to catch the late showing of *There's No Business Like Show Business*. Old movies are always nostalgic. In the heart of China they are emotionally overwhelming.

The West Lake and the pavilions and pleasure domes of the Southern Song court are now the park and Sunday pleasure ground of crowds of Chinese tourists, gawping, photographing each other with hired cameras, scattering peanut shells and honeymooning in tin paddle-boats at two fen an hour. The lake and its landscape remain beautiful, across the water hump-backed stone bridges, long walks shaded by willows and the intricate silhouettes of small pavilions crowning the green islands. The surrounding hills, covered in deep forest, were blurred in a haze of heat. It is only a faint shadow of what it must once have been but the shadow is a satisfying and beautiful one.

Solitary Hill Island is opposite the hotel. It has a road running around it and is linked by a long causeway to the northern shore. There are many buildings on the island, restaurants, pleasant tea-houses and one or two delapidated memorials to the former cultural life of Hangzhou. I liked best the old garden and pavilions scattered up the hillside which were the headquarters of the local society of calligraphers and seal engravers. The gardens were charming and the paths led up between flowering azaleas and softly drooping wistaria growing over heavy wooden trellises. Everywhere there were beautifully inscribed memorial tablets, ponds and rocks, and at each level a new view of the lake. Inside some of the pavilions were fine examples of calligraphy and in one pavilion were two young craftsmen engraving seals in the traditional way.

We should not have noticed this charming place with a private-looking entrance had it not been for another encounter with a Chinese eager to practise his English. This time it was an elderly man on a bicycle who stopped us just as we were passing the garden. He had been trained as an electrical engineer and had learned English at a missionary school in Shanghai early in the 1940s. Now he was living in Hangzhou and translating technical magazines. I should have liked to ask what had happened to him in between, how he felt when the communists came to power in 1949, what had happened to him during the Cultural Revolution, why he had moved, or been moved to Hangzhou. Each time we had one of these brief and tantalising conversations I had to struggle not to ask the interesting questions. He had certainly kept up his English well and said that it was a great pleasure to live in Hangzhou. As he left he recommended us to cross the road and visit the seal society.

Down the road from the hotel, by a confusion of bus stops and old-fashioned shops mainly for the crowds of Chinese tourists, is the Mausoleum of General Yue Fei, a national hero who, in a conspiracy in 1141, was falsely accused and executed. With one of those adjustments that Chairman Mao was good at, the twelfth-century general is now made to appear as an early hero of the Revolution. The mausoleum is like a large temple with courtyard gardens, huge crowds and a memorial hall occupied by a clumsy modern statue of the general and crude murals showing scenes from his life. In an inner courtyard are older stone statues of the four evil conspirators who caused the death of the general. They are shown realistically bound and kneeling in disgrace before his tomb. Even today many visitors slap their stone heads but there is a notice above the offenders requesting visitors not to express their disapproval by spitting. The notice did nothing to deter this activity elsewhere.

Some way further along the lakeside is the ancient temple called Lingyin Si with the cliffside opposite covered in Buddhist carvings. The temple was built originally in AD 326 but was destroyed many times. The buildings that remain today are restorations of the Qing Dynasty. It is said that the temple and the cliff sculptures were saved during the Cultural Revolution by the decision of Zhou Enlai. Today they are rather seedy but interesting and packed with sightseers. There are many signs of devotion with forests of candles and sticks of incense in front of the main altars but there are only a handful of aged monks to look after the place and to keep it in some kind of order. For all the bustle of the sightseers there is a forlornness about these neglected temples which once must have enjoyed such magnificence and splendid ritual.

The sculptured figures on the side of the Feilai Feng hill are highly interesting and some of great beauty. I thought they were the finest works of art I saw in southern China, with little competition. After weeks of tawdriness, it was intoxicating to look at something of real quality. The earliest sculptures date from about AD 950, a group of three Buddhist divinities to the right of the Qing Lin cave. Altogether there are some 330 sculptures carved in the rock face at different levels. It would take hours to examine them all properly, not least as the precarious paths are choked with Chinese holiday-makers struggling to line their wives or girlfriends in front of a suitable Buddhist deity for a souvenir snapshot. But fortunately the rather coarse, pot-bellied, laughing Maitreya is a far greater attraction than the delicate Buddhas who sit in the lotus-position remote in their sanctity and serenity.

As you leave the temple, on the left are large tea-plantations producing the famous and delicate green tea of Hangzhou. It provides the perfect oriental scene with which to leave Hangzhou. The low bushes stretch away across the rising ground to the forest beyond. Here and there, bending over the squat, neatly shaped bushes, are girls in wide straw hats, with deep woven baskets slung from their hips. Rapidly but meticulously they pick the young budding leaves of spring which produce the best green tea. Looking at this scene, one that even the Southern Song Dynasty could still recognise, I was reminded how those small green leaves had for centuries been the most important link between East and West. The ships of the East India Company came primarily for Chinese tea, also carrying back Chinese porcelain teapots and teacups for the wealthy to indulge this new fashion, a fashion that in Britain was to turn into a national habit. Other ships carried tea to Portugal and Holland while for several centuries the camel caravans took bricks of tea to Russia. Perhaps at one time or another tea from the fields of Hangzhou found its way into the cups of Europe.

I have been to Shanghai five times and each time I have failed to fall under the spell that enchants many people; so many that I know I must be wrong. Those who praise Shanghai most strongly have almost all lived there and I have always felt that one could not begin to come to grips with China's largest city of 11 million people without living there. I feel a Scrooge about Shanghai as I dislike just about everything that others admire. I think the much-praised Peace Hotel is one of the gloomiest places in the world. People despair that its fine lobbies have been spoiled by intrusive partitioning. I find it an academic question as I can see no sign of anything to spoil. As for all the admiration that is now poured on the jazz-age architecture of the Bund, the main street along the river . . . those, clumsy, provincial out-of-place little skyscrapers? More and more we live in an age where taste does not distinguish between the bizarre and work of quality. I find the buildings of the Bund entertaining, like the Chinese restaurants in London's Shaftesbury Avenue.

I did enjoy the standard steamer trip that runs from a jetty on the

Bund and takes one down river to meet the Yangzi just before it flows into the sea. The view was mostly boats of every shape, type and size but far better was a mid-trip entertainment in the ship's theatre by a Chinese juggler followed by a Chinese conjuror. Since the theatre was packed with an enthusiastic audience, clearly everyone else was also surfeited with boats. The juggler was excellent but the afternoon belonged to the conjuror, a small, ordinary-looking man who was skilled at his tricks and even more skilled at handling his audience. By good chance, when the inevitable moment came for the magician to seek an assistant from the audience, who should he find in the front row but an enormously tall and wonderfully good-humoured black African. Inevitably, the gold watch was borrowed, wrapped carefully in the white cloth, and smashed to seeming smithereens with a hefty wooden mallet. I suspect that the African had never seen the trick before and the look of dismay on his face, of total uncertainty, and the way the small conjuror hopped about stirring up the audience and playing on the fears of his victim were simple theatre at its best. The conjuror looked so utterly insignificant yet had an enormous and beguiling personality which he got across in total silence to a multilingual audience. I found his performance a more interesting link between East and West than those ill-proportioned monuments on the Bund. Next time I might circumnavigate Shanghai by taking the boat down the Grand Canal.

24 The Imperial Palace

BEIJING

25 The last emperor

26 The Great Wall

27 A new generation

BEIJING

28 The Temple of
    Heaven

29 Bamboo baby carriage

Interlude: The Other Republic

TAIWAN

'We want to apply for visas for Taiwan.'

A stocky Chinese woman thumbed her way through every page of my passport, wincing twice. 'You have two visas for mainland China.' Her disdain was tangible.

'Yes.'

'Why did you have to go there twice?' She made it a matter of shame.

'Well, I went as a tourist.'

'There is nothing to see.' The conviction was invincible. 'Are you going again?'

'No, there is nothing left to see,' I lied obediently.

I was rewarded with the application forms.

Yuki-san had only one mainland Chinese visa in her passport. She got away with a scolding about the Chinese jade amulet she was wearing, in fact bought in Hong Kong.

Taiwan, the Republic of China, has no formal diplomatic relations with Japan. We had to obtain our visas from their thinly disguised consulate in Osaka, the Association of East Asian Relations. Such euphemisms help to keep mainland China happy and ensure the continuing development of the massive trade between Japan and Taiwan. Since President Nixon brought the People's Republic of China back into the international diplomatic fold, most countries have set up similar 'have your cake and eat it arrangements' with Taiwan. But this partial loss of identity has left the Taiwanese more sensitive than ever about the People's Republic of China. The Chinese leaders' declaration that sooner or later Taiwan must be reunited with communist China has increased the tension.

In 1949, the Kuomintang army routed by the communist forces, Chiang Kai-shek fled to the Chinese island of Formosa and set up the Republic of China. Taiwan now has a population of about 19 million, with the 300,000 neglected aborigines living in poverty down the east coast while the Chinese population enjoy the highest standard of living of all the smaller and booming Pacific economies. The more that is revealed about Chiang Kai-shek, and the vastly wealthy Song family he married into, the more of a fascist monster he appears. He is now dead but the tradition of right-wing government he established, Confucian embellishments and all, continue. That government has brought miraculous prosperity to this small island but little democratic freedom.

I have been to Taiwan three times and always I have disliked the atmosphere there, a mixture of rampant materialism and the sense of a police state. This feeling has been confirmed by various Taiwanese I have met in Japan and only a few weeks ago I had a long conversation on an aircraft with a Taiwanese in his late twenties studying in Europe for his PhD. He confirmed everything that I had ever felt and he had just made up his mind to leave Taiwan for good and settle abroad. I returned to Taiwan while writing this book to make some comparison between these two Chinas, one rich and minute, the other vast and poor. After travelling all round the island I came to the conclusion that the two societies have grown so far apart, comparisons are not of much significance and the development of Taiwan is no pointer to communist China's future.

In a necessary but unplanned scramble for prosperity the 'beautiful island' that the Portuguese admired so much in the sixteenth century has been littered everywhere with industrial development, reaching a crescendo of horror in the glistening nuclear power station which now overshadows the beautiful southern beaches of the island and the forests of Kenting Park. It is becoming difficult to escape from industrialisation anywhere and even the famous beauty spots like Sun Moon Lake, Mt Ali and the Toroko Gorge are marred by tawdry commercialisation and overcrowding.

There is enough in Taiwan to make one visit worthwhile and if you are seriously interested in Chinese culture and art, then a visit to the fabulous National Palace Museum on the outskirts of Taipei is essential. It contains some 600,000 Chinese works of art smuggled out of China by Chiang Kai-shek, and includes a large part of the former imperial collection combined with other collections. The collection's size is rivalled only by its quality and its removal has, in effect, left mainland China without any major collection of Chinese art, particularly painting. In defence of the 'theft' one must ask how much of this collection would now survive if it had remained in China, every piece so vulnerable to the vandal. It has been sumptuously housed and immaculately cared for in Taiwan where it is made available to the public and serious scholars from all over the world. Parts of the collection are exhibited in rotation and it is said that it would take ten years at least to see everything. If, by any chance, you are disappointed by the art you see in China, arrange your next holiday in Taiwan and allow yourself time for at least two days in the National Palace Museum where you can feast on the greatest Chinese paintings, ceramics, bronzes, lacquerwork, textiles and enamels in the world.

The museum does have some supporting attractions. Taipei has some spectacular temples, a marvellous range of delicious Chinese food, not all expensive, and a tempting selection of cheap pirated cassette tapes and books which *theoretically* are not supposed to be taken out of Taiwan. I would warmly recommend two places outside Taipei. Although it will be crowded in summer and you will pay an extortionate price to sleep in the nastiest kind of hotel, make the journey to Mt Ali. Alishan embarrassed the Japanese when they absorbed Taiwan into their empire since it was tactless enough to be several metres higher than sacred Mt Fuji. However, the mountain compensated for this impertinence by being covered in magnificent and rare timber which the Japanese forested by building an intriguing small-gauge railway which still winds its tortuous and impressive way almost to the peak. The journey up and down is beautiful and around the peak there are walks among the great forest and a sunrise for those who like rising early.

Alishan forms part of a range of mountains that runs down the centre of the island which for centuries isolated the east coast from the more populous western half of the island. Since the Second World War a road was tunnelled through the mountains creating the spectacular Toroko Gorge, the wonder of Taiwan, where a series of tunnels winds through varying coloured marbles, the road breaking out of these tunnels into magnificent mountain views. Beware of the package tours to the gorge since some of them take you through only a small section of this great mountain road. It will cost you less and you will see more to take an ordinary bus from Taipei which will go the whole way through to the east coast where you can spend the night. The next day do the same bus ride in reverse back to Taipei. Those two days and the Song landscapes in the National Palace Museum will make you glad you came to Taiwan, and, for better or worse, the island is another face of China.

8

Seat of Power

BEIJING

I had no wish to be met at Beijing airport. It seemed an unnecessary expense. But in China you can never win. The CITS neatly turned it into a necessity by refusing to disclose the name of my hotel until I met their courier at the airport. The Chinese can wring blood out of the stoniest-hearted traveller. I consoled myself that at least I could get some useful information from my guide. By some bureaucratic confusion the owlish-looking courier did not speak one word of English and at the airport was holding up a placard with my name written in Japanese.

We drove in silence along the narrow road from the airport in an elderly and battered Citroën. The verges on both sides were densely planted with trees and shrubs, shutting out any view. The young driver lit his third cigarette and slipped a tape into the cassette-player. Suitably enough, the car was filled with old and evocative French film music. I felt disoriented, without a view yet held between two worlds. I began to imagine myself blindfolded, being whirled along to some unknown destination. It was the first time that I had travelled in China alone. For the past week I had been feeling apprehensive and now subconscious nerves were playing games with my imagination.

The screen of trees ended abruptly, the road widened into a broad highway and a vast modern housing development spread before us. The new apartment blocks, hard and bleak against the sky, were scattered over the huge and rough building site which surrounded them. The arms of tall cranes stretched out over half-finished buildings. In between, scarred, dusty sites waited for the first foundations. Although it was early afternoon, there were few people about, no children playing in the streets and for kilometre after kilometre few shops or any other sign of life. The new buildings were shoddy and the touches of decoration emphasised only the poor design. But no doubt these apartments seemed luxurious to their new occupants. It was a raw and anonymous area, depressingly suburban except that it spread right into the centre of Beijing. It was a bleak introduction to China's ancient capital.

All my life I have heard people who lived in 'Peking' before the Second World War describe it as the most fascinating city in the world. It is hard to believe now. Little remains of that exotic and colourful world except the old street names. A few of the great monuments remain but apart from them Beijing has been reduced to one of the most characterless capital cities in the world. I cannot bring my memories of Beijing to form a coherent plan. I picture it as a number of unrelated areas and places held together only by the bus routes. There are the scattered palaces, parks and temples, the drab confusion of avenues and traffic around the railway station, the empty expanse of Tiananmen Square, the sudden magnificence of the Forbidden City, and the dreary shopping streets where cabbages are piled on the kerb. My main impression is of a few superb buildings set in a sprawling, ugly and essentially provincial city. The streets are cleaner, the people better dressed, the traffic policemen smarter than in Chengdu or Chongqin but mostly Beijing is just another big Chinese city.

Man has lived in this area for a long time. In the 1920s the remains of the famous 'Peking Man' were discovered about 40 km south-west of Beijing. Half a million years ago this early man was already using simple stone tools. But until the second century BC Beijing was only a small village. It was during the Qin dynasty, when China was first centralised, that Beijing developed as a trading centre between Korea, Mongolia and the area south of the Yellow River. After the collapse of the Tang dynasty in the tenth century, it became the capital of the Liao dynasty under the name of Yanjing. In 1115 the Jin dynasty defeated the Liao and enlarged the capital, renaming it Zhongdu. During the Mongol invasion Zhongdu was largely des-troyed but when the Mongols established the Yuan dynasty the old capital was rebuilt on a much grander scale and was called Dadu or great capital, and was the winter capital of Kublai Khan. Marco Polo came here in the thirteenth century and marvelled at all he saw, calling the great city 'Khanbalik', Khan's town. Dadu was a little to the north of the present inner city where one can still see fragmentary remains of its walls.

What is now left of the old layout of the city and its surviving great architecture date from the Ming period. At the start of the Ming dynasty they moved the capital to Nanjing but the third Ming emperor, Yong Le, moved north again and renamed the old capital Beijing, the northern capital. The Ming emperors made the city larger and grander than ever. The imperial city remained in its former position but the inner city was moved south. Beyond, a new outer city was created. In 1535 the great surrounding walls and gateways were faced with brick, a feature which became the architectural signature of the Ming builders. It was a long period of peace and prosperity and the power and wealth of the Ming emperors is demonstrated by their building works. The dynasty collapsed in 1644 and the last Ming emperor fled through the northern gate of his great palace to hang himself from a tree on Coal Hill. Heaven had clearly withdrawn its mandate from the Ming dynasty.

The Manchurian Qing dynasty took over the capital and though both the emperors Kang Xi and Qian Long did a considerable amount of building in what remains of the old capital the basic Ming plan remains unchanged. Beijing was seriously damaged during the Boxer Rebellion in 1900 but it was Chairman Mao who was mainly responsible for destroying both the basic plan and the character of the old city. His bulldozers demolished the old walls and gateways and other buildings to make way for the great empty avenues that now divide the city. It was a new kind of imperial dream and one must be grateful that so much survived the whims of Mao and the mindless destruction of the Cultural Revolution. Today, a saner regime is hastening to restore the damage and neglect which Beijing's palaces and temples have suffered with much already achieved.

I cannot pretend to find Beijing either a fascinating or a sympathetic city but it does contain China's most splendid architecture which alone would justify a journey across the world. In that respect a visit to Beijing is memorable, particularly as it will include a tour to the Great Wall. There is an abundance of local colour in other Chinese towns. Only Beijing can offer you the Forbidden City and the Temple of Heaven.

I explored Beijing in a haphazard way and I shall describe it in the same way. Many of its sights are scattered and obscurely sited, tucked away down muddy alleys or isolated by highways and modern development, highrise apartments or a towering hotel, all bronzed metal and tinted glass. Mostly I walked, occasionally taking a bus when I knew where I was going, although the hotel usually gave me the wrong bus number. If I was walking to some extremity of the city I made a note of the buses on that route so that I could use them if I came back the same way. My map was diagrammatic and I was surprised by the actual distances. On foot Beijing is a big city but, like everywhere in China, the pedestrian's view is the best.

My hotel was in the eastern section of the city. My courier had delivered me safely but had demanded 40 yuan for the car ride. I was furious since I had already paid for this in advance but I had no receipt to prove it. Several weeks later, returning to the airport in a taxi far grander than the old Citroën, I noticed that the correct fare was 25 yuan. However, I was grateful to have a hotel room. September and October are now the high season in Beijing for tourism and conferences and I heard several times that the city's accommodation was about 30 per cent overbooked. When I asked my hotel if I could have a room for one night before leaving China, the girl at reception simply laughed at me. It had been the same on my first visit to Beijing. We had spent three hours touring the city in a taxi trying to find hotel rooms. Eventually, we were banished to a former Russian hostel in the outer suburbs. This time I heard of groups who were accommodated 50 or 60 km outside the city and brought in each day for their ration of sightseeing. It was impossible for them to get any personal view of Beijing or to sample its nightlife, opera or disco.

The first morning I set off it was already over 32°C, far higher than I had expected for September and miserable for sightseeing. The hotel was just by the north-west corner of the pleasant Ritan Park, adjoining one of the three embassy compounds of Beijing, sited well to the east of the famous Legation Quarter of the Boxer Rebellion days. Another modern compound lies to the north of Ritan Park while the Soviets live in splendid isolation in a compound slightly to the west of that. I had not come to Beijing to study diplomatic architecture but from passing glimpses it would not have been a stimulating study. Each urban-suburban embassy was fronted by tall gates and a wretched Chinese sentry trying to appear alert in the hot, humid sunshine. A gaggle of fruit-sellers on one corner brought a touch of life and noise to these slightly solemn streets.

At the far end I stepped into a noisier, larger world. I was faced with broad avenues alive with bicycles and rumbling buses, and I was plunged into the noise and dust of central Beijing. At this point the roads, the underpasses and the roundabouts dominated the scene which otherwise was largely uninhabited. Even the flow of traffic was inadequate for these great highways. I turned right towards the centre of the city, following the path alongside the road, moving almost shoulder to shoulder with the column of cyclists drifting past. Shimmering slightly in the heat and the dust, Jianguomenwai Street stretched into the distance leading towards the Forbidden City.

At the first big intersection, across the traffic, in the distance I saw what looked like a small fort with intriguing astronomical instruments sticking out above the battlements. Dodging bicycles and buses I crossed the road and approached Beijing's ancient observatory. It was built in 1296 at the south-east corner of the Yuan capital and rebuilt in 1522 on the same site by the Ming emperor, Jia Jing. For centuries the Chinese emperors were deeply concerned with astronomy and geomancy, not only for the accurate measurement of the calendar but for the correct and auspicious siting of the capital and its ceremonial buildings.

The Mongol emperors employed Muslim astronomers when they established the imperial observatory. They continued to run the observatory until 1629 when they were replaced by the Jesuits. These resourceful Europeans, led by the Italian, Matteo Ricci, arrived in China in the late sixteenth century and rapidly captured the confidence of the emperor through their learning and Western skills, not least in astronomy. In 1610 the Muslim astronomers made a serious miscalculation in predicting an eclipse and before long the observatory had been put into the hands of the Jesuits. Some of the astronomical instruments now displayed on the roof may include some designed by the Jesuits while one is said to have been a gift from Louis XIV. However, since all the instruments were taken to Germany after the Boxer Rebellion and were returned to China in 1919, there is some doubt about the authenticity of all the instruments now on display. But they do recall the Jesuits' considerable influence at the Chinese court and China's longstanding willingness to make use of foreign skills and knowledge.

The dark brick observatory once formed part of the Ming city walls which explains its fortified appearance. Inside, to the right from the inner court, low buildings surround a pleasant garden, and, to the left, you climb the tower by a narrow stairway. The observatory was closed for some twenty-five years. Standing above Beijing's new subway it nearly collapsed but was recently restored and opened as a museum. The displays on the first two floors remind the visitor that astronomy was important for Chinese marine navigation but that in some other areas for centuries there was no hard and fast line between astronomy and astrology. Marco Polo commented on the thousands of astrologers and soothsayers in the capital whose predictions could give anyone a peep into the future for a fee of one groat.

On the roof of the observatory, set out on raised platforms, are various large astronomical instruments, each of bronze and some 3 metres high. Several are lavishly decorated with writhing dragons and other exotic ornament which did not interfere with their accuracy. There is a giant celestial globe, an elegant, scrolled sextant, an altazimuth and several kinds of armilla. They are fascinating objects of scientific sculpture; they are also a vivid reminder of that small band of Jesuits, brave yet slightly comical in their mandarin robes as they appear in contemporary prints. Their influence at the imperial court lasted over a century when it was finally eclipsed in 1722 by attacks from Europe and the withdrawal of the emperor's favour. Soon afterwards Christianity was suppressed in China until pressure from Britain in the later nineteenth century opened the door to a variety of missionaries.

I started walking west again. Although this is the main avenue running across Beijing from east to west, most of it is dreary and featureless, a ceremonial route without a ceremony. The cyclists, like the poor, are always with us and I never cease to marvel at the ingenious ways in which the Chinese exploit this simple form of transport. The girlfriend or the wife perches elegantly side-saddle on the back. Clusters of distraught hens or ruffled ducks are strung either side of the handle-bars. Two small children are lodged on the crossbar and, occasionally, by some mysterious levitation, an armchair or a small sofa balances on the carrier. The bicycle has become the pack-horse of China and without it life might come to a halt.

Elsewhere along the avenue was evidence of Deng Xiaoping's encouragement of a partial return to capitalism, both to stimulate the economy and to provide employment for the alarming number of jobless young people in the large cities. In the patches of shade along the walls small traders sell glasses of tea, tawdry plastic trinkets and a selection of dark glasses, the last being a sign of 'with it' fashion among the young. This 'street corner capitalism' has spread all over China. Its larger manifestation can be seen on the corners of Beijing's main intersections where large hoardings, strident and naïve, advertise television sets, refrigerators and cosmetics. As incomes rise the government struggles to increase the supply of consumer goods and to improve their quality. The growth in production during the last two years has been dramatic. When I came to China in 1983, most people's ambition was to own a bicycle and a transistor radio. These are becoming commonplace and many Chinese are now raising their sights to television sets, fridges and small washing machines. Such goods are now advertised regularly on television and are usually available in the department stores in the larger towns.

Although the average income in China is still extremely low, many families have more than one member working and they share the cost of buying a television set or other expensive pieces of household equipment. The Chinese leaders are reluctant to use the word 'capitalism' in connection with their revised, pragmatic approach to the economy, but whatever they choose to call it, it is becoming an economy which recognises the demands of the individual consumer and the political wisdom of supplying them. Such pragmatism comes naturally enough to the Chinese which is one of the reasons why their communism is different from that of Russia. In the heat of the revolution everything had to be sacrificed. Today out-of-date dogmas are being replaced by policies that fit the realities of human nature and China's economic problems.

An enormous building loomed ahead. It was the famous Beijing Hotel where several well-known foreign journalists had lived and worked before and during the Cultural Revolution. A number of foreign organisations also keep a permanent room there to assure accommodation for their staff visiting Beijing. This probably explains why the hotel always seems to be full. The original building, still in use, dates back to the early years of this century and was a focus for the foreign community in the 1930s. It has a splendid, if under-used, sprung ballroom floor. The modern extension was built in 1975 but already has acquired that dowdiness which seems to overtake all large Chinese hotels within months of their completion. Now several international hotels have opened in Beijing but the Beijing Hotel remains a centre for foreigners, its large lobbies always packed with young and old tourists sipping milk shakes and Coke. It is also one of the few places in central Beijing where one can be certain of picking up a taxi fairly quickly.

Not far beyond the hotel I entered the vast area of Tiananmen Square, the heart of the capital. On the north side lies the Forbidden

City. The square takes its name from the outer gateway of the imperial city, Tiananmen meaning 'Gate of Heavenly Peace'. The massive gate has five arched entrances. Above the central arch, originally used only by the emperor, hangs a portrait of Chairman Mao. It was here that he proclaimed the People's Republic on 1 October 1949. Since the end of the Cultural Revolution the accompanying portraits of Marx, Engels, Lenin and Stalin have been removed. Personality cults are now out of favour in China. It is interesting how Deng Xiaoping rules China from the shadows, occupying seemingly less important official posts. But everyone knows who is in charge.

For the multitude of Chinese tourists who flock to Tiananmen Square it seems obligatory that they are photographed beneath the benign portrait of Chairman Mao. The whole area in front of the wide gateway is occupied by professional photographers. They stake out their studio with lengths of string which corral the groups and keep spectators at bay. I suspect that most Chinese tourists go through this ritual more out of curiosity than in a spirit of political homage. Mao has become a part of the tourist round.

To the west of the square is the Great Hall of the People, completed in one year in 1959. This enormous building is the central seat of government and the stage for state occasions. It was here in 1985 that Margaret Thatcher and Premier Zhao Ziyang signed the agreement about the return of Hong Kong to China in 1997. On that occasion Zhao told Mrs Thatcher that she was seated in the equivalent of 10 Downing Street. Mrs Thatcher observed that the *whole* of 10 Downing Street would fit comfortably in the hall where they were sitting. The building is vast with a concert hall holding 10,000 people and banqueting facilities for 5000. It was here that Chairman Mao lay in state after his death. But despite its political functions, the Great Hall of the People is open to the public like all the official buildings around Tiananmen Square.

On the eastern side of the square is the Museum of National History, also built in 1959, which includes the Museum of the Revolution. Not surprisingly the presentation in both museums has obvious political overtones. In recent years it must have been difficult for those in charge to keep abreast of changing policies and degrees of status among the party leaders. But the museum is interesting as a reflection of Chinese politics and political thinking.

The long queue stretching across the centre of the square leads past the Monument to the People's Heroes, built in 1958. In 1976 it was the centre of the 'Tiananmen Incident'. Many people, sickened by the excesses and chaos of the Cultural Revolution, expressed their feelings by bringing wreaths here in honour of the late Zhou Enlai, who, in the popular imagination, remained a symbol of sanity and moderation. The police removed the wreaths which led to a huge demonstration here against the tyranny of the Gang of Four.

Beyond the Monument is the Mausoleum of Mao Zedong for which people are endlessly queuing. It was built between 1976 and 1977 and his body is still displayed here, draped in a red flag inside a casket of crystal. When the mausoleum was reopened in 1983, two museums had been added commemorating the lives of Zhou Enlai and Zhu De and Liu Shaoqi. Making Mao Zedong share his mausoleum with other national heroes was part of the process of lowering the pedestal on which Mao had placed himself. Throughout China the official photograph of Chairman Mao is far less common than it used to be.

It is impossible to predict the place Mao Zedong will eventually take in Chinese history. It is always difficult to appraise those great war leaders who in victory move into ordinary political life where frequently they fail to sustain their martial genius. Wellington, Churchill and Eisenhower are obvious examples. Mao's position was less conventional. He was an inspired and indomitable revolutionary and it has been suggested that he only felt at home in a state of revolution. The pragmatism and compromise of Liu Shaoqi's faction, essential for the rebuilding of China, seemed to Mao a betrayal of the ideals that had sustained them through the revolution epitomised by the agonising hardships of the Long March in 1935. But the fact remains that while Mao's heroic efforts during the revolution liberated China, from 1949 onwards he made a series of catastrophic decisions reaching a climax in the unleashing of the Cultural Revolution which almost destroyed the country.

Mao's faith in manpower over mechanisation was wrong, his agricultural policy was wrong, his concentration on heavy industries was wrong and his attempt to eradicate growing bourgeois and bureaucratic abuses by creating anarchy came close to a national disaster beyond his control. How far Mao may have become senile in the years before his death in 1976 we shall probably never know, like so much else at the heart of the Cultural Revolution. For the future, if China continues its present progress, with its economy expanding and the standard of living rising, some wounds will heal and the wounded themselves will die. In time history may concentrate on the achievements of Mao's revolutionary leadership with less emphasis on his later vanities and political mistakes. One thing is certain. Good or bad, he must remain a giant character in Chinese history, his mixture of success and failure mirrored in the lives of several great Chinese emperors. Like those great emperors he lived out his life on a grand and turbulent scale.

Chairman Mao is gone but in and around Tiananmen Square the power of the central government lives on, spread out in the shadow of that former seat of power, the Forbidden City, which housed both the Imperial Palace and the imperial administration. But I find Tiananmen Square and its official buildings a depressing example of totalitarian architecture, particularly in comparison with the marvellous design of the Forbidden City. The Great Hall of the People is a massive, solemn building but lacking any real character. And despite its size it fails to command the great square which has no sense of occasion like the great ceremonial squares of Europe and, indeed, the courts of the Imperial Palace. The scale is inhuman and the buildings are boring. Communism everywhere has failed to produce an imaginative style of architecture. Perhaps its architects are nervous of showing some allegiance to older styles with the wrong political associations. With relief I turned my back on the present and looked at the dark red wall of the Tiananmen Gate supporting its long tower and the sweeping lines of the double tiled roof.

The Forbidden City is an enormous complex of palaces and official buildings, several now housing interesting museums. On grounds of size alone I would number it among the marvels of the world but it does require at least two whole days to see it thoroughly. The Forbidden City, in its present form, was built in the Ming dynasty between 1417 and 1420. It covers 73 hectares and, largely as a result of frequent fires, much of it was rebuilt or heavily restored in later times. It is said to contain 800 buildings and 9000 rooms. By around 4 p.m. your feet will not argue with those statistics. It was designed both as the emperor's palace, with additional accommodation for the members of his court, and as the seat of government. It is a confusing labyrinth of great ceremonial buildings, palaces large and small, courtyards and linking alleyways, each palace enclosed within its own walls and the whole imperial city surrounded by a rectangular, crenellated wall pierced with huge gates at the four points of the compass. It is one of those complexes that look comparatively simple from the plan in your guide book yet when you stagger out at the end of the day you feel that you have missed a great deal. And you are probably correct.

Roughly speaking, the Forbidden City is divided into three sections running from north to south. The buildings of the Imperial Palace occupy the centre while the east and west sections are made up of a variety of smaller palaces and other buildings with special functions. Each time I have visited the Forbidden City I have been overwhelmed by it. The splendour of its overall design and the architecture of the main buildings is obvious enough but it is harder to recapture much sense of the ceremonial life that was lived there during the Ming and Qing periods. The sumptuous framework has largely been stripped of the detail necessary to arouse the imagination. Parts of the complex, particularly in the western section, are still under restoration but the main central palace and the museums in the eastern section will keep most visitors well satisfied, not least the wretched groups who are rushed through the whole complex in under two hours.

The Tiananmen Gate is the outer entrance to the Forbidden City whose actual walls start at the Meridian Gate. From the Tiananmen Square five white marble bridges, matching the five entrance archways, cross a small stream. I was impressed to see two men in a boat fishing for cigarette packets and other litter. Beijing is working hard to be a clean city. Everywhere there are notices forbidding spitting, printed rather surprisingly in both Chinese and English. Beyond the Tiananmen Gate there is a large open space, a last stop for refreshment and fun before the Chinese tourist undertakes the sightseeing marathon. To the right is a line of stalls selling food and souvenirs and, among them, the professional photographers whose cardboard cut-outs instantly transform you into a Ming noble or a Qing princess. In the thin shade of the trees to the left groups of Chinese squat and chatter while they picnic. You will be seeing the Forbidden City in the company of hoardes of eager Chinese sightseers. The trickle of foreign groups is hardly noticeable.

Moving forward through the holiday crowd I passed under the great Meridian Gate and entered the Forbidden City. Before me was a magnificent courtyard dominated on the far side by the enormous Gate of Supreme Harmony. The poetry of the names by itself does much to conjure up the overwhelming scale of everything. On massive bastions of brickwork the raised gate towers, huge but elegant, spread their two-tiered roofs like the gorgeous wings of magnificent yellow dragonflys. High, enclosing walls surround you and the expansive stone-covered courtyard is crossed from east to west by a silvered stream curving in the shape of a Tartar bow. All around the towering walls, the ceremonial buildings and the extravagance of space is broken up and lightened by a chain of carved, white marble balustrades that define the outline of this sumptuous conception.

Before I go further, let me try to stimulate historical imagination. For all its present architectural grandeur, there is also something forlorn about this great palace where weeds stipple the courtyards and most of the imperial apartments have been stripped of their furnishings and treasures. Even where these remain, the frayed and faded furnishings of the late Qing dynasty do nothing but cast a late nineteenth-century dowdiness over these state apartments which give no idea of their earlier magnificence. It is now an empty stage from which the fabled extravagance of imperial life and ceremony has vanished. One must struggle to people it once again with an emperor all-powerful, surrounded by his silk-clad ministers, his scheming eunuchs, his court scholars and the stream of suppliants from across the empire seeking imperial favour.

Although Marco Polo wrote of the palace life in the thirteenth century, in the reign of Kublai Khan, his descriptions of court ceremony help to give life to the Imperial Palace as we see it today. There is a rich colour and an immediacy in his descriptions which is further enlarged by his constant amazement at the size and lavishness of the oriental world, the splendours of his Venice paling in comparison. Faced only with the empty shell of the Imperial Palace, I marvel exactly as Marco Polo did 700 years ago. It is but a shadow of what he saw but enough remains to allow us to share his amazement.

He first describes various parts of the palace, walls covered with gold and silver and decorated with dragons, birds, animals, horsemen and lively scenes of battle. The main hall of the palace was so large it could accommodate a banquet for 6000 people; shades of the Great Hall of the People, and, like me, he was bewildered by the number of surrounding chambers. He describes the 7 km of surrounding walls, their towers full of munitions, harness, arms and armour. Behind the main hall were apartments for the Khan's wives and concubines, set in a parkland of soft lawns where gentle deer walked and grazed. Twelve supreme lords supervised the great army and lower lords supervised the provinces, with a judge and clerks to administer justice for each area. The Khan was supreme in everything, the final court of appeal. There is a great sense of busy coming and going as the emperor considered military affairs, taxation, local government and legal cases with the aid of his carefully ranked advisers. In between times the great Khan found time to consult with and reward his astrologers and, on occasion, to distribute alms to the poor of the capital.

By the time of the Ming dynasty, the emperors lived a more cloistered life, an imperial seclusion which led to the Imperial Palace being called the Forbidden City. The Son of Heaven lived in the most splendid isolation. On the few ceremonial occasions when he left the palace, he moved with a vast and totally silent procession along deserted streets since it was forbidden to look at his imperial person. His whole life was ritualised with a proper time and place, and a proper building for each imperial function. In the centre of the palace, raised on a high terrace and approached by marble stairways, are the three main and most magnificent buildings. The Hall of Supreme Harmony stands in front overlooking an enormous courtyard. The magnificent architecture reflects the title of this great building. There is perfect harmony in the three rising terraces of white marble, the flat arches of the main façade and the sweeping lines of the vast double roof. The filigree of the carved and pierced marble balustrades makes a perfect setting and foil to the massiveness of the huge hall, whose splendour is set off by the final rich harmony of yellow tiles, red walls and the tumbling skirt of white stone. This was the throne room where the emperor dealt with the formal business of government. Behind is the Hall of Complete Harmony, the imperial retiring room where the emperor prepared himself to give audiences.

The northern building, the Hall of Preserving Harmony, was reserved for receiving envoys from vassal states or foreign countries. Under the imperial system, envoys from anywhere were treated as vassals and were left in no doubt of their inferiority to the Chinese. When the Earl of Macartney arrived in 1793 to negotiate better trading terms for the British, he was soon cut down to size by Emperor Qian Long. Macartney arrived in the capital with 600 packages containing splendid gifts from George III. Macartney was confident that this array of Western riches would impress the emperor. The Chinese reacted differently, treating the gifts as *tribute* and thereby reducing Britain to the role of another vassal state.

Their attitude was confirmed by the imperial edict thanking the British monarch for his 'respectful spirit of submission'. The edict continued even more patronisingly: 'The virtue and prestige of the Celestial Dynasty having spread so far and wide, the kings of myriad nations come by land and sea with all sorts of precious things. Consequently there is nothing we lack, as your principal envoy and others have themselves observed. We have never set much store on strange or ingenious objects, nor do we need any more of your country's manufactures.' Such words reflected the imperial attitude to all foreign barbarians and were not intended as a particular snub to George III. The imperial will was not to be seduced by British clocks and other ingenious Western toys. Fifty years later the British realised that the emperor was best persuaded by gunboats. The concessions that Macartney failed to obtain with gifts were taken by force during the Opium Wars. In the eighteenth century the emperor was still able to stand firm. It is said that in disdain of foreign barbarians, many gifts were never even opened and that these are still stored somewhere in the Imperial Palace. The idea of a museum of unopened parcels is certainly intriguing.

I stood in front of the Hall of Supreme Harmony and looked out over the great courtyard before it, large enough to hold 100,000 people. Behind me was the throne room of the Son of Heaven. This had been the centre of power of the Chinese empire. Here, as in Tiananmen Square, size was the symbol of power. But in this great Ming palace imagination and artistry had shaped size into a marvellous harmony between the buildings and the space that contained them. For all their grandeur, they retain a human scale where one may feel humbled but not lost. Everywhere there is rich detail; the elegant balustrades, grimacing bronze lion-dogs, intricate roof finials and those huge slabs of marble carved with a writhing dragon, the ramp for the emperor's palanquin. But in the end I remember the harmony of those great buildings where massiveness, a basic simplicity and space are counterbalanced to form one of the most overwhelming architectural experiences in the world.

Behind the three Halls of Harmony are other gates and further halls which served the personal needs of the imperial family. At the extreme north is the imperial garden, definitely not maintained to imperial standards, laid out around the Hall of Imperial Tranquillity. Just beyond is the north exit and the Gate of Inspired Military Genius. By this point I was hot and exhausted. The temperature had risen and I had been in the Forbidden City for nearly four hours, unable to find a seat or a drink. Everywhere was crowded with eager Chinese tourists, some eager for sightseeing, quite a number eager to practise their English on me.

At last, in the shade of one of the gateways, I found a seat on a crowded bench. Next to me was a girl of seventeen and her mother. The girl spoke reasonable English but it was her mother who insisted on asking all the questions. Before long a small crowd had gathered round and the girl was interpreting for everyone. She had taught herself English with the help of the radio. Many Chinese wish to learn English but there is a great shortage of teachers in the schools, particularly those outside the big cities. People asked all the usual questions. Where did I come from? How many children did I have? What did I think of China? After that interest focused on the new computerised Japanese camera I was carrying. The Chinese are fascinated by new technology and have developed a particular passion for photography.

As in all halting conversations of this kind, nothing of importance was said but there was some significance in the freedom of the situation. I gathered that most of these people were on holiday from other parts of China. This is another new development. Good workers and, no doubt, the more senior cadres and their families are now allowed to take short holidays and to travel to the famous sightseeing places in China. Everywhere I found far more ordinary Chinese moving around. These are all pointers to the changes now taking place with the government's more flexible policies.

With the help of the girl and her mother I found the only place in the Forbidden City where one can buy a drink. I thought that I had bought a bottle of beer but it turned out to be insipid lemonade. But in that dehydrating heat anything was welcome and it gave me the energy to start unravelling the maze of minor palaces and museums which make up the eastern section of the Forbidden City. There is a great deal to see here but poor signposting makes it easy to miss places of interest.

Each of the minor palaces is set in its own walled enclosure, linked by wide walks or narrow alleys. Here the women of the imperial household lived, a palace for the empress, for the heir-apparent and for the favourite concubine. This hidden world was supervised by an army of eunuchs who ran the imperial household besides controlling the imperial harem. Still today an atmosphere of intrigue lingers in this part of the palace. It must have been a claustrophobic and often cruel life. In the final years of the Qing dynasty the notorious Dowager Empress Ci Xi was the centre of palace politics, scheming to keep power in her own hands and her son, Emperor Guang Xu, as her puppet. The emperor's favourite concubine, the 'Pearl' Zhen Fei, tried to persuade the young emperor to stand up to his mother. Zhen Fei was found mysteriously drowned in a small well which can still be seen. Such harem politics must always have been part of the pattern of life in the Forbidden City.

The Chinese government is obviously spending a great deal of money to increase the Forbidden City's value as a tourist attraction. General restoration of the buildings has been carried out and several excellent small museums have been opened in various parts of the eastern section. The objects are attractively displayed but I wish there could be fuller labels in English. I discovered eight museums, not all mentioned in my guide book, and I may have missed some. I had the feeling that more museums will be opened in the future. But at the end of seven hours, whatever I had missed, I came away satisfied. Several of the museums contain specialised displays of Chinese art objects: ritual bronzes, elaborate Chinese jewellery in an oriental-Fabergé style, gorgeous imperial costumes, richly ornamented weapons and a collection of elegant Chinese musical instruments. I recommend them all, not least because they are less crowded. To see them you must pay an additional fee.

There was a good collection of musical boxes and automata but what fascinated me most of all was an enormous display of ornate Chinese, French and British clocks. Emperor Qian Long may have asserted that 'he had never set much store on strange or ingenious objects', but this breathtaking display of French and British eighteenth-century artistry and mechanical ingenuity belies his statement. And surely some of the late eighteenth-century British clocks on display, alive with dancing figures, singing birds and spiralling glass waterfalls, must have come out of the Earl of Macartney's 600 packages. Others of these European masterpieces, probably made specially for the oriental market, were ordered through foreign merchants in Canton.

My final surprise, for I stumbled on it down the narrowest

passageway, was the emperor's private theatre, a two-storey and elaborately decorated stage, no doubt with elaborate machinery for flying gods and raising devils. Like an Elizabethan theatre it was set in a open courtyard. The imperial family watched the performance from the privacy of the building facing the stage which now houses a small museum of theatrical costumes and stage designs. The main stage was raised above the courtyard and the theatre was as elaborately decorated as a grand temple with huge circular pillars supporting the upper storey and the heavy roof. I would have given a lot to see a Chinese opera performed in that splendid theatrical setting.

Instead, when eventually I got back to the hotel, I watched television. The film must have been one of the programmes commemorating the fortieth anniversary of the end of the Second World War in 1945. It was gruesome and uncompromising in its portrayal of Japanese military brutality during their occupation of China. Somewhere in the countryside a group of sick, undernourished Chinese peasants waited expectantly in a barn. They had been told that a Japanese army doctor was coming to see them, hopefully to give them medical attention. The doctor arrives and makes a brief examination. In pathetic ignorance they thank him for coming to cure them. They are loaded into a truck by a group of Japanese soldiers, sinister in white anti-germ masks. The doctor proves to be their judge, not their physician. They are driven to a remote place where a large grave has been dug. The soldiers, helped by their bayonets and two Alsatian dogs, herd the now screaming peasants into the deep pit. The earth is shovelled over them, covering their writhing bodies and trickling into their still screaming mouths.

The film left me nauseated and puzzled. It was blatant anti-Japanese propaganda. It matched China's recent and vigorous protests against the Japanese Prime Minister's official and controversial visit to the Yasukuni shrine in Tokyo where Japan's war dead are enshrined including a number of war criminals. The visit was criticised in Japan and throughout South-East Asia but the Chinese objected most strongly. It all leaves one wondering what the Chinese and the Japanese think of each other. The Chinese have much to remember and seem to have no intention of forgetting. When the Japanese captured Nanjing in 1943, it is estimated that they massacred over 200,000 Chinese, a greater number than all the Japanese killed by the atom bombs dropped on Hiroshima and Nagasaki. You will find no mention of this telling fact in the rather one-sided display at the Hiroshima Peace Museum. But the Chinese do not forget. Nor, I suspect, do they forgive. They have too deep a sense of history.

I have long been puzzled by Japan's attitude to China. Their whole culture was altered and inspired by contacts with China during the Tang period and by the introduction of Buddhism. Japan's cultural debt to China is as great as Western Europe's debt to Greece and Rome. But the Japanese show no obvious sense of gratitude or affection towards their mother culture though they live with it every hour of the day in their written language. They tend to emphasise that all their borrowings from China were soon given a new Japanese identity and mostly they prefer to dwell on China's present poverty than on the great culture which so enriched Japan in the past. Despite this I have always felt that the Japanese still feel inferior to the Chinese or, at the least, nervous of them. And, despite Japan's wealth and technical superiority, I am certain that most Chinese feel superior to the Japanese.

Today each country has much to offer the other. China needs Japan's industrial skills and investment. Japan needs raw materials and hopes for a large share of China's potential market. If, in the new mood of pragmatism, they can forget their differences, it should be a fruitful partnership. The Chinese are clever negotiators with a gift for putting the superior party into an inferior position. They share with the Japanese that oriental shrewdness but the Chinese also have a Western flexibility and a more extrovert character. In the present pragmatic mood the Chinese would probably do business with the devil, on their own terms.

There is an amusing and apocryphal story told about the first postwar visit of a Japanese prime minister to China in 1972. When Mr Tanaka stepped off the plane at Beijing he was welcomed by Chairman Mao Zedong. The Japanese prime minister gave a deep bow and launched into a ritualistic apology for all that Japan had inflicted on China during the war. Tanaka was confused when Chairman Mao interrupted him.

'There is no need to apologise,' cut in the Chinese leader. 'Whatever you may have done to us, it was nothing compared to the two great burdens we inflicted on you.'

Tanaka was completely mystified and probably ruffled at being interrupted in the middle of his carefully prepared speech.

'What do you mean? What did you do to Japan?'

Mao paused, enjoying the other's discomfiture.

'Well, we inflicted on you the Chinese writing system and, if that were not terrible enough, we went on to teach you Confucianism.'

Mao's joke showed a distinctly Chinese sense of fun and that ever-present Chinese sense of history.

China has had centuries of experience in foreign policy. With so many turbulent tribes on her borders her policy has been a mixture of armed suppression and appeasement. I was reminded of this when I was exploring the northern section of Beijing and visited the colourful – garish might be more accurate – Yonghegong or Lama Temple. The architecture and decoration were an exotic mixture of Chinese, Tibetan and Mongolian. It was built originally as an imperial palace but in 1745 was turned into a temple for visiting monks from Mongolia and Tibet. Tibetan Buddhism had spread into Mongolia and various Tibetan-style temples were built mainly to please the Mongolians. The Imperial Summer Palace, north of Beijing at Chengde, was lavishly built by the Qing dynasty during the eighteenth century. One of its most spectacular buildings is a replica of Lhasa's Potala Palace and there are other temples in the Tibetan style. At that time Tibet was being used by the Chinese to maintain a balance of power with the Mongolians. This was architectural diplomacy on the grandest scale.

It was obvious that my taxi driver had no idea of the exact whereabouts of the Lama Temple. He dropped me off in the wrong street but after wandering around for a while I saw the extensive temple buildings rising above a high wall and was guided to the obscure entrance by the top of a brightly painted archway which stood out against the sky. Inside, a long path led under this ceremonial gate to the main temple buildings, passing through informal gardens of flowers and fruit trees and, beside, low pavilions selling souvenirs and unappetising refreshments. The place was swarming with Chinese sightseers. There were many family parties, the children, as always, dressed as if they were on their way to a party. Many of the little girls wore fanciful headdresses of gauze, ribbons and spangles, clearly the handiwork of mother and grandmother. The swinging youth of Beijing were equally with-it in their loud T-shirts, leather jackets and inevitable dark glasses. Many had acquired a layabout manner and a few carried mammoth and blaring radio/cassette-players – 'ghetto-blasters', as they're known in the West. In the ticket kiosk there was a hunched, leather-faced old monk whose toothless grin spread up behind his ears. Despite the fact that I was festooned with cameras he thrust a selection of faded transparencies at me. I felt mean for not buying some. There were several other old and decrepit monks tending the altars and sweeping the temple precincts. Despite the presence of these lamas I saw nobody praying or making offerings at the many altars.

There was the usual range of temple halls, one behind the other, with ornate, tawdry decoration and Tibetan-style sculpture, bizarre rather than beautiful. There were a few bronze prayer wheels and many inscriptions in Chinese, Tibetan and Mongolian. Some attractive Tibetan-style wall paintings in one hall were the one thing in the whole temple that brought back an echo of Lhasa. In one courtyard I came across a middle-aged couple dressed in Mongolian national costume. The man shambled over to me and said that I might take their photograph for the price of two yuan. His hat was askew, he swayed in his thick boots and I could smell alcohol. Raising his voice his invitation became unpleasantly persistent. Mongolian drunks are no less embarrassing than others. His miserable wife caught his arm and tried to drag him away and I slipped away into the next hall. He was one of the few drunks I saw during my travels in China.

I knew that somewhere to the west of the Lama Temple was the largest Confucian temple in Beijing. Looking for some grand approach and unable to read the discreet Chinese signpost, I twice walked past the muddy lane that led to the main entrance of this huge complex. I might have spared myself the effort since the temple was closed for restoration and the gate keeper became extremely restless when I had a look through the open door. Inside was a huge enclosure where beneath the trees were row upon row of stele engraved with fine Chinese characters, perhaps commemorating success in an examination or other notable events. On the far side steps led up into the main temple. The whole place looked gloomy and neglected and most certainly in need of conservation.

I walked back through the north-eastern section of Beijing and for the first time I saw the ordinary life in the city. It was a drab area but the streets were lined with shops which serviced the local people who lived in crowded warrens down the many side-alleys. The display of goods in the shops, including the foodshops, was meagre and of poor quality. In the foodshops the women and girls who served wore cylindrical caps of white cotton, pulled down low to protect their hair. It gave the foodshops a strangely clinical air, nurses gathering for a major operation. The Chinese housewife is a demanding shopper. They rummaged through the wilting cabbages and fruit blackened with bruises. It was early autumn and a season of comparative abundance. Though the quality was mostly poor, there was some choice of fruit and vegetables. Whenever I tried to buy fruit in China it was usually too bruised to eat, probably because of lack of packing materials. The only fruit I found in good condition was watermelon, protected by its own thick skin. The shoppers shouted and the shopgirls shouted louder. They are poorly paid and work on the basis of take it or leave it, the motto of all who serve in China.

The next day I walked to the south of the city to see the so-called Temple of Heaven, the most beautiful group of buildings left in China. It is the masterpiece of Ming architecture. It was here that the emperors came with their gorgeous but silent processions to check the calendar and pray for abundant harvests. The enclosure is nearly 5 km long on each side. Within, each part, each building, each linking causeway has a symbolic significance based on Chinese belief, geomancy and magic superstition. To the north stands the building that has become the symbol of China, the Hall of Prayer for Abundant Harvest. The circular temple is raised high on a square marble terrace, the circle symbolising heaven, the square earth. It is the roof that is unforgettable, a three-tiered crown of deep blue, glistening tiles topped by a golden finial. Here at last is a building that fulfils one's dream of China, simple yet exotic. Inside, four great wooden columns support the domed roof, richly decorated with an imperial dragon encircled by clouds.

Overwhelmed with admiration, I turned again to my guide-book only to be informed that the original Ming masterpiece had been burnt down in 1889. The tree trunks used for the reconstruction of the great pillars had come from the United States. Such replicas turn aesthetics on their head. In Kyoto it is commonly said that the 1955 replica of the ancient Golden Pavilion is more beautiful than the original. I confess that the Hall of Prayer leaves me wholly satisfied.

The emperor came here each spring to pray for a good harvest, first carrying out the necessary rites in this building and later proceeding to the southern Altar of Heaven to make further offerings. I followed the crowds through the gateway and along the causeway enclosed by white marble balustrades. Once again the new passion for photography was evident. Cheap cameras are now flooding the Chinese market and have become one of the most popular of the newly available consumer goods. Everywhere pert girls were posing against the carved marble posts, while young soldiers, in bedraggled khaki drab, stood stiffly, singly or in heroic groups, staring into the lens as if it were the cannon's mouth.

At the end of the causeway, enclosed by a circular wall, is the charming, more miniature Temple of the Imperial Vault of Heaven. I feel there must have been some small ministerial department of poets composing these fanciful names. It is a delicate, octagonal building with a single roof of the same dark blue tiles, elegant as a paper umbrella and an architectural daughter of the great mother-temple which dominates the northern view.

For most of the Chinese there the temple was not the attraction. They were fascinated by the strange echo in the surrounding wall. People at opposite ends can whisper to each other and be clearly heard. Young and old, they pressed their ears to the wall, their faces gaping with astonishment as the messages passed mysteriously through the brickwork. It is certainly more efficient than the Chinese public telephone service. It had taken me over one hour to call the airline office 1 km from my hotel. Nearby was another attraction which I saw all over China: adults and children crowded round a tall bronze incense burner and tried to press small coins onto the vertical metal surface. Usually the coins fell off but a few stuck to the bronze, a sign of good luck. The children's round faces were tense with concentration, black fringes over creased eyes. One small boy had given up. Withdrawing from the crowd, he squatted on the ground and sunk his small teeth into a large roasted corn-cob.

Walking south again I came to the Altar of Heaven from which the whole complex has been misnamed by foreigners as the Temple of Heaven. This is an open-air altar raised on a huge marble terrace formed by three concentric circular terraces again symbolising heaven. This was the most sacred part of the whole temple. Here, the emperor, surrounded by priests and sacred musicians, performed the final rites of the spring supplication. Everyone present must have watched him anxiously as the slightest mistake would be read as an ill omen for the coming year. The altar was considered so sacred that it was not open to the public until 1912. Even now, with the curious crowds, the playing children and the clicking cameras, it retains the atmosphere of a sacred place.

I had now been walking the streets of Beijing for three days and as

I wandered back to the main road to the north of the Temple of Heaven I tried to analyse the life of Beijing. It is certainly cleaner than other big Chinese cities and generally the people appear slightly more prosperous and the women and young men more fashion-conscious. Certainly much of the uniformity of dress has gone and nobody is ashamed of bright blouses or Western-style T-shirts. Everywhere the Chinese are well behaved even if in most places they are noisy. I have lived so long in an oriental country that I am completely used to Asian faces. As I watched a Chinese crowd I saw their faces in terms of character rather than nationality, and in most cases I doubt if I could tell a Chinese face from that of a Korean or a Japanese. Like passing crowds anywhere, the Chinese are uniform and unexotic. The occasional robed lama at a bus stop, the occasional obvious Mongolian or, for that matter, the unusually overdressed woman, such exceptions stood out as they would anywhere.

The Chinese crowd is made up of round faces, long faces, sad eyes, laughing mouths, smooth cheeks, anxious wrinkles, withered age, the anonymous crowds of China like the crowds of London or New York. Attempts at individuality are breaking through in the rash of jeans, bright sports shirts and plasticised zipper-jackets, the latter worn without regard for the heat. The mood of the crowd is self-contained. Families and groups of friends go about their pleasure seemingly relaxed. More and more the young hold hands. In shady if not particularly private corners boys lie with their heads in girls' laps. The girls tend them by cleaning their ears and other intimate if not particularly romantic attentions. The people of Beijing are struggling for a higher standard of living and they are slightly ahead of the rest of China.

But so far any ethnic communities had eluded me. Somewhere in Beijing there must be pockets of minority people, colourful, different, even photogenic. I looked at my map and saw that to the west was the Old Mosque of Beijing. That seemed promising and I started walking again. I passed through a market devoted to horticulture, from potted plants and packets of seeds to gnarled and venerable bonsai. Keen gardeners were loading their bicycles with new treasures for the balcony and the backyard. I then tried a shortcut and found myself in a noisier market selling nothing but jeans and dark glasses. I walked on through wider streets lined with dull shops, the traffic all bikes and buses and grandmothers pushing small children in homemade bamboo prams.

I felt I must be getting somewhere near the Old Mosque which lay to the south of this main avenue. There was a bewildering choice of narrow sidestreets. At a large intersection I found two traffic policemen but although I had the name of the mosque written down in Chinese they could not help me. I took a chance and turned left. It was at least a relief to be away from the dust and noise of the big street. It is one of the pleasures of Beijing that when you turn off the main street, you usually move into a quieter and smaller world, sometimes almost rural. Here the side street soon narrowed into a lane where crazed mud walls enclosed crowded huddles of small houses, shaded by tall trees. Their brown and crinkled tiled roofs sprouted weeds, tufts of grass and the occasional flower. Through the narrow wooden gates hens and small children shared the dust while women struggled with large buckets of water. Along the top of the crumbling walls plants were potted out in miscellaneous containers: flower pots, discarded cooking pots, enamel bowls, rusted tin cans and the occasional dented spittoon. The gateways to some of these compounds were fronted by low marble pillars which suggested grander days. Today only the overcrowding was obvious.

I kept walking south, becoming a little worried as I had come much further than I had expected. But suddenly, through the trees, I saw a large green dome and five minutes later I was standing in front of the Old Mosque of Beijing. Despite its name it was a modern, dreary building, a factory or a school with a large dome perched on the top. It was also shut. Across the street from the main entrance five old men sat in the shade smoking, eyeing me with disapproving curiosity. They looked disappointingly Chinese as did the whole neighbourhood. I had enjoyed the long walk but the nearest I came to anything ethnic the whole way was a shop selling jars of yoghurt.

The bus excursion to the Great Wall starts with a Chinese puzzle. In central Beijing an office offers the tour at a price highly inflated for foreigners. Exactly across the street at a small window you can buy tickets for the identical tour at around one-tenth of the price. At the Great Wall, 70 km from Beijing, there were enormous crowds, Chinese in holiday mood and tourist groups of many nationalities. We struggled up the hill from the bus park and a young American pointed out the wild hashish growing by the path. We bought our tickets and the next moment we were on the wall, its steep, paved roadway undulating over the mountains in either direction. It is one of the great sights of the world, functional yet magnificent architecture, the most audacious engineering and now, much of it ragged and crumbling, an integral part of the dramatic mountain landscape. The builders ignored the near-impossible contours of the mountains. The wall plunges up and down, finding a precarious way along the narrow ridges and over the steep crests of the winding ranges, a spectacular landscape where man has dominated nature.

The Great Wall stretches 5000 km across northern China from the Shanhaiguan Pass on the east coast to the Jiayuguan Pass in the Gobi Desert. It was started 2000 years ago in the Qin dynasty when the separate walls of various independent kingdoms were joined together. Hundreds of thousands of workers were employed. Many were political prisoners and many, who died on the job, were buried in the wall. In places the wall is 8 metres high and about 6 metres wide and often so steep that it is hard to climb the paved slope without the help of the recently installed handrail. It is difficult to understand how horses could have negotiated these sections. But the wall proved more useful as a highway and line of communication than it ever did as an effective defence against the barbarians from the north. Genghis Khan observed that the wall was only as effective as the men who manned it.

Organised tours in China never allow the visitor enough time to see anywhere properly. I just managed to reach the watchtower high on the wall, struggling through a crowd as dense as spawning salmon, when I realised that I would have to hurry back to catch the bus. But there is no hurrying on the Great Wall. I had to queue to descend the narrow tower stairway and make my way through the groups struggling up the slopes, avoiding the photographers, the breathless and, all the time, trying to catch final glimpses of the Wall snaking up and away into the distant mountains. I had been before but it is one of those rare places that seem even more spectacular when visited a second time.

Most tours to the Great Wall return through the wide valley containing the tombs of the Ming emperors. Only the Dingling tomb has been excavated. Its cavernous but hot and humid underground vaults have a certain grandeur. The approach to the tomb entrance is through a complex of terraced buildings and you finally descend, having paid a hefty additional fee, by a modern iron stairway to Emperor Wan Li's underground palace of death. Here he was buried with his two wives, each in an enormous sarcophagus. Although most of the objects now shown in the tomb are replicas, they give you an idea of the solemn scene revealed by the excavations in 1956 which were completed in 1958. Each time I have been there I was impressed by the scale of this great mausoleum but somehow found it as unappealing as some echoing morgue.

Back in the fresh air I found another of those ingenious professional photographers who had the most romantic cut-out figures I have seen. Here you could be photographed as a brawny warrior wrestling with a Manchurian tiger, as an armoured knight astride a prancing horse or your choice from four other historical phantasms. It was a small but perfect dream factory with a queue of eager customers. Along the ceremonial avenue approaching the tombs were older flights of fancy. These were splendid stone figures of helmeted and grim-faced soldiers, twice life-size, and charming stone animals, graceful seated horses, lions, bulging elephants, camels and more mythical unicorns and squatting griffin-like creatures. Along the avenue ambled real ponies hauling small carts, oblivious of their petrified relations by the roadside. But the amateur photographers swarmed around the stone creatures, men, women and children scrambling to be snapped riding a Ming camel or elephant.

I cannot leave Beijing without some account of my hotel there. I do not wish to overburden readers with the daily problems that face the individual traveller in China. They might be led to believe, quite correctly, that I became obsessed with these obstructions and anxieties. But I do wish to alert the intending traveller with some examples of the fate they are likely to share which, if not worse than death, does stretch the patience at times. Superficially the hotel appeared pleasant enough with an attractive lobby, efficient people at reception, two lifts both working and everything seemingly well above China's usual hotel standards. My room was comfortable even if the furnishings were awful in their tastelessness. The desk lamp, frilly shade and sub-Dresden chrome pink, was so perfectly out of accord with the bedside lamp, writhing steel arms supported on concertina-tubes of black plastic. Forty per cent of the curtain rings were missing and the carpet was a horrible stained mosaic of other people's orgies. The flasks for hot and cold water were empty. When I took them to the service counter, the boy filled them, pushed them at me and returned to his magazine. The signs were all there. It was self-service again.

It must have been two in the morning. Somewhere there was an extraordinary noise. Half-asleep I thought it came from outside, a monotonous electronic whine. It persisted, dragging me awake. It was inside the hotel, it was driving me mad and I must get it stopped. Angrily I headed for the service counter wearing only a pair of underpants. The noise was not only inside, it was on my floor. The service station was deserted except for a flashing red light on a large metal box which was obviously the fire alarm. The hotel was full and it was amazing that all the others guests slept through this insistent noise. There was no sign of any night staff and no sign of a fire. That left the noise to be extinguished. Neither lift was working so I charged down six flights of stairs and arrived near-naked in the lobby which appeared to be as deserted as the rest of the hotel although the whine of the alarm was still loud and clear. Stumbling around I found two youths snugly wrapped in blankets and fast asleep on two bench seats. I succeeded in waking the *night staff* only when ruthlessly I rolled them both onto the floor. It took me another five minutes to make them aware of the alarm and persuade one of them to come up to my floor and reset the alarm with his special key. I climbed back into bed. The silence was beautiful but as I lay there I thought of the 700 sleeping guests and the night when it was not a false alarm.

The frustrations in obtaining my railway ticket lasted longer, throughout my whole week at the hotel. I wanted to go by train from Beijing to Datong. When checking in I had seen a notice saying that the hotel would buy air and rail tickets. The next day I found a charming girl at the desk who seemed to speak good English. She agreed to get me a ticket but asked to write down all the details on a piece of paper so that the ticket could be bought immediately. When I saw her the following day she assured me that the booking was in hand. My nervous inquiry on the third day was met with smiles and further assurances.

The fourth morning the girl looked as if she had never seen me before. She asked if I had yet seen the man in charge of transport. I agreed to meet him at 2 p.m. I presumed that he would have my ticket. In seconds it was obvious that he had never heard of my request and he asked me to write down the details to avoid any delay. The pretty girl had vanished from the desk and I never saw her again.

In most such negotiations in China the key figure disappears at the critical moment. I suppressed my irritation and wrote everything down again. The young man asked for 50 yuan in advance and promised to leave the ticket at the front desk the following afternoon.

The next day I returned to the hotel at six. There was no ticket and no message. I was getting worried since I was due to leave for Datong the day after tomorrow. It was a long overnight journey and soft sleepers are hard to get. I knew that I could not keep my hotel room. The boy at the desk promised to telephone my room if he heard anything. At seven-thirty he rang to say the man had returned. I found him in the lobby and asked for my ticket. He had forgotten to tell me that I needed a permit to go to Datong and without it he could not buy me a ticket. Datong is a main tourist attraction and it never entered my head that I needed permission to go there but it seems that the town is in a sensitive military area. It meant that tomorrow I must go to the Public Security Bureau who would not issue the permit until the morning of my departure to Datong. Again suppressing my anger, I agreed to meet the man the day after tomorrow at ten, to collect the permit and go together to the station to try and buy a ticket. He urged me not to be late for our meeting. Even before things had gone wrong I had found him unsympathetic. By now I loathed him.

The Public Security Bureau is to the east of the Forbidden City and I was there at opening time. A pleasant policeman assured me that my permit would be ready at nine the following morning. In my limited experience the security police are the only officials who are efficient and reliable. Next morning the permit was waiting for me. In any other capital city these journeyings would have been nothing. In Beijing getting a taxi can take an hour or more. This large hotel had no certain means of booking or calling a taxi. One simply queued with other guests on the front steps hoping that a taxi would come to drop off another fare.

Frustration was intensified by the fact that the hotel forecourt always had at least eight taxis standing idle, several with their drivers inside, resting. Nothing would persuade them to accept a fare. They worked to some quota of hours or kilometres each day. Since their pay was fixed and they received no tips, there was no incentive to work once they had filled their quota. They preferred to sit idly in their taxis and smoke. I cannot blame them but for guests in a hurry or with planes to catch it meant trying to get a taxi at least one hour before you needed it, with the hazard that you might arrive at the hotel steps to find three people ahead of you. There are one or two hotels in the centre of Beijing where usually you can get a taxi fairly quickly but nowhere have I ever been able to pick up a cruising taxi. The journeys to the Public Security Bureau did nothing to improve my temper.

At ten sharp I was waiting in the hotel lobby to go with the young man to collect the permit and to buy my ticket. He strolled in at ten-thirty and without any apology asked for my permit. I reminded him that we had agreed to pick it up together before going on to the station. He started to tell me that he was very busy and that it would be better for me to collect the permit and to meet him later at the hotel. I reminded him that I was due to leave for Datong that night and that he had already agreed to come with me to the Public Security Bureau. He busied himself pushing his papers into the plastic briefcase, assured me again that he had several appointments and got up to leave.

Six days of frustration, incompetence, fecklessness and time-wasting pushed me over the top. I also got up, hot with anger, and grabbing his arms I snarled into his face, 'You're bloody well not leaving my sight for one bloody second until we've bought that ticket!' The shaming fact is that it worked. If a Chinese can pale, he paled, while I got redder and redder. He agreed to come with me and stood on the hotel steps until we got a taxi forty-five minutes later. The permit was ready, the taxi took us to the station, I got my soft sleeper reservation and I was ready to say farewell to Beijing. My week there had been hard work but mostly rewarding. The hotel will remain unforgettable.

30 Xuanggong Si, the Hanging Monastery

DATONG

31 Cave temple Buddha

32 Huayuan Monastery Buddha

33 Hard seat to Hohhot

34 Fancy dress and plastic yurts

35 Tibetan-style temple at Wulantuger

9

Buddhist Sanctuaries

DATONG

The train arrived at Datong, 300 km west of Beijing, just after 6.15
a.m. In front of the station a young Chinese asked if I was Swedish. I
knew who he was looking for since I had met a Swedish couple on the
train. I pointed them out. He went over and spoke to them and
returned to ask if I would like a lift in their car to the new hotel. I
accepted with pleasure. I didn't know that there was a new hotel and
would have set off in the wrong direction. Also the morning was cold
and a long, uninviting avenue stretched away from the station into a
haze of smog. Datong is a large industrial centre and an important
coalmining town. That morning it looked bleak with smoke from the
factory chimneys smudging the sky. The town is mostly a raw and
featureless place but just outside are some of the most famous
Buddhist cave temples in China which draw many tourists to
Datong.

During the drive to the hotel I discovered that Carl and Inge
wanted to see the cave temples and other Buddhist temples further
afield. We agreed to share a car for the day. They had to return to
Beijing the next day so we agreed with the young Chinese, who was a
local CITS official, that he would send a car to the hotel immediately
after breakfast since we had a long drive ahead of us. The hotel had
been open for only three months but it already looked as if it might
disintegrate by the end of the year. The water-garden in the centre of
the lobby was now coated with a crazed green crust of drying slime.
The carpets were stained and everywhere was dirty. It was the usual
story of no proper management, ignorance and instant neglect.
Undoubtedly the staff were poorly paid and had no incentive to raise
their standards or anyone to teach them how. But that must be a
common situation in many Chinese industries today.

We set off at eight in a glistening Japanese car, obviously the pride
and joy of the elderly and careful driver. I learned that Carl was a
particle physicist, obviously a distinguished one, now working in one
of the most prestigious research centres in the world. He had been

sent to China to advise the Academy of Sciences about setting up a fabulously expensive piece of equipment in China. The project would cost billions of dollars but evidently it had the personal blessing of Deng Xiaoping and, as Carl said, in the long term might offer important industrial benefits. But perhaps the truth is that all poor countries have their vanities. China has not yet achieved a reliable telephone service or a regular electrical supply, even to its laboratories, but no money or talent is spared to make an atomic bomb or to put up a satellite. These things can be achieved by creaming off the best people and vast sums of money but are they really the top priorities for a country that can barely feed itself? And for that matter did Carl, Inge and I need to be driving about the Chinese countryside in an expensive Japanese car with electrically operated windows? The carts we passed on the roads all day didn't even have proper springs.

I was interested that while Carl and his wife were receiving extremely modest hospitality from the Academy of Sciences, the government for which Carl was now working had paid his airfare to China and were subsidising his month of absence from his own laboratory at no cost to the Chinese. Without doubt the Chinese are masters at exploiting the notional potential for trade with industrial nations. All over China I met foreign experts of the highest calibre who were advising China at their own country's expense. And while the Chinese are no longer in quite a position to treat such foreign aid as the due tribute of vassal states, they are always careful to suggest that it is an exchange of ideas between equals. Carl and Inge were happy enough. They simply wanted to see China.

The Yungang caves are 16 km west of Datong. In the middle of the fifth century AD, the Northern Wei dynasty had established their capital at Datong where it remained until it was removed to Luoyang in AD 494. Nothing remains of this important period for Datong except for the famous Buddhist caves. There are fifty-three caves cut deep into the cliff face running 1 km east to west. The caves and the many niches around them are said to contain over 50,000 statues. Most of the caves were carved during the Northern Wei dynasty between 460 and 494. When the capital was moved to Luoyang, the art of cave sculpture continued there. The concept and art of cave temples derived from India where it reached its highest achievement in the masterpieces of Ellora and Ajanta. Despite the poor condition of the Yungang caves, they are the best preserved in China, though local pollution from the chimneys of Datong presents a grave threat to their future. They are among the earliest stone carvings in China and the decoration shows Chinese mixed with Hindu and Persian influences.

The first two caves are at present closed for restoration but all the first four caves, at a much later date, have been enclosed by an elaborate wooden monastery façade which rises up the cliff face in several storeys. This later façade darkens the caves and distracts from the bold simplicity of the earlier design. Much of the sculpture in these first caves is painted in polychrome colours, both the huge single figures and the intricate carved wooden decoration. I found the great standing and sitting Buddhas wooden and unmoving. The surrounding decoration with naïve scenes from Buddhist legend and flying angels was charming but a kind of folk art rather than great sculpture.

I was more impressed by the open caves where the plain rock provided an impressive setting for the huge figures without cramping them. At cave 20, at some time the whole front has collapsed leaving the famous seated Buddha and the two accompanying figures out in the open. The huge figures, given room to breathe, have a tremendous presence, both dramatic and spiritual although it looked as if the heads of all three were replacements. Many of the smaller figures carved in the surrounding niches have a more ethereal quality, their faces thin and delicate, their bodies elongated and delicately draped, sculpture full of grace and spirit. In many other places the rock is carved with row upon row of miniature seated Buddhas, each in his own tiny recess. The mere repetition has a charming votive quality. It is certainly a distinguished complex and a striking display of devotion.

I have to confess that I was disappointed. I had come expecting great religious sculpture to be measured against the best Indian or Gothic art and it was not there. Centuries of damage and the present bleakness of the site are against it. Over your shoulder Datong stains the sky and you breathe the sour air of pollution. That atmosphere must be further destroying the sculpture every minute but how can you encapsulate a kilometre of caves against the dark breath of an industrial city? Chinese tourists swarm everywhere, ignoring the many notices forbidding photography. We met a bizarre Chinese painter, dressed in a loud dogtooth jacket and a tartan deerstalker hat with a watermelon grin to match. He was eager to show us his paintings, all 200 of them, but we were more eager to continue our journey. We faced a long drive to the intriguing Xuanggong Si, the Hanging Monastery, 80 km in another direction from Datong.

It was a pleasant drive through the countryside. In places it was flat and dry, elsewhere lush with rich, red soil and quaint farmhouses, white plaster contrasting with the gold of the autumn harvest. The Chinese peasant wastes nothing, not even other people's energy. The roads were spread with dried crops which the passing vehicles helped to thresh. Our driver was nervous for the paintwork of his immaculate Toyota and swerved away from the piles whenever he could. Ahead lay a dark, craggy range of mountains and everywhere erosion had split the red earth into sharp little ravines, gullies, twisting river courses and deep trenches, water running everywhere. Here the adobe farmhouses had neat façades of black brick and luxuriant green gardens brightened by huge sunflowers.

We came to the western end of the steep Jinlong canyon. At the other end a high dam contains the Hengshan reservoir. The Hanging Monastery is high up on the south face of the canyon, a wall of the Hengshan mountains. Despite the concrete dam and scattered earthworks on the northern side of the canyon, it is still a dramatic setting for the fragile monastery which hangs high up on the rockface, supported on wooden pillars little more than poles, wedged into the rock below the narrow terraces. The monastery stretches out tight up against the cliff in three sections. At the east is the entrance gateway and courtyard and westwards the main monastery housed in two three-storey buildings linked together by narrow walkways. It hangs in the air, each building with a charming and intricate tiled roof, reminiscent of chinoiserie garden pavilions.

It was originally built more than 1400 years ago during the late Northern Wei dynasty but has been rebuilt many times since then. Most of the present structure probably dates from the Qing period. The dam was built in 1958 and the leaflet we were given assured us that the massive concrete wall 'adds to the charm of the scene'. I didn't see it that way myself. It remained a fascinating place but I would rather have shared the original view of the Northern Wei monks though it must have been an isolated retreat.

Today you park at the bottom of the canyon several hundred metres below the monastery. You cross the river on a swaying suspension bridge and climb by paths and steps to the entrance. From inside the peculiarity of the structure is even more obvious. It is joined precariously to narrow terraces cut in the rock. The hanging wooden façade covers chambers in the cliff, the narrow building partly supported on joists wedged into the rock and partly by angled wooden stilts wedged several metres below. Many of the floors, worn and warped, showed the long drop between the boards along the outer balconies which were enclosed only by low and flimsy railings. The monastery is said to contain forty halls, each minute and crowded with crude figures of the Buddha with a clutter of altars and tawdry devotional objects.

I saw no monks but the occasional visitor had left an offering of money or food. It was not easy to move about, like being on an overcrowded boat. Narrow steps, little more than short ladders, led from one floor to another. I had to go up and down crabwise. The carpentry was intricate and the woodwork carved and painted with lively patterns. Despite the additional load, the roofs were elaborate with beasts crouching in rampant anger at the end of the ridge tiles. It was not great architecture, despite its ingenuity, but it had the bizarre charm of some architectural toy, suspended magically in space; more suitable for a harem than a hermitage.

After another longish drive we arrived in a small town in Ying county, now famous only for its towering Wooden Pagoda, the oldest and highest still standing in China. It was originally built in 1056 during the Liao dynasty. It stands isolated in a compound surrounded by dusty trees and gardens. It is an impressive structure rising through six hexagonal roofs to a sharp pinnacle on top. But its great height lightens its massiveness and it has a surprisingly elegant profile. One cannot enter so I could see only the outer part of its complicated structure. The carpentry was elaborate with the interlocking system of brackets supporting the flying eaves of the roofs and tying them to the main frame. In the history of Buddhist architecture nothing is more fascinating than the development of the pagoda from the first simple stupas. The town around the pagoda was a dusty and wretched place, built mostly of mud bricks. A group of lively children were playing round the legs of a tethered donkey. The moment I raised my camera they scuttled off through a doorway. Seconds later five grubby faces were peeping out at me from their place of safety.

We drove back to Datong and straight into another bureaucratic fracas. To be accurate, we drove first into a police trap on the edge of the town where our driver had his licence confiscated for driving over a double white line. He was endangering nobody and was only trying to pass a column of horses and carts overloaded with coal. But in China you do not argue with the police. He drove us back to the CITS office since the guide who had organised the car had promised Carl and Inge to buy their return tickets to Beijing.

Needless to say he did not have the tickets. He now said that Carl must go by car to the station to buy the tickets. He must also pay an extra twenty yuan for the car ride. Since the man had promised to get the tickets and since we had already paid heavily for our car to deliver us back to the hotel, not surprisingly Carl was irritated. The man explained that since our driver had lost his licence, with the implication that that was our fault, he was disqualified from driving. The twenty yuan was to hire another car and driver. The whole thing was childish, the money involved trifling but when you suffer the same kind of treatment day after day, it can get under your skin. I could see Carl getting tight with anger.

I tried a long shot, mostly out of curiosity. I drew the man aside and asked him if he realised how foolish he was being. He already knew that Carl was a distinguished guest of the Academy of Sciences, a famous physicist. But did he know that Carl had come to China at the special request of Deng Xiaoping? I don't know whether he believed me. Perhaps he was hedging his bets but immediately he became more reasonable and Carl responded with a compromise solution. I think that most situations of this kind are caused by the total inflexibility of the bureaucratic system which is always loaded against the tourist.

When I drew my curtains next morning I looked out on a bleak world. Overnight the temperature must have dropped to freezing and a Siberian wind was stirring the dust. Even in sunshine the surroundings of the hotel would not have raised my spirits. I looked down on a mess of churned earth and rubble spreading to a derelict factory building, broken windows and a crumbling chimney. To the right was a mountainous heap of coal. The loading of old lorries blackened the air with coal dust. I went down to breakfast and a day of sightseeing in Datong.

Gone was the grand Toyota and after abortive inquiries about a bus I set off down the cold and windswept avenue. This end of the town was deserted. It was grey and depressing except for beds of bright cosmos daisies that lined the street, their heads torn by the wind and their colours an absurdity in this bleak place. Further on marigolds, dahlias and morning glory mocked the sudden winter. I hurried on, dust in my eyes, the cold creeping down my neck.

I was heading for the Huayuan Monastery which is just east of Datong's central crossing. Although the roofs were visible from a distance, it was not easy to find the entrance tucked away in a side street. The monastery is large but it has become surrounded by the town since it was first built in the tenth century AD during the Liao dynasty. The monastery is divided into the upper and the lower temple. Everywhere was dilapidated and conservation was in progress. It suffered during the Cultural Revolution but now the elderly blue-robed monks are back in residence, shuffling between the buildings in narrow, pointed slippers. Most of them looked bad-tempered, piggy faces with screwed-up little eyes, pottering about their gardens and carrying firewood. Anyone might look sour after what they had probably experienced during the last twenty years, not to mention the abject poverty that now faced them for the rest of their lives.

The decayed atmosphere of the place was somehow appealing. It had a sad but touching quality. Steep stone steps led up through a gateway to the inner court and the main hall of the Upper Huayuan Temple, Precious Hall of the Great Hero. In the centre of the court was a charming bronze pagoda 2 metres high. Near the top quaint little figures leant over the balustrade. The hall is impressive from the outside and inside richly decorated and housing fifty-two Ming statues of the Buddha and Bodhisattvas made of wood and clay. I thought the sculpture and the Ming and Qing murals were disappointing despite a glowing description in my guide book. The same book gave scant attention to the Lower Huayuan Temple. When I finally found it in a separate compound to the north of the main monastery, I had a wonderful surprise. Again I climbed steep steps to reach the Buddha hall and inside I found the most beautiful collection of sculpture that I saw in all China.

The hall was built in 1084 to house a large library of Buddhist sutras, still stored around the walls. The twenty-nine figures are shown in three groups, a low altar in front of each. They are made of clay and date from the Liao dynasty. They were originally painted but much of the colour has gone and time has blackened the rest, leaving the figures austere and emphasising their graceful lines and the remote, sublime shadow of expression on their faces. It is hard to describe great sculpture and to capture the inner feeling created by the outward appearance. These standing and seated Buddhas, some resting on gilt lotus flowers, and the tall, ethereal Bodhisattvas were mysterious with the inner mystery of faith. They were strange, worn and ancient yet somehow their original inspiration was still alive and deeply moving. I had seen nothing so compelling in any other temple. For the first time I could sense the early Buddhist faith of China.

These sacred treasures were guarded by two formidable old women, their grey hair chopped short, hard fringes above square faces. There were notices everywhere forbidding photography but the guardians were absorbed in gossip and tailoring a pair of trousers with large scissors on the furthest altar.

Hell, I thought. If they can cut out trousers on an altar, I can take a photograph. I retired behind a pillar to fix my flash. When I emerged the two tailoresses were bent over the 'cutting table'. My flash exploded and before the light had died the guardians descended on me howling like banshees, their old faces burning with indignation. I thought they might try and snatch my camera but I stood my ground and let them shout. Eventually they got bored and with great arm waving showed me the door. I went, proud possessor of one photograph, a contemplative Buddha resting on a golden lotus flower.

To the west of the monastery lay the old quarter of the town, a picturesque contrast to industrial Datong and the monotonous avenues. The main street was lined with old shops supported on bright red pillars, the roof tiles held firm by layers of clay. It was still cold and the street traders had vanished. A team of women in white cotton caps swept the street and the pavements. The shops sold a variety of food, clothes and other necessities. One was a unisex barber's and beauty salon. The window was dressed with photographs of trendy hairstyles and a selection of cosmetics and toiletries. In the chair just inside the door a man was having the last blow-wave fixed by a girl with an old-fashioned hair drier. At such moments the Cultural Revolution seems a century away.

Further down the street was a Ming Nine Dragon Screen, a long wall with nine fighting dragons depicted in coloured tiles. There is a similar screen in the Forbidden City. In China the doorways to temples and houses were often masked by some kind of screen which one had to walk around. The Chinese believe that evil spirits can travel only in a straight line.

Datong boasts one of the only factories left in the world still making steam locomotives though it is said that prodution will be phased out in this decade. There is a factory tour twice a week which can be booked through the CITS office. Travelling the railways of China, steam locomotives are still commonplace though diesel locomotives have largely taken over the long-distance passenger trains. Once you have obtained your ticket, the rail service in China is admirable. With the size of the country, the vast areas of mountains and the number of trains running every day, the standard of punctuality and basic efficiency is commendable and not matched by any other public service in China. I have caught trains at every hour, often from minor stations and they are seldom more than a few minutes late, often on a run of twenty-four hours or more. During my last journey to China I found the domestic airlines so unreliable, I found it easier to travel by train.

I had one last amusing experience in Datong. I needed to change a traveller's cheque and the hotel told me to go to the Bank of China. It sounded very grand. The bank seemed to be near the hotel so once again I set off into a midday gloom and cutting wind. I came to a large intersection and, following the sketch plan provided by the hotel, I turned left. I expected to find a substantial bank building not far along this road. Within 100 metres I had moved down the social and traffic scale into a world of horses, mules and bucolic carters. The road turned to mud, the gutters were choked with the debris of a vegetable market along the pavement and the road was congested with horse, mule and donkey carts. Some were slowly on the move, most hitched to trees while the carters refreshed themselves at a series of bivouac-restaurants across the road. I dodged between the restless flanks of these animals, picking my way through the mud and the splashes and pyramids of dung.

It seemed an unlikely area for the Bank of China, but China is an unlikely place. Even allowing for that, there were not any substantial buildings in this Dickensian quarter of Datong. One could hardly house the Bank of China in a torn canvas bivouac. I kept going, leaving the street activity behind. I seemed to be heading out into the country with only the wind for company. Suddenly, on my right and out of nowhere, appeared a decaying apartment block. I would have ignored it if it had not had slight pretensions to being substantial. More important, an armed guard stood at the gate. Here a small notice announced BANK OF CHINA, together with the opening hours which were not generous.

I had missed the morning session by two minutes and would have to return at three. The bank had turned out to be a mere hour from the hotel. Necessity brought me back at three. The bank occupied one corner of the ground floor of the building. There was a stout, beaming woman behind the counter busy calculating the fortunes of China on an enormous wooden abacus. She was so fascinated by my British National Health half-lens reading glasses that she fetched her colleagues out of the back office to examine them.

The richer by several hundred yuan, yet again I wended my way through the mud and excrement, past the cosmos daisies and windswept dahlias, up the long empty avenue which had bus stops but no buses and back to the hotel to pack.

10

The Grasslands Tour

HOHHOT AND INNER MONGOLIA

There ought to have been something romantic about Inner Mongolia. I had long awaited to see the great grasslands and its nomadic life. This was the home of the ultimate barbarian, the great Genghis Khan, whose horsemen had secured an empire stretching half across the world. But not all my motives were so high flown. In my racy but usually reliable guide book I had read a hilarious description of the CITS 'Grasslands Tour'. It proved to be accurate to the last awful detail, though the authors were not to know of the special experience that awaited me in my Mongolian tent.

Every traveller in China has his or her own tales to tell about hard seat train journeys. For myself, provided that I could get a seat, often unbookable, and the carriage was not too crowded, I found a daytime journey of up to ten hours quite bearable. Usually the view and one's travelling companions compensated for most of the discomfort. Beyond ten hours and at night it starts to be a different matter. It was a mere five hours from Datong to Hohhot, the provincial capital of Inner Mongolia. I did not have a reserved seat but I found a young man spread luxuriously over two seats who grudgingly moved up.

We trundled north-west across a sandy and treeless landscape. Between the dry river beds and the brown hills in the distance there were patches of miserable cultivation. So much of northern China has been damaged by deforestation. The government has encouraged widescale planting of trees and wherever they have flourished the improvement is very noticeable. After an hour we passed through an area with more trees and nearer the Yellow River. Here, wide bands of wheat stretched from the railway up across the sloping floor of the valley to where small adobe villages were sited along the ridge. Trees had been planted thickly creating oases of moist soil which were planted with tall wheat and flourishing vegetables. Animals were grazing everywhere: sleek horses, cattle, mules, donkeys, sheep, long-haired white goats and huge, snuffling, black pigs. The harvest was half-in and the remaining lanes of golden wheat were matched by the red earth of the early ploughing. In the village yards the winnowing floors were busy; on some donkeys were dragging metal rollers around and around, on others a man and his wife sweating with hand-flails.

It was hard to choose between this autumn view and the restless life in my compartment. The train was packed and many people stood the whole way. Everyone was friendly and I was pressed to fruit, biscuits and bits of bread. About every half-hour a woman attendant circulated with a huge kettle replenishing our mugs with boiling water which everyone drunk without any addition. Even tea is expensive for the ordinary person in China. My instant coffee and powdered milk drew quite a crowd.

Across the corridor was a young father travelling alone with his two-year-old daughter. He nursed and fed her with touching care and tenderness. Everywhere the Chinese love of children is evident. At each stop food-sellers climbed on the train, offering ice creams, apples and lunch-boxes full of greasy rice and little else. A few seats away was an old man who both fascinated and irritated me by his obvious complacency. He addressed his two friends non-stop, like a public meeting, stabbing the air with a lean finger. He had short grey hair and a huge nose which amply supported his spectacles. In his rare moments of silence he leant back, a superior and knowing smile playing about his lips. I could not understand a word he was saying but his companions looked horribly bored.

On the seat immediately opposite me were, I presume, two brothers. There was a strong resemblance. I would guess that the elder brother was about sixteen and the younger twelve. Both had a smudge of moustache on their upper lips. They spent most of the journey locked in an emotional embrace. Such an open display of physical, even if brotherly, affection in a public place would certainly have given rise to curiosity in the West. But as they hugged, nuzzled and stroked each other, the Chinese took not the slightest notice and there was a complete innocence about their behaviour. It did remind me of some of the comments I have read about sexual life in China. It is officially stated that homosexuality does not exist though gruesome stories of homosexuals being punished have leaked out. The statement is doubly surprising when all early heterosexual relations are discouraged and most people are forced to wait until their late twenties to get married. One might have supposed that such conditions would encourage at least adolescent homosexuality.

I once had a homosexual neighbour in Japan who had come there after four years in Shanghai. I cannot believe that they had been celibate ones or that he had confined himself to non-Chinese partners. In China it is commonplace to see youths wandering along hand in hand and no doubt much sexuality is unconsciously suppressed. Perhaps the greatest regulator of all forms of sexual activity is lack of opportunity. Even for married couples it is sometimes necessary to reach an agreement with other members of the family living in the overcrowded apartment to stay out shopping a little longer.

We arrived at Hohhot at 12.30 p.m., another large town stretching away from the railway station almost endlessly in every direction. I thought the Friendship Hotel was near the station but the motor bicycle rickshaw shot off at high speed in a different direction taking me to the place to which the hotel had recently been moved, several kilometres from the centre of town. It was one of those confusing compounds with several large buildings that must have been a hostel or a hospital before it was turned into a hotel. In such complexes, since there is never any signposting, it is difficult to find the reception desk. I had dragged my luggage twice round every building before I discovered the receptionist in what had appeared to be an exhibition hall right by the main gate. She said that the hotel was almost full and she could give me only a poor room in Block 8. She waved her hand in a northerly direction and returned to her knitting. I completed another circuit before I found Block 8, concealed behind a decrepit boiler-house and mounds of coal.

Block 8 was a suitable name for this grim building, and I had indeed been given a poor room. It must have been the office or nursing station for this floor. The whole of the corridor wall was a glass partition. Since I was exactly opposite the lavatories and bathrooms for the whole floor and the public telephone was immediately outside my door, I was glad that I had planned to leave early the following morning for the silent grasslands. It was worse than I had expected. The Chinese are growing addicted to the telephone though personally I have seldom succeeded in getting a connection. However, as the night wore on, I learnt that the Chinese are still under the impression that the telephone works on the same principle as the speaking tube, and the greater the distance the louder you must shout. Around 1.30 a.m. there seemed to be several long-distance calls. Equally, it could have been bad lines or simply the Chinese enthusiasm for new technology.

Outside the CITS office, housed in one of the hotel buildings, was a poster advertising the thrills and spills of their 'Grasslands Tour'. This time I seemed on target for an ethnic group, complete with untamed stallions and camel rides. We would penetrate the heart of the grasslands, feast on Mongolian dishes, rub shoulders with nomadic herdsmen and spend a romantic night in a genuine yurt, the Mongolian circular tent. True or false, it was not to be missed.

While booking for the tour I acquired a sympathetic ally. This was Diana, an assistant Attorney-General from a large American city. A shared sense of the absurd was to help us both through the next two days. She was in China with her brother, a photographer for a leading American magazine who had come to Beijing in the hope of being allowed to photograph the big party conference then taking place. He had declined to accompany Diana to Inner Mongolia on the grounds that it might be uncomfortable. I thought foreign correspondents were meant to be rugged, and he was only thirty-five.

We boarded the CITS bus the next morning in the company of twenty frenetic young tourists from Hong Kong. Our bus vibrated with Cantonese and squeals of excitement. With the microphone turned to full volume we suffered a long spiel in Chinese from the local guide followed by 'Tie a Yellow Ribbon to the Old Oak Tree' by some Chinese cousin of Tom Jones. We drove out of Hohhot where only the occasional flock of sheep peopled the dry and undulating landscape that led to the grasslands. The base for our Mongolian safari was a settlement called Wulantuger which had obviously been developed as a centre of tourism. This had stripped it of its genuine Mongolian identity turning it into something between a dude-ranch and provincial operetta. Youths and maidens hobbled around in heavy leather boots and knee-length tunics. And there stood our yurts, set out in ten neat rows, romantic as caravans in a seaside car park. The yurts were the right size and shape but authenticity stopped there. They were not only covered with a modern plastic material but this was held in place by modern metal fasteners used to secure the waterproof covers of expensive speed-boats. Concrete paths led up to each door, and although at the end of the enclosure there was a stinking yurt-shaped public convenience, the back of each yurt had been fitted with a tin cubicle containing a basin and a lavatory. These had been so neglected that they were almost unusable. When I glimpsed the chocolate brown stains on our basin, I retreated to the heavy ammoniac air of the public convenience.

By the time Diana and I had finished our inspection of the tents of Mongolia we realised that most of the yurts had already been occupied by the Hong Kong students on our bus and two others that had come behind. We were just about to try and find an unoccupied yurt when a voice asked, 'Would you like to join us?'

Meryl was seventy, grey and about as broad as she was stumpy. The effect was increased by a chunky home-knitted cardigan which ran out of wool just above her knees. The determined line of her jaw and mouth prompted me to refuse her offer but Diana had already accepted. I think she lived to regret it.

The weakness of this story is that it centres on an enigma which I never solved and never shall. The situation was tragic but, I must confess, intriguing. We had just finished thanking Meryl for her invitation and putting our bags inside the yurt when down the concrete path came a tall, young Chinese pushing a collapsible wheelchair containing Bill, Meryl's paralysed husband. Bill, slightly older than Meryl, had had a bad stroke six years previously. It had left his mind permanently blurred and his body almost totally paralysed. Seated or lying he could not move without help though, put into a standing position, he could remain upright long enough for someone to get his wheelchair in position. In other words he was helpless.

'The trouble is', Meryl assured us, 'Bill is just crazy about travelling.'

It may have been true. But most of the time Bill seemed unaware of what was being said and incapable of expressing a point of view. But the surprising fact was that Meryl and Bill were on a ten-month world tour. The more we heard the stranger it all seemed. Bill's first wife had died shortly after his stroke and Meryl, the wife's spinster cousin, had taken Bill over. She was wonderfully patient with him but it was as if Bill had been entered for some paraplegic marathon and Meryl was the proud and unrelenting trainer. As she mopped up the dribble on his chin or unzipped his pants and thrust the urinal on him, she found it necessary to say to the reluctant audience of these sad indignities:

'Bill's such a sport. Only happy travelling.'

Bill lay on the yurt floor, his face a grey mixture of tiredness and bewilderment. Undoubtedly, Bill was a sport, but perhaps not quite as Meryl saw it.

The 'Grasslands Tour' was carefully organised to pass much of the time simply hanging about. The whole circus could have been compressed into a long morning, and as for the night in the yurt, I think I would have settled for a shorter stay over morning coffee. I have little to say about the food at Wulantuger except that it was unspeakable and mostly uneatable. I have no difficulty in recalling the smell of the ethnic boiled mutton. But the meals served a valuable function in occupying two hours of the unhectic programme. At three we returned to our bus to visit a Mongolian farming settlement. If that sounds contradictory in this land of nomads, the Chinese government is trying to make the nomads settle in small communes. Perhaps it is easier to keep track of them that way for the grasslands eventually meet the sensitive Mongolian-Soviet border. The commune we were taken to was pure Hansel and Gretel. At one end of a line of houses we were led into a spacious and spotless interior where a shrewd-eyed peasant served the local tea laced with camel's milk. This delighted the Hong Kong youth to whom it was as exotic as the remotest herdsmen's encampment.

The grasslands were genuine enough, vast, quiet and stretching away to an undulating line of low hills. It was a still and empty world. In the autumn sun the grass was brown and lifeless but the long grass and wild flowers of late spring must be beautiful. We drove to a nearby hill where a mound of rocks fronted by three rough stone altars marked an old shaman sacred place. The herdsmen gathered here for seasonal rites and it acted as a rough compass for the wandering nomads. Up on this hill and looking over the still view, suddenly a genuine horseman galloped flat out across the middle-distance, the horse wild as the wind, bringing for a fleeting moment the old reality of Mongolia.

When we returned to Wulantuger we were shown the only genuine thing there, a temple in Tibetan-style, complete with a kindly old lama who showed us round. The main hall was brightly painted with a large throne at the far end. Behind this hall was the temple with three altars and three large gilt Buddhas draped in votive scarves. The surrounding walls were painted in Tibetan-style with ferocious gods and esoteric charts of paradise. The grizzled priest tended the altar lamps with reverence, a frail figure in a threadbare robe. In reality the temple was garish but it had an atmosphere of continuing devotion and the smell of the lamps carried me back to Lhasa.

The temple must have been large at one time. When we went to

36 Mosque by the Yellow River

LANZHOU

37 Music in a temple garden

38 Muslim street restaurant

LANZHOU

39 Street library

dinner I saw that the complex of courts which now accommodated the dining rooms were built in the same style as the adjoining temple. Wulantuger had been reorganised for the tourists. Dinner was no more appetising than the mutton bones at lunch. Diana and I retired to the yurt, ate some cheese and crackers she had brought from Beijing and went for a twilight walk on the edge of the grasslands.

A concert of Mongolian music and dance was advertised for seven in a small concert hall behind the yurts. Diana bullied me into going and, to my surprise, within minutes of it starting I was captivated. Everything was of a high standard and authentic. The dancing was charming with attractive costumes, the music enthralling and the show given an edge by the enthusiasm of the performers, all of whom were genuine Mongolians. The two girl dancers were strikingly beautiful, tall, strong featured and moving like proud animals. Everything reached a climax with a haunting flute solo, the strange, intricate music played with great skill. The music evoked a genuine Mongolian culture which made the tour some kind of insult. The trembling notes of the flute spoke eloquently of the old way of life of the grasslands. It was beautiful, but it was also sad in making one aware of what was being destroyed. The flute player and the galloping horse had given us two glimpses of the real Inner Mongolia.

The next day we had to suffer the last act of the farce while each Hong Kong youth, screaming with wonder and delight, took turns to ride on the backs of two intellectual-looking Bactarian camels who, when they put their woolly heads together, looked deep in learned conversation. After that it was the same thing with two beautiful Mongolian ponies, all speed and muscle. Obviously Wulantuger was working with a small cast. Two of the previous night's male dancers appeared the next morning as camel handlers while the talented flautist and a fellow musician rode the ponies.

On the way home we did stop at two of Hohhot's sights. The Temple of the Five Pagodas, dating from the eighteenth century, now consists only of a pleasant courtyard garden and the impressive gateway topped with five small pagodas, their bases surrounded by panels with charming, lively figures carved in relief. I shall never forget those panels. Shortly before I had left Hohhot my electronic typewriter had burnt out. Now my new camera went 'on the blink'. Since it was computerised there was no chance of having it repaired in China and I had weeks of travel ahead of me. Suddenly I had an inspired thought – dust. After a thorough clean it was back in working order. More miraculous, two days later, the electronic typewriter, unaided came back to life. Should all this seem rather high-tech, I do assure you that I also travel with an ordinary toothbrush.

The last stop was the tomb of Wang Zhaojun, concubine of Emperor Yuandi of the first century AD. As a monument it was of little interest but the compound was planted with a sprawling, abundant garden, colourful and as unruly as an English cottage garden. On the far side was a small hill with a view across the fertile surroundings to the town in the distance. Although it was advertised, we never saw the Chinese-style Great Mosque. That is the way of official itineraries in China and one of the reasons why I would never restrict myself to a package tour. Frequently I met members of groups who had not been given what they had been promised, be it a first-class hotel or cabin on a steamer, or an excursion to places listed on their itinerary. Travelling alone is often frustrating but to some extent you are in control of your own journey.

Places like Hohhot, a little off the beaten track, are particularly frustrating. One accepts the 'Grasslands Tour' for what it is, and enjoys bonuses like Meryl and Bill and the flat-cheeked flautist. But the infuriating fact remains that somewhere out there in those silent grasslands the traditional way of life goes on: real herdsmen live in yurts of beaten felt, milk their mares and play that enthralling flute music under a cold night sky. But unless you are an official guest of the government, you won't get near it. There is no transport, and even if you had the transport you would not get permission to wander in an area so close to an alien border. The CITS does offer a four-day tour which takes you to other grassland areas but this is a place one wants to explore independently. The traditional nomadic life is dying, or being killed off. Having come so far I would have given so much to see more. But I felt the same feelings of frustration in Kunming, Chengdu, Lhasa and other places where the surrounding countryside offered interest and beauty, all unattainable.

11

Along the Silk Road

LANZHOU

The confusions of individual travel in China give rise to unexpected ironies. I had no interest in Lanzhou. I went there only as a stepping stone to the cave temples of Binglingsi. I failed to reach the caves but fell in love with Lanzhou, walking the streets of the old town for four days. But first I had to get there.

Lanzhou is twenty-four hours by train from Hohhot, going south-westwards across the bleak provinces of Ningxia and Gansu. I had reserved a soft sleeper and my train was due to leave Hohhot at 11.30 p.m. The car insisted on leaving the hotel early so I found myself at Hohhot station at ten with an hour and a half to wait. Large Chinese railway stations, particularly late at night, are not attractive but give one a glimpse of the lower end of life. The main waiting room was large and filthy and so crowded that I was forced to sit just by the entrance to the men's lavatory where the air was acrid. It was a restless spot as people streamed in and out of the lavatory, probably the only public convenience for miles.

Most of the benches were taken up by men lying full-length, their heads supported on huge bundles. How many of them were actually waiting to catch a train I have no idea. At this hour of the night the derelicts and the bewildered creep out of the woodwork, no doubt attracted by the warmth of the station. This is a face of China not included in the travel brochures. Mixed with the genuine travellers are the ragged down-and-outs, grimy beggars putting out a tentative hand, the occasional drunk and a few trembling and twitching creatures who, in most countries, would be in mental homes. With all this and the filth on the floor and the sharp stink in the air, it was a Hogarthian scene.

Sitting next to me were two engaging ragamuffins, each about fifteen, one of whom wore his khaki cap at a jaunty angle. They were also on their way to Lanzhou. Their only luggage was an old army haversack which contained their toothbrushes and two small and bedraggled white pigeons enmeshed in a string bag. Whether these birds were pets or for the pot I couldn't discover but they were shown off with great pride. I had my doubts if they would survive the twenty-four-hour journey. Both the young men had a tremendous sense of humour and with the aid of little drawings we communicated for about an hour. Suddenly, a shadow fell over us and there was a sour-faced station policeman. He ordered the boys to clear off. Whether he was protecting me from them, or them from me, I have no idea.

Five minutes later, having rounded up a couple of micreants, he was back demanding to see my ticket. He beckoned me to follow him and I was led away to the boring isolation of the soft seat waiting room. It was the only time in all my China travels that a policeman interfered with my movements and for all I know the man may have intended to do me a favour. Soft seat waiting rooms always alarm me lest nobody comes to lead you to your train. Twice I had nearly been left behind. This time a kind young Chinese took me through the huge station to my carriage and made sure that I found my sleeper. It was lucky he did. My ticket had been filled in with the wrong carriage number.

I shared my compartment with three friendly minor officials, two of whom seemed to have wives elsewhere on the train. I went to bed immediately, looking forward to the long journey across Ningxia and Gansu the next day, my first glimpse of the Silk Road. The landscape that I watched for twelve hours the next day gave me an entirely new and considerably less romantic picture of that famous trade route. Popular television programmes, by their careful selection – the brilliant silks of Hangzhou, a brightly tiled mosque, the refreshing greens of an oasis, a river sparkling between the mountains – do not emphasise the main part of that long road which runs for thousands of kilometres through the kind of bleak desert I watched from the train, though this was only the first stage of arid emptiness that faced the caravans.

There was occasional relief with patches of fertility nearer the Yellow River which allowed the irrigation of maize, vegetables and sunflowers but the desert soon absorbed the landscape again into a bleaker view. The desert was enclosed in the distance by dark, shadowy mountains, while nearer, humped sand dunes ran down to flatter land, pocked with dead grey-green scrub. The occasional patch of vivid yellow and purple wild flowers thrilled the eye like precious stones. Everything was dusty, dry, brittle, the narrow tracks, the thorny plants and the cracking red and grey soil. The slightest break in the monotony was welcome: telegraph poles, an occasional flock of scrawny sheep, the patterns of pebbles on the railway embankment, even the black smoke of our engine as it drifted back over the train darkening the afternoon sun. Always dust moved in the air. The landscape was like arid architecture; hard, unrelenting lines and forms, drab harmonies of colour, functional for drought. The merchants on the Silk Road had months of this, and worse.

From time to time we stopped at remote stations. In Ningxia we were passing through one of the poorest and most arid regions of China. The importance of the railway is indicated by the number of lines, sidings and waiting freight cars at these isolated stations. There is little else but a compound surrounded by high red brick walls shaded by tall trees. Two women were lowering makeshift buckets into a deep well. The few people on the platform watched the train. A pig-faced man stared emptily into our compartment. He was chewing sunflower seeds, pulling them out of his pocket with the monotony of someone telling their beads. He frequently looked at his watch but clearly he was not going anywhere. He will probably be in the same place tomorrow and the day after that. Little can happen here to break the domestic routine except for the arrival and departure of trains. Yet even here, in this godforsaken corner of the world, modern male fashion has found its way. Down the platform strolled two youths in the tightest jeans and leather jackets, set off by white plimsolls. China is on the move, in one direction or another.

A compressed hiss of steam, a metallic jerk and we were off again, leaving the rough buildings behind and re-entering the dry desert world. The momentary intervals of farmhouses and metalled roads continued but always we were soon back into the land of dry scrub, the dark mountains closing in on both sides. Darkness fell, my three companions began to put their possessions together, a varied collection of plastic cases, neat cloth bundles, string bags and other containers. Most of it seemed to be food, perhaps the specialities of Hohhot which I had failed to notice. The wives came into the compartment to put the finishing touches to the packing. The train finally pulled into Lanzhou at 11 p.m.

When I came out of the station it was dark and there were few lights in the town. The main road leading from the station disappeared into blackness. There was no transport of any kind. I had no map and no idea where the hotel was situated in this town of two million people, now asleep. As I looked down the empty street I thought how this situation offered a test to anyone considering travelling alone in China. Although it is totally safe, at such moments it can be dauntingly lonely.

I slung my bags on my shoulders and started walking. A few people lurked in the shadows, against the wall or under the trees but I thought it unlikely that I could extract information from such night birds about the location of the hotel. I was simply hoping that I might be lucky, looking out for a splash of lights which at this late hour might indicate a hotel. I had no choice and I knew from experience that often hotels are at the opposite end of the town from the station. I was lucky. After walking for about twenty minutes I saw a large roundabout and to one side an exceptional amount of light. It was the Lanzhou Hotel and a pleasant woman at the reception desk gave me a room, promising that the bathroom had hot water. A youth led the way, leaving me to carry my bags while he continued chewing nuts and spitting out the shells with abandon. There was no hot water and not much cold. I fell into bed, dirty but relieved.

After a good breakfast I followed my golden rule and before doing anything else asked about booking a train to my next destination, Xi'an. The clerk seemed to say that the line was closed because of a strike and said that I must fly. A strike seemed unlikely and I learned later that the line between Lanzhou and Xi'an had collapsed following a rainstorm and it was closed for three days. Luckily, the CAAC office was only a few minutes from the hotel. I queued behind a young German who was told, to my dismay, that the flight I wanted was already full. Mysteriously, but typically, when my turn came, with a straight face I asked for exactly the same flight as the German and was immediately sold a ticket. The wretched German had to stand there arguing for another hour before he was allowed to buy his ticket for the same flight.

My heart was still set on the cave temples of Binglingsi. I knew that excursions were organised by the Lanzhou CITS and I found their office on the third floor of an obscure building at the back of the hotel. There were five Chinese seated round a table, drinking tea and chatting. There was not a piece of paperwork in sight. I asked about their tours to the cave temples. They grinned and sipped their tea. They regretted that their office was too busy to organise tours for individuals. Could I join another group? There were no groups going. Perhaps I could hire a taxi? Impossible, the office had no time to organise transport. However, I might care to try the municipal travel service. Another grin and their heads closed ranks as they returned to their tea and gossip. I know a brick wall when I see one.

I returned to the reception desk and asked there if they could arrange for me to hire a car. They then explained that I could get to the cave temples only by car and then by boat as the caves were at the end of a reservoir. I then asked if they knew about the municipal travel service. Yes, that was in the lobby of the Victory Hotel on the other side of town and they marked the place on the map. This rigmarole had taken the whole morning, typical of how the individual traveller eats up his or her time achieving nothing. I decided to leave the Victory Hotel until after lunch.

I found a bus that ran from near my hotel to the Victory Hotel on the other side of town. The Chinese bus service is excellent once you get used to the struggles to get aboard, the crush inside and the butch girls who sell the tickets. I got into such muddles trying to explain where I wanted to go that I soon gave that up. Instead, I stood in stony silence refusing to communicate until I reached my destination when I took the opportunity of unloading my dirtiest bank notes on the girl at the seat of custom. En route often I had to put up with strident demands for payment which caused everyone in the bus to stare at me but I got used to that. The Chinese are overt starers so I had plenty of practice, on and off the buses. At least it made me feel less guilty about my intrusive camera.

We arrived at my destination, in fact the end of this particular route. I cannot comment on the town at this stage. The main disadvantage of standing in a bus when you are tall is that you see nothing except the handrail and your neighbours' hair condition. I looked around. The Victory Hotel sounded both large and grand, something with wings and a flag. There was nothing like that in this seedy neighbourhood. I had the name written in Chinese on a piece of paper and was directed up the hill to what seemed the crumbling edge of the town. Street vendors lurked under the trees and old men shuffled by the wall smoking thoughtfully. After two more false starts I was confronted with a tenement-like building, every window draped with washing and the lobby, for this was it, as busy as a railway station. The benches were packed, the floor piled with baggage, a crowd around reception and people queuing restlessly for the lavatory. It was a low-class and highly popular hotel.

Easing my way through this crowd, by now convinced that no one here would speak English and that I was heading into another language confusion, I found the desk of the municipal travel service. The truth is that when I set out I did not believe that I had the slightest chance of finding it. The girl not only spoke reasonable English but was very helpful. My hopes were raised. Yes, the travel service ran tours to Binglingsi which I could join. Better and better. The next tour would go in four days time. I knew deep down that I was a loser. I could not stay in Lanzhou that long. I thanked her warmly and turned my attention to the streets of Lanzhou. A few intriguing glimpses while searching for the Victory Hotel had already whetted my appetite.

The next day I followed yesterday's bus route on foot. It had been grey and chilly and I had seen autumn in the brown and brittle leaves of several trees. Today it was bright and warm and the town looked cheerful as I walked along the main avenue, busy with buses, bicycles and a surprising number of cars, many of them stately old black sedans, their back windows and bureaucratic occupants shrouded from the common gaze by brownish net curtains. Lanzhou is capital city of Gansu province, a settlement with roots going back to neolithic times and later an important town along the Silk Road and a base for defending the Gansu Corridor leading out to the main desert routes to the west. With its large Muslim population and Muslim quarter in the old town I found in Lanzhou more atmosphere of the Silk Road, with its exotic trade and its intermingling of cultures, than anywhere else. It was not strong but here at least one could see the slight remains of that great trading culture among the stalls of the Muslim butchers and on the street corner where a jaunty Tibetan was selling peacock feathers.

At first sight Lanzhou is just another large, industrialised, polluted Chinese town with smoking chimneys and the demolition gangs at work clearing away the debris of history to make room for the harsh façades of more apartment blocks and government offices. Wide, tree-lined avenues sweep north and south and east to west across a basin surrounded by steep and rugged mountains. The surging Yellow River races across the northern boundary of the town, a fierce tide of surging, muddy water. But behind the new concrete façades, at the western end of the town, lingers an older Lanzhou. Maybe it was my delight in at last finding a genuine and readily identifiable ethnic group or that it was perfect autumn but I was captivated. However, I should confess that there were few foreign tourists in the hotel and two young Americans I spoke to were wasting no time in 'getting out of this dump'. I can only say that it was my kind of town.

Walking westwards the first kilometre or two leading to the bleak central square, grandstands for May Day parades and all, were simply dull. Immediately after the square the avenue suddenly changes into a narrow street creating a chaotic bottle-neck for the buses and cars. This was the start of the old town. That fact was not entirely obvious since many of the old façades had been modernised but every few metres gateways and narrow alleys gave glimpses of a more haphazard world. The archways framed small courts and narrow pathways lined with tiny ramshackle houses and outbuildings, their rough brickwork leaning uncertainly among festoons of laundry and struggling patches of garden whose vegetables stretched up to reach vines, morning glory and other plants straggling down from pots lined up on every ledge.

Some of these alleys receded some way lined with ten houses or more, their inhabitants scrubbing, planting, cooking, shampooing and mending bikes cheek by jowl. Occasionally a larger archway revealed a crumbling temple and, once, a brick pagoda sprouting weeds like a bottle-brush. One temple was being restored by a large team of workmen. The youths did not give the impression of great skill. At the mouths of many of these old alleys the householders were launching out into private enterprise: a tray of cigarettes and matches, half a dozen home-knitted pullovers, a pile of the famous Lanzhou melons, three spivvy youths selling six cheap suitcases and a bearded Muslim with glasses of tea. I was particularly intrigued by one larger stall where a whole family were selling exquisite paper cut-outs in brilliant crimson paper of a variety of Chinese scenes and dragon-filled decorations and lengths of Chinese characters which no doubt brought the owner good luck. All were charmingly designed and executed with skill.

The ordinary shops and the lively markets down the side streets were full of interest. I saw windows of cosmetics, brilliantly wrapped fireworks, a busy tailor's shop where three cheerful young men were cutting a suit and, just down the road, a large shop window with several rigid dummies, their faces like bad waxworks, displaying the latest crudely made ladies' high fashions. In the street markets, as so often, the stalls laden with jeans seemed to predominate. Before long jeans will have replaced the Mao-style jacket and cap as the national dress of China.

Nearer the river the Muslim population becomes more obvious, serving in their own pavement restaurants, bakeries and kerbside food stalls. The men, bearded in different styles, wore knitted white caps or caps of white cotton. The older women wore something like the veil of a nun, covering the head and hair with an oval opening for the face. The younger women and the children wore the cotton caps. A few ancient men had rusty velvet caps, their spotted knuckles clutching nobbly sticks and I saw a few men bound up in wide black cummerbunds which supported their baggy trousers. The beards varied from dense sproutings of white hair down to thin wisps on adolescent chins. The men had that fierce, intense look common to the Muslim world, though the few I spoke to usually broke into genial smiles.

Of course, they were first and foremost Chinamen even if old Islamic blood ran in some veins. Over the centuries many local people had been converted to Islam, just as many Mongolians had been drawn to Tibetan Buddhism. But there was a distinct mingling of different cultures in Lanzhou. It was symbolised by the White Pagoda Temple, spread up the steep hillside, rising above the green dome and minarets of the large mosque below the hill, surrounded by the clustering houses of the old Muslim quarter. Despite the physical dominance of the Buddhist temple this area was the heart of Muslim Lanzhou.

As I crossed the narrow bridge I could see the real power of the Yellow River, a force that has brought floods and destruction to China for centuries. There were no boats on this racing water. It swirled along, its flat, circulating eddies full of sediment, surging against the piles of the bridge and breaking free in exploding waves of white foam. On the north side of the river there were two mosques, a more modern one by the water's edge just below the old mosque. Immediately over the bridge, stretching out along the street that ran east and west, was a lively Muslim market. There were stalls shaded with canvas sheets with mounds of fruit and large baskets of nuts. There were vegetable stalls, clothes stalls and, tucked in between, noodle restaurants and men grilling kebabs. The butchers' stalls were segregated on the other side of the bridge where bearded, hard-eyed men hacked at fly-kissed lumps of dark mutton. Pathetically, across the street, six sheep were tethered to a telegraph pole, unsuitably right by the entrance to the Buddhist temple. But these days there are few Buddhists and everyone eats meat, when they can get it.

I climbed the steep steps that led to the entrance gate of the White Pagoda Temple. It is built on a series of large terraces reaching up the hill, the Ming and Qing gateways and pavilions linked by pleasant gardens, steps and steep paths to reach the older and lopsided white pagoda at the top. All the way up and down one has fine views over the temple roofs, across the river to the main part of the town where, on the far side, distant mountains rise sharply behind Lanzhou. The temple halls and pavilions and small kiosks perched on the viewing-points are all attractive in their setting though the place has more the atmosphere of a public park than a Buddhist temple. It also offered an unexpected open-air concert.

On the lower terrace there was a shady garden with walls, steps and dark cypress trees. As I approached the western end of the garden I saw an open pavilion and a considerable crowd of people gathered around a group of six musicians preparing to play. It was a delightful scene. The orchestra was surrounded by several old men, comfortably seated in home-made deckchairs, tugging on their beards and chewing small cheroots. A man in a cummerbund and baggy trousers served tea by the cup. Others sat on nearby benches or on the low walls of the pavilion. The leader of the orchestra, a shaven-headed and genial percussionist, saw me loitering on the edge of the crowd and beckoned me to sit on a bench near the players. Everyone was welcoming and it soon became obvious that this was a regular meeting of amateur music lovers. I was given a cup of tea and the music began.

It is hard to say whether the players or the playing were the more fascinating. Even the instruments were exotic though I had seen similar two-stringed fiddles in Mongolia, their small, cylindrical sound-boxes covered in snakeskin. But the orchestra was dominated by the percussion. The leader beats out a complex basic rhythm on three small drums with one hand, playing a pair of elongated 'castanets' with the other, really two unattached lengths of wood which are clicked together. The cymbalist was the character of the group. He sat throughout the afternoon clashing away, his peaked cap pulled low over his dark glasses, a black cigarette in a long, rustic holder clenched between his teeth. Between pieces all the other musicians changed places with other players in the audience. The cymbalist gave up his seat to no man. The third percussionist played a variety of 'castanets', bone and wood. The percussion and the three wailing fiddles wove in and out of each other's rhythms, the stretched notes of the fiddles able to ride over the top of the heavy percussion. The lady singer who suddenly joined the ensemble could have ridden over the top of anything.

This elderly but well-built lady howled and screeched her way through a long song. The audience obviously enjoyed it thoroughly and I could presume only that my ear was not yet attuned to these oriental strains. She gave way to a battered-looking man in drab blue workman's dress. He rose from his chair, rubbed the back of his hand over his unshaven chin and broke hoarsely into a song intense with emotion like a kind of oriental flamenco. It all came from deep in the throat and as he increased both feeling and volume I could see the neck muscles stretching. To loud applause he resumed his chair, a slightly smug 'follow that' expression all over his face. The middle-aged lady who came next certainly did her excruciating best.

The musicians changed and changed again. Fat, grinning men played the drums. Thin, serious, bespectacled young men sawed away at the three fiddles. There were Muslims and non-Muslims, men and women, young and old. I have no idea how often the concerts were held, but everyone knew everyone and everyone knew what to do. Their pleasure and sense of relaxation was obvious and the friendliness of the group spilled over on to me. It was an unexpected afternoon and one of the most enjoyable I spent in China.

I had supper that night with a young Swiss glaciologist who had been sent by the Swiss government to the Institute of Glaciology in Lanzhou to teach them the latest methods of measuring glaciers. A Chinese scientist had already spent a year or more in Switzerland and this was also a return visit. He had spent a rough four weeks camping on a glacier out west beyond Urumqi but welcomed the opportunity as it enabled him to study glacier formations unique to China. It seemed that Chinese ideas of camping were equally unique but since they did nothing but work, eat and sleep he hadn't had much time to think of the primitive conditions. In any case, he was an experienced mountaineer so he was used to large doses of discomfort. He was now back in Lanzhou for several weeks to process their fieldwork on the local institute's computer. I had had supper with him each evening and every day he had suffered the same frustration.

They hardly started work in the morning before the power failed, the computer went down and for the rest of the day they sat chatting around a black screen. He said that he enjoyed working with the younger Chinese scientists, but the older ones were incapable of flexible thinking. As usual, basically to stimulate trade, his government had paid for his visit to China though in this case he was acquiring valuable new experience.

The next day, as Lanzhou is 70 km from its airport, the result of lack of suitable flat land nearer the town, I had to catch the bus at 2.30 p.m. I decided to spend the morning visiting the local museum which was said to have interesting archaeological finds. It needed two long bus rides to get to the extreme west of the town and when I finally found the museum it had obviously been converted into a trade show centre. The building was tightly closed but over the entrance was a long banner proclaiming, 'Exhibition Centre of Gansu Economic and Technical Cooperation with Foreign Countries'. I liked the use of the word 'cooperation', another echo of that old imperial attitude to foreign vassal states. It looked as if they were building a new museum next door but it was some way from completion. It was perhaps suitable that my visit to Lanzhou should start and finish with frustration, with so much fulfilment and pleasure tucked in between. I made the long bus journey back to the hotel to check out before leaving for the airport.

The flight for Xi'an was due to leave at 5.20 p.m. and the bus left the CAAC offices punctually at 2.30, the drive to the airport taking just over two hours. Most of the way we drove through a strange red and pink landscape, a world devoted to making bricks from the local clays. Everywhere there was deep erosion with deep flat-bottomed valleys or narrow ravines like miniature Grand Canyons, with twisted peaks and pinnacles of red earth left free-standing. Grass and plants grew in the ravines and in the wider areas stood rectangular and oval kilns with many doors, stretching alongside the road for kilometre after kilometre. By the kilns were piles of dark, leather-hard bricks ready for baking and elsewhere huge stacks of fired bricks, some being loaded into lorries.

It was a strange landscape on a large scale, the erosion following small rivers and great red cliffs rising up behind the brickworks far below the road in their valleys. Caves were cut into the faces of the ravines and the cliffs and the people lived here and there in adobe houses. The colours were striking in the afternoon sun and I thought of the rose-red cliffs of Petra. These musings were interrupted by our arrival at Lanzhou airport and the news that our flight for Xi'an would not be leaving as scheduled. Indeed, no one knew when it would be leaving.

12

Early Capitals

XI'AN AND LUOYANG

It was the delay at Lanzhou airport which led me to meet the three Chinese who were to give me such an unusual introduction to Xi'an. The sky around the airport crackled with lightning and it was the lingering storm that was threatening our flight and others. Probably because their provincial airports lack sophisticated navigational equipment, the Chinese do not fly unless conditions are near-perfect. A spot of rain or a thin layer of ground mist and all flights are delayed. The airport lounge was packed since three full flights were due to leave. Passengers' tempers were not improved by the total lack of information. One group of Chinese passengers seemed about to stage an uprising and were noisily storming the airport manager's office, their spokesman trembling with anger. It seemed that the group had been at the airport since seven that morning. Two planes had come in heading for their destination but in both cases, as a result of booking errors, the flights were already full and they had been unable to board. Now they had heard that there was unlikely to be a plane for them until the next day. A red-faced manager appeared from his office and tried to calm them down.

'At least it's better than it used to be,' a youth sitting next to me explained. 'The inefficiency is still bad but now at least they feel free to complain and, most important of all, the head of the airport comes to apologise and to explain the problem. Until recently nobody was prepared to take even that much responsibility.'

The speaker was a Chinese of about twenty-one who was going with his older companion for a two-week engineering course to Xi'an. He spoke reasonable if broken English while the older man just smiled. The young man came straight out of a famous Chinese painting, a portrait of a boy with a huge grin and a pudding-basin haircut which stuck out around his head like a frayed straw hat. His warm character was in his eyes as well as his grin and talking to him made the long wait a pleasure. I had also met up with a pleasant young backpacker from Hong Kong who was bound for Xi'an and he occasionally acted as interpreter when the other Chinese boy got stuck.

It was now 7.30 p.m. and still no news of our flight. It was pouring dense rain and the three Chinese were pessimistic. We retired to the airport restaurant and consoled ourselves with a reasonable meal and some excellent beer. Finally, six hours late for this one-hour flight, at 11.30 p.m. we were squeezed into a small plane which arrived at Xi'an airport around 12.30 a.m. I waited to collect my baggage, wondering how far we were from the centre of Xi'an and if there would be any transport to the hotel at this hour of the night. Outside the airport building it looked suspiciously dark. I found my bag but my three companions had vanished. I presumed that they had gone their own ways.

How wrong I was. All three were waiting anxiously for me outside the airport where a small bus was standing.

'We wonder if you have anywhere to stay or if you would like to come with us?'

It was pouring again, I was exhausted by the long delay and with no idea where to go I think I would have accepted a bed in the road. We climbed aboard the bus which I presumed was going somewhere into Xi'an though I was puzzled by the trifling fare. We rattled along through total darkness for no more than a kilometre or so and came to a sudden halt. I got out and we still seemed to be in the middle of nowhere though there was a high wall on the other side of the bus. A gate opened throwing some light out onto the wet road. My friends led the way and as I passed through the door I saw a small notice: XI'AN AIRPORT HOTEL. The title was a euphemism. I was intrigued. To one side of a muddy yard was a small office and we queued while each Chinese showed his small red identity card. The particulars were entered in a large notebook and he paid three yuan. My turn came and the girl took my passport while the young Chinese translated the necessary details for her which she entered in her register. I also paid the modest charge. My Chinese friends led the way along a path past several low buildings and at the end turned into a bleak dormitory containing twelve iron bedsteads packed tightly together around the walls. In the centre of the room was a table and a few chairs. A few beds were already occupied. By the remainder two soldiers and a number of workmen were getting undressed. I made up my bed from the rough but warm quilts and slipped between them, deeply grateful to have a bed for the night.

40 Terracotta soldiers guarding the tomb of Emperor Qin Shihuang

XI'AN

41 The Great Mosque

42 Small Goose Pagoda

43 Grilling kebabs

XI'AN   LUOYANG

44 Abacus-seller   45 Heavenly king at
                                      Longmen caves

I was fascinated by the thin man in the corner in a tight, worn grey suit. His movements were slow and deliberate as he tidied his clothes and possessions with obsessive precision. He had a nutcracker face in which the elongated chin came to a sharp point, stretching his skin tight over his bony face. Despite his narrow jaw, from his mouth he extracted a fearsome and livid pair of dentures which he dropped neatly into a jam jar of water. They lay there grimacing through the glass. He arranged himself for bed with the care of an old spinster, finally draping his emaciated body in a knee-length, old-fashioned vest.

In the morning his obsessiveness was more clearly revealed as he packed and repacked his two small suitcases, rearranging rolled-up socks and moving notebooks and papers from one plastic folder to another until it was all ordered to his pernickety satisfaction. He spoke to no one, looked at no one. He was safely isolated in a world of his own, perhaps a world he had retreated into during the persecutions of the Cultural Revolution of which he may well have been a victim.

After the lights were turned out I lay thinking of the kindness of my Chinese friends and even more, how unexpected it was to be lying there sharing a dormitory in a workers' hostel with two soldiers and nine artisans. My surprise had nothing to do with the primitive conditions but with the fact that I was allowed to sleep there, signed in like everyone else, paying exactly the same charge and wholly accepted by my fellow guests, most of whom had hardly given me a glance. It was a small sign of a very great change that has taken place in China during the last two years. My presence in the Xi'an Airport Hotel would have been unthinkable, indeed illegal, until recently.

When I first visited China in 1983, not only were non-Chinese foreigners completely segregated from the Chinese, even overseas Chinese from Hong Kong, Taiwan and other places had their own hotels which were out of bounds to Westerners and to mainland Chinese. All that has been swept away with the government's more pragmatic attitudes and probably because of new pressures on accommodation as the Chinese themselves travel more and more, some on business, others holidaymaking. Apart from this hostel, which was rather unusual, in many hotels I was the only foreigner on my floor, the other rooms all occupied by mainland Chinese.

In the morning the other three were ready and asked me if I would like some breakfast. The young man led the way, out of the hostel and down some streets which led through blocks of old apartment houses. On a corner was a hovel with a roof and a back wall and smoke drifting from a chimney. The owner was frying those long Chinese doughnuts which we were served at the communal table with bowls of hot soya-bean cream sweetened with sugar. The breakfast was warming and delicious but to my dismay the two Chinese insisted on paying for mine. Considering how little they must earn it was a generous gesture.

Back at the hostel we had to part as they were due to start their course at nine. They told me that there was a bus at the bottom of the road into central Xi'an. We said goodbye and the Hong Kong Chinese and I headed into town. At the end of the road we were both surprised to discover that we were already in the inner suburbs of Xi'an. I had remained under the impression that both the airport and the hostel were miles out of the town. Ten minutes on the bus and we were passing the massive Ming belltower which stands in the centre of Xi'an. We got off the bus and found our way to the huge Renmin Hotel.

The woman at the desk hardly looked up to inform us that the hotel was full. After five minutes' argument, mostly by my Hong Kong friend, I was given a room. That hotel remains a mystery to me. Everyone I spoke to had been refused a room on arrival and after anything from five minutes' to one hour's argument had obtained a room, or at least a bed. One morning I was walking through the lobby where I met four young Austrians, exhausted after twenty-seven hours on hard seats. They had just been refused rooms and thought that the girl had not been able to understand their poor English. The two girls were on the verge of tears with exhaustion and they asked if I could help them. I did so with interest as I had a small trump card up my sleeve which I thought might help me to discover the reason for this absurd charade.

'Excuse me, but please find these four people a bed. They are exhausted. They don't mind sharing or sleeping in a dormitory.'

'The hotel is full.'

'I know that. It always is. But please find them a bed.'

'The hotel is completely full.'

'Yes, you told me exactly the same thing when I arrived but five minutes later you put me in a room with two empty beds.'

'You were lucky. Today the hotel is full.'

'But you say that to everyone and then you find them a bed.'

'Today is different. I have checked all through the hotel and there is not a single bed. We are completely full.'

I played the small trump; more of a tiny lever to slip in the cracks of bureaucracy.

'So there is not a single bed in the whole hotel.'

'I have just told you that I checked.'

'Well, I think you'd better check more thoroughly. Just for a start there is an empty bed in my room. The American checked out an hour ago.'

A slightly disconcerted look showed that the lever was in place. I leant on it.

'What's more, another American checked out this morning from the room next door. That's two empty beds in your "completely full" hotel.'

One telephone call to my floor and five minutes later the four young Austrians all had beds. Of course, nobody ever checks anything. There is no regular communication between the front desk and the staff looking after the bedrooms. Since guests pay in advance for their rooms they do not have to check out at the front desk. Guests are not given room keys since the keys are kept by the floor staff, so when a guest leaves the front desk has no way of knowing until the room staff eventually remember to tell them, or someone like me puts the pressure on, forcing the desk clerk into the trouble of ringing round. It is a maddening non-system by no means limited to the Renmin Hotel, Xi'an, and it makes life particularly difficult for those foreigners who speak neither Chinese nor reasonable English, and reasonable English includes the ability to understand the peculiar English spoken by many Chinese.

After I had obtained my own bed I asked my Hong Kong friend if he would like to share my room, part of a four-room dormitory with a shared bathroom. But no, he had decided to save money and stay on at the Airport Hotel. I suddenly realised that he had come all this way through the rain simply to make sure I was all right and to help me get a room. I was touched by the kindness I had received in the last twenty-four hours.

Xi'an is the capital of Shaanxi province and the Wei River valley has nurtured civilisation from the neolithic era. Intermittently it was the capital of the Chinese empire for over 1000 years being named Changan, City of Everlasting Peace, by the first emperor of the Han dynasty around 206 BC. Under the Tang dynasty it became one of the greatest cities in the world, the massive rectangle of its walls, said to measure 10 by 8 km, enclosing a population of over one million people. It was the starting place for the Silk Road to the far West and its trade led to the establishment of many foreign communities free to follow their own religion and culture. This cosmopolitan background and the flow of fine objects from the Middle East stimulated the already vigorous Tang culture which became one of the most vital periods in Chinese history, not only in art and architecture, but in government and general administration, a pattern to be closely copied by both the Ming and the Manchu emperors.

All contemporary visitors were overwhelmed by the scale and magnificence of Changan, its power, its wealth, and the community of foreign traders, Muslims, Zoroastrians from Persia, Nestorian Christians from Syria, each with their own quarter and their own temples, mosques and churches. Among the various foreign missions were ambassadors and Buddhist priests from the imperial court of Japan. Already strongly under the influence of Chinese culture, in AD 794 they modelled their new and splendid capital, Kyoto, on Changan, creating a more modest version of the Chinese layout and grid street plan which remains in both cities to this day.

As the power of the Tang dynasty weakened Changan began to decline and with the final collapse of the Tang dynasty in 907 it ceased to be the capital of China. It was rebuilt during the Ming dynasty as a palace for one of the imperial princes but the building was on a reduced scale and the great town never recovered its former importance, slipping into the dusty obscurity of a remote provincial centre. Its present revival is due to communist efforts to stimulate the economy of chosen inland provincial centres, to counterbalance the economic dominance of the coastal trading centres and by the growth of the tourist trade, stimulated mainly by the sensational archaeological finds in the neighbourhood, with the promise of more to come. China lost most of the imperial collection of paintings and art objects when hundreds of packing cases were audaciously smuggled out of China to Taiwan by Chiang Kai-shek in 1948, now forming the unrivalled collection of Chinese art in the National Palace Museum in Taipei.

The Chinese will never forgive this act of 'looting'. Their answer has been a great deal of archaeological work which among the mass of material excavated has produced a few headline-catching items, two of them now providing the main draw to Xi'an for the average tourist. Certainly I would not have gone there had it not been for the neolithic village of Banpo and the treasures found in the area surrounding the tumulus tomb of Emperor Qin Shihuang who united the Chinese empire for the first time shortly before his death in 210 BC.

Even though I had not expected too much of the city of Xi'an, I was still disappointed. Apart from the small area around the Great Mosque there is nothing left in the town to suggest the cosmopolitan atmosphere of Changan. Xi'an is now a large, rather drab and dull provincial city encumbered with a few massive Ming remains which lose the impressiveness they once had in their isolation among dense traffic encircling concrete hotels, office blocks and large stores. The streets are busy: abacus-sellers, old women selling ice cream, youths in baseball caps grilling kebabs and the magazine stalls besieged by young readers and the mass of the crowd surging slowly along the huge avenues. The department stores were packed, the cinemas were packed, I had to queue for a table at the big Sichuan restaurant. The population is around the two million of the Tang period but the old magnificence of Changan has gone and there is not a trace of the exotic Silk Road. This inland Venice of the East has sunk beneath the waves of history. Imagine Florence with two or three fragmentary churches and its railway station or Oxford with little left but the clutter of Saturday afternoon shopping along the Cornmarket. One could not even describe Xi'an as a shadow of its former self. It is depressing when such a great monument of world history disappears so completely.

I went first to the Great Mosque, to the north-west of the Ming belltower and, nearer, the drum tower. The mosque is tucked away in the side streets of the old Muslim quarter, alleyways of mud houses, children playing in the narrow yards. The Great Mosque is as large as its name implies though it would easily be mistaken for a Buddhist or Confucian temple. The site may go back to the time of Changan but the present wholly Chinese-style buildings and gardens are probably not earlier than the eighteenth century and not of great architectural distinction. You wander past the great triple gate at the entrance, through a series of smaller gates, low buildings lining the long courtyard gardens, the woodwork decorated with typically Chinese lattice patterns, until you reach the main garden with a central pillared kiosk standing before the main hall. This end of the mosque was in disarray with many carpenters and their assistants working on the complete restoration of this large building. The hall and half the garden were barricaded off. There seemed to be no sign of services or personal prayer though an old man sitting by the gate told me that there are still 18,000 Muslims living in Xi'an. Walking around the pleasant gardens I saw many inscriptions on buildings and gateways, almost all in Chinese. Here and there, on the stone gates, Arabic inscriptions had been cut into the stone. I couldn't help wondering if those written on more fragile materials might have been destroyed.

The following day I found a shop near the hotel which rented out those 'iron horses' the Chinese call bicycles. The rental service was run by two cheerful girls and a shy youth with an incipient moustache whom the girls teased mercilessly. They took a lot of trouble in selecting a large bike and raising the saddle and off I steamed (glided would not be the right word) heading south for the Small Goose Pagoda. Xi'an was mostly flat and a bicycle was the ideal form of transport in the pleasant autumn weather.

With the help of the bicycle I was able to see all the main sights in Xi'an in one day. Although the Small Goose Pagoda and the Big Wild Goose Pagoda to the east – each about 4 km south of the Ming city walls – are remnants of the great Tang Buddhist culture they now look forlorn without their original temple setting. In the time of the larger Changan, the Small Goose Pagoda stood in the centre of the city. It was built in AD 707 and is a square and elegant tower, now fifteen storeys high since the two top storeys collapsed after an earthquake in 1555.

The Big Wild Goose Pagoda is a simpler design, a square brick building of only seven storeys but 64 metres high, 23 metres higher than the other. It was originally built in AD 652 to store the precious Buddhist sutras brought back from India by the monk, Xuan Zang. His great journey is the central episode in the delightful sixteenth-century novel known to the Western world as *Monkey*, brilliantly translated by Arthur Wailey and more recently enchantingly inter-preted in a television cartoon. The pagoda now stands alone, a notable landmark, but its small arched doorways at each level make it slightly reminiscent of a towering dovecote. It seems a popular area for Chinese holiday-makers and on some rough ground nearby were stalls selling food and drink, an itinerant conjuror and, inside a large canvas enclosure, a travelling song-and-dance show.

There are a few other minor attractions and a museum housed in a large Confucian temple, all worth a glance, but the two major attractions of Xi'an are combined in a one-day bus tour to the east of the city. Ten kilometres along this road is the neolithic village of Banpo, first excavated in 1954, the earliest known settlement of what is called 'Yangshao Culture'. Of the excavated site 3000 square metres have been covered over and now form the main exhibit of the museum, the reconstruction giving a vivid idea of how these hunting, fishing and gathering villagers lived some 6000 years ago. The whole site consists of a residential area, an area for making pottery and the burial ground. There are the remains of forty-five houses and other buildings, more than 200 storage pits, six pottery kilns and 250 graves, seventy-three for children who were buried in earthenware pots. The village dwellings are surrounded by a large, excavated moat, 2 metres wide, 2 metres deep and 300 metres long.

I usually find early archaeological sites boring, incapable of bringing back any real sense of the life that was lived there thousands of years ago. At Banpo one is aware of the struggle of these primitive people to survive against the forces of nature, marauding animals and sickness. The great moat, an extraordinary achievement in itself, and the pathetic child burials both remind one how precarious their life must have been. The archaeologists have succeeded in making this remote way of life absolutely real to the modern visitor. I did wonder about the full reconstruction of the wooden buildings, including roof structures. In excavating this kind of site, nothing remains of wooden houses but their post holes which do little more than give the archaeologist a ground plan. Without some external evidence, which is unlikely to exist at Banpo, the wooden reconstructions are pure guesswork though there is nothing at the site to tell the visitor of this fact. The whole reconstruction is presented as proven fact.

More and more, all round the world, government archaeologists are being pressured by their tourist authorities to produce 'remains' that are complete enough to draw the ordinary tourist. For example, since I first saw them twenty-five years ago, certain famous Mexican sites have been 'tarted up' out of recognition, and out of the realms of scientific archaeology. With some of the world's most fascinating sites ahead of them, it will be tragic if politics interfere with and distort archaeology in China for the sake of tourists' foreign exchange, but it is probably inevitable.

The terracotta army which has guarded the tomb of Emperor Qin Shihuang for over 2000 years needs no cosmetic treatment. Unadorned it stands as one of the most spectacular and dramatic archaeological discoveries of all time while its presentation is un-usually imaginative. Without question it is now one of the eight wonders of China.* The moment I saw it I was glad I had come to Xi'an.

Emperor Qin Shihuang succeeded in defeating the rival warring states and, under the short Qin dynasty (221–207 BC), united China for the first time, ruling with exceptional cruelty and tyranny and making use of vast armies of prisoners and dispossessed peasants for such public works as the Great Wall, and his own tomb which was started immediately on his ascent to the throne. The tomb was covered with a great mound of earth 40 metres high which can be climbed. This central tomb has not yet been excavated though reliable old records suggest that it contains almost unimaginable treasure. Chinese archaeologists are also convinced that it has never been touched by grave-robbers. Legend says that loaded crossbows cover the entrances, spring-loaded to kill intruders. Modern surveys have confirmed old reports that the inner tomb area has a circumfer-ence of 2½ km and the outer walls are 6 km around. The inner tomb is said to be a magic palace of gold and silver and precious stones, with rivers and seas of flowing mercury. After the emperor was laid within his new kingdom, all the craftsmen who had worked on the mausoleum were buried alive to ensure total secrecy. At present there is no sign that the Chinese intend to intrude on the First Emperor's privacy, but if and when they do, it may prove to be the El Dorado of all time. What has already been revealed is almost beyond imagination.

In 1974 when some peasants were digging a well some 1500 metres east of the main tomb they came across a huge vault which later excavation proved to contain an army of life-size and extraordi-narily realistic soldiers, modelled out of terracotta, all armed and marching with horses in battle formation. In 1976 two similar vaults were discovered. The first and largest vault is 62 metres from north to south and 210 metres from east to west. About 5–7 metres below ground-level and running east to west are deep passageways divided

* See Introduction, which includes a list.

by walls, the terracotta army marching in ranks eastwards down these long corridors, bowmen in front and soldiers with a variety of hand-weapons following them. Among the troops are thirty-five horse-drawn chariots. Each figure is different, with individual faces and holding real weapons, the quality of the swords denoting rank. It is estimated that this vault contained some 6000 figures though many were in fragments when they were dug up.

Today, as you walk around the perimeter and across the central aisle of this great hall, you can look down on this ghostly army marching eastwards, rank upon rank. In the huge front section the soldiers have been perfectly restored and they stand ready to defend their emperor as on the day they were placed there. As the eye travels down the rows of soldiers – as though on some archaeological battlefield, where both time and war have brought havoc – the state of the figures deteriorates until in the large back-section, hardly excavated, the mutilated fragments of these warriors lie scattered, limbs, trunks, heads severed and half-buried.

The degrees of excavation and repair create a sense of drama and bring extraordinarily moving reality to the complete soldiers in the front ranks, their grave expressions battle-scarred by the corrosions of time. The panorama of this ancient terracotta army immediately brought back to me the vivid description of the battle that opens *Macbeth*. In another strange echo from the past, I was suddenly a boy again watching grey-faced soldiers returning up the Portsmouth road after Dunkirk. That even one figure should have been sculpted with such emotive powers would be praiseworthy but to have created over 6000 such striking warriors makes them a wonder of the world.

If the terracotta army suggest the huge scale of the Qin emperor's tomb, the horse-drawn carriage shown in the adjacent building suggests the quality. The group consists of the covered two-wheel carriage drawn by four horses with two drivers. This beautiful object is about one-third lifesize and perfect in every detail. But despite its accuracy and realism, its quality of workmanship, elegant design and exquisite detail make it a considerable work of art. It has the perfection of goldsmith's work with the vitality of great sculpture, not least in the virility of the four horses.

On the way home, and a strong anticlimax, we were taken to Lishan, Mountain of the Black Horse, hot springs, now little more than an overcrowded public park with walks up the hillside around large and small terraced ponds. It is said that Yang Guifei, the

'Precious Concubine' of the Tang Emperor Xuan Zong, used to bathe here and I was amused to see that the usually prurient Chinese were jostling each other to get through the door into her private bathroom, a bleak and wholly antiseptic marble pool.

One person who must have long remembered Lishan was Chiang Kai-shek who was caught here by the communists after he had been betrayed by one of his generals. This 'Xi'an Incident' is recorded in a collection of photographs in a pavilion here. Chiang Kai-shek was released after he promised Zhou Enlai to join forces with the communist troops against the invading Japanese. This was in 1936.

Another few hours on a hard seat across another eroded landscape where many houses are built into the cliff-face and I was in Luoyang, another city that had been capital on several occasions, during the Zhou, Han and Tang dynasties when Xi'an was threatened by invasion by barbarians from the West. Once a great city and centre of the arts and learning, little is left in the present industrial town with a population of over one million. The two places of interest lie outside the town though both are easily accessible by local bus.

The White Horse Temple, the Baimasi, lies isolated about 15 km east of the town. According to tradition in AD 68, during the Western Han dynasty, two Indian monks came to Luoyang on white horses bringing with them Buddhist sutras, the story supporting the claim that this was the first Buddhist temple in China. The arrival of the monks is commemorated by two stone horses that stand before the main gateway. If only a symbol of the founding of Buddhism in China, it is sad to see such a historic and revered temple now so dilapidated and without any distinct odour of sanctity. A group of temple buildings, none of them earlier than Ming and probably mostly Qing, are handsome in a way but the neglected interiors and the leering, overcoloured statues are a travesty of this great faith. The hangings on the altars are garish, the robes of the few old monks who hobble about are threadbare, their faces mean and ill-tempered. I believe that many old people come here to pray around the New Year but while I was there the whole temple had a secular, sight-seeing atmosphere.

Along a track about 1 km east is the Pagoda which Reaches to the Clouds, the Qiyunta. It is a simple, square, thirteen-storey structure of ancient but unknown date, reaching up among the trees like an elongated beehive. It had some dignity, forlorn yet venerable. I walked back along the track where two men tried to persuade me to have my photograph taken astride a horse, no doubt with the pagoda in the background. I passed the two stone horses and turned left to the small square and the bus stop. My mood was ambivalent. I was disappointed but at the same time I was glad that I had come.

The great attraction of Luoyang is the Dragon Gate or Longmen cave temples carved between about AD 494, during the Northern Wei dynasty, to 850, the end of the Tang dynasty. The caves are about 12 km south of Luoyang cut in the cliffside on the north bank of the Yi River with a pleasant promenade running along the river beneath them. There are less famous cave sculptures on the other side of the river. The Longmen caves are said to include a staggering 2100 grottoes and alcoves, over 100,000 Buddhist statues, forty pagodas and 3600 inscribed tablets.

The general concept is grand, helped by the fine position along the river. The several large groups have suffered less damage than the smaller groups and figures, most of which have been defaced, quite literally, and some actually cut away from the rock face and stolen by foreign museums and collectors in the past. Hundreds of niches are now empty. I searched right along the cliff-face and I could not find a single smaller figure with a complete face. I do not know if some of this damage was done during the Cultural Revolution but some may have been the result of time and erosion, particularly from the water that seeps through the rock in places.

I was deeply impressed with some of the larger groups but the general layout speaks more of an act of devotion rather than some planned work of art and architecture, but the complex was developed over a long period. The large groups bear no relation to the smaller ones and the alcoves and niches seem to have been carved at random with no regard to the surrounding sculpture already completed. But one must remember the great skill required to carve these enormous figures out of the solid rock of a cliff-face. The flat Northern Wei style, particularly in the solemn treatment of hanging draperies, is easily distinguished from the fuller, more rounded Tang sculpture, the figures standing out in three-dimensions from the rock face. Admitting the attractive site here, I was more impressed by the sculpture of these Longmen caves than that at Datong. The famous Tang period Fengxiansi group, which now stands in the open, its cave roof having collapsed, is splendid both in size and as an expression of the Buddhist faith. The great central seated figure of the Vairocana Buddha, 17 metres high, almost floats in an aura of inner calm, in contrast to the humanity of the accompanying disciple and a more delicate, ethereal quality of the crowned, slightly gothic Bodhisattva. There is a further contrast with the group on the right side of the Buddha, fierce, lively guardian gods trampling an evil spirit underfoot. In an extraordinary way the figures in this group both exploit the power given them by their enormous size but at the same time express a delicacy of spiritual feeling one usually finds in a small carved ivory. In the earlier Wei dynasty figures, their mysterious, flat form gives them a transcendental feeling. I left the caves with the dominant feeling that it was incredible that working in stone on that scale sculptors could produce figures of such grace and beauty.

13

Places of Pilgrimage

QUFU AND TAISHAN

More by chance than by design, the two places that most intrigued me were the last on my tour of China. They were Qufu (pronounced 'chufu'), birthplace of Confucius, and, a short way north, Taishan, most sacred of China's five holy mountains. I was looking forward to both of them and on the map the journey from Luoyang to Qufu looked simple enough but the reality proved a little different. From Luoyand I had to go to Zhengzhou, a major railway junction. Having said that, there is nothing else to add about Zhengzhou. I arrived there, checked into the main hotel and discovered from the CITS office that there was a direct, overnight train to Yanzhou, the nearest station to Qufu. But, as I had feared, they said I must wait two days for a soft sleeper.

For two days I lurked in the gloomy hotel, writing a few letters and reading the last of my dwindling supply of books. In an attempt to lose myself in someone else's adversity I started reading Graham Greene's *Lawless Roads*. It must be one of the most depressing books he has written. Those endless nights in sordid Mexican villages where it never stopped raining and the cockroaches skittered about like mice did little to raise my spirits. Our situation was completely different but our sombre moods were too close and, following Mr Greene's own example, I turned to *Barchester Towers*: Mrs Proudie is cockroach proof and certainly a great deal more entertaining than Chinese television. Punctuated by meals where the set menu always seemed to be the same, the days passed.

On the afternoon of my departure I got my soft sleeper ticket. The train was due to leave Zhengzhou at 6.23 p.m. and the man in the CITS office said it would arrive at Yanzhou at 10.10 the following morning. He wrote both times for me on the bottom of my ticket, copying them from his own timetable. My spirits lifted. The timing was ideal. It would give me a restful night on the train, arriving at Yanzhou in good time to catch a bus for the short ride to Qufu. I looked forward to the journey with pleasure.

A car drove me to the station and I was taken to the soft class waiting room. It was another of those silent mausoleums over-crowded with upholstered sofas and chairs but almost empty of people. I started to get restless ten minutes before the train was due to leave. There were three bulky women officials gossiping in an adjoining office. I showed them my ticket and they waved me back to my seat. The time of departure passed and I started to sweat. I knew by experience that Chinese officials are not infallible and I had no wish to spend another two wasted days in Zhengzhou. There were three elderly Chinese in the waiting room besides myself and they disclosed that they were catching the same train. It was late arriving but they would take me with them in a few minutes. Shortly, they gathered up their luggage and I followed them out into the station.

The several platforms, and the tunnel which joined them, were chaotic with swarming crowds pushing in opposite directions. With a screaming whistle or a moaning siren, huge steam locomotives and long diesels pulled in and out from the crowded platforms. Passengers ran, pushed and fought trying to reach their trains but in all the confusion there was not a single notice about arrivals and departures. My three elderly guides were as lost as I felt. Up and down we went, trying platform after platform. They sought information from other passengers who had too many problems of their own to answer, and from bored station officials who were simply indifferent. I was amused that these senior cadres commanded no more respect than anyone else.

We had made inquiries on six of the station's eight platforms before we learned that our train was unusually late and was still due on Platform 2, which we had already visited twice. We stood waiting where the sleeping compartments would stop, staring down the line of the track. At last a pinpoint of light broke the dark distance, turning into a Cyclopean headlight as the monster rumbled into the station. The drama of night trains never palls. A pleasant young woman in charge of my sleeping car took me to an empty compartment and the train was soon under way again. A girl from the dining car came to ask if I would like dinner. She told me to come along at eight o'clock. I basked in the thought of dinner and a night's sleep. Qufu already lay within easy reach.

I wondered why the girl had told me to come to dinner so late. When I arrived I saw the reason. The other passengers had left and a table had been specially laid for me, complete with the rarest of items, a clean cloth. I was served a delicious dinner which included a large river fish in a sauce spiced with fresh ginger. It was the best meal I have ever had on a Chinese train and among the best meals I have eaten in China. Three sweating cooks hung out of the kitchen door watching anxiously. Under the eye of this professional audience I felt obliged to over-eat. Before I left the girl asked if I wanted breakfast and I agreed to return at 8.30.

Before I went to bed I thought it would be wise to check with the attendant that she would give me a call in the morning. She was in her office but she looked puzzled when I started to talk about breakfast, a word she seemed to understand. A premonition suddenly went through me like an electric charge. I showed her my ticket and pointed to the arrival time written on it by the CITS clerk. She looked even more puzzled. I wrote the arrival time in Chinese characters opposite the word 'Yanzhou' on the ticket. She shook her head, took out a pencil, crossed out 10.10 and write in 2.44.

What did she mean? Morning or afternoon? From the map it seemed too far to reach Yanzhou by 2.44 a.m. but the girl made it clear that she would be giving me a call in five hours time, at 2 a.m. There would be no breakfast. I returned to my compartment still wondering if I had misunderstood her. The CITS clerk had copied the time off the official printed timetable. For the next few hours I lay tense in a state of uncertainty and ragged sleep which was ended by a brisk knock on my door sharp at two. 'The man of wisdom is never in two minds,' says Confucius. 'The man of benevolence never worries.' I hurriedly pulled on my trousers.

The train had caught up with itself and arrived at the small station of Yanzhou at exactly 2.45 a.m. With a firm push I was decanted onto the platform by the attendant who probably thought I was out of my mind. At least I had arrived safely at Yanzhou, even if four hours before the first bus left for Qufu. The powerful Kong family, the descendants of Confucius, earlier this century had refused to allow the railway to pass through Qufu lest it disturb the revered master resting in his ancient tomb. So Qufu remains a half-hour bus ride from Yanzhou.

The station was dimly lit but by no means deserted. There was a large-roofed, but otherwise open, waiting area where I found a seat. I soon discovered that it was too cold to sit and I began to pace up and down between the long lines of benches. These were occupied by muffled bundles of humanity, their heads pillowed by their baggage, the breath from their sagging mouths clouding in the cold air. I picked my way among the peanut shells, the smears of spittle, the crumpled newspapers and the odd pool of vomit. It was scruffy, it was bleak, it was smelly and the time passed agonisingly slowly. Somewhere in a tree above a cicada, a leftover from warmer nights, hissed huskily. The sound was at odds with the dead sky and a few cold stars.

The moon was full and white, a night moon holding back the dawn. I continued walking. Crabby old women in quilted black jackets peered at me with blatant curiosity and added me to their gossip. One ragged, wild-eyed old fellow ran his filthy finger around the seams of my bag, while over the fence what appeared to be a party for young people in a restaurant turned into a fight with the crash of breaking glass and screams from the girls. It had been the Moon Festival and this was probably the tired end of the celebrations. It was something to watch, to distract from the penetrating cold and from the minutes that never seemed to pass.

The dawn came and eventually the sun rested on the horizon in warm splendour. I found a bus and we headed into the countryside. The roads were busy with people and vehicles on their way to work, men urging reluctant mules and donkeys into a new day. It was a beautiful morning with the sun throwing beams of trembling light across the road matching the shadows of the trees. Mist rose like thin steam over the river, the streams and the still ponds. Here and there heavy lotus leaves gave an exotic touch to the late autumn morning but mostly it was a simple, rustic picture, the everyday, demanding round of the Chinese countryside.

As we drew near to Qufu, I started to think again about Confucius. It is an extraordinary story. Confucius – the latinised form of Kong Fu Zi, Master Kong – is said to have been born in Qufu in 552 or 551 BC and to have died and been buried there in 479. Little is known with certainty about his life. Although he came of a good family, he lived in obscurity and poverty, his teachings exercising no real influence until centuries after his death. Confucius lived at a time when China had disintegrated into a number of warring states. His moral and political philosophies were devised as a solution to contemporary problems and for several years he is said to have visited various rulers trying to persuade them to achieve peace and prosperity by following his precepts. He met with no success and returned home at the age of sixty-eight where he devoted his last years to

46 Court in the Kung mansion

47 Tomb of Confucius

QUFU

48 Noodle-maker

49 Blacksmiths

50 The 6000 stone steps of the pilgrims' path

TAISHAN

51 The west route to China's most sacred mountain

52 A guardian lion outside a temple on the west route

teaching a small group of followers. He was buried a short way outside Qufu.

What happened after that is uncertain. We shall never know exactly how his teachings survived or how far what was eventually written down around 200 BC accords with the original words of the philosopher. However, there is plenty of evidence in the oriental world of the accuracy of the oral tradition and it is quite possible that a line of disciples managed to preserve at least the heart of the master's teachings. In fact, relatively little survived. *The Analects*, or sayings of Confucius – his complete works – in English fill a mere 101 pages in the Penguin edition. Nor do we find there a tight-knit moral and political system but only dozens of brief comments, often enigmatic, scrappy, biographical and wholly unsystematic. Nevertheless these moral and philosophical scraps altered the course of oriental history. Confucius must be numbered with Christ and the Buddha as one of the men who has exercised the greatest influence on the human race, an influence which lives on in Asia.

It was under the fifth Han emperor, Wu, who came to the throne in 147 BC, that Confucianism was made the cornerstone of Chinese government and a growing religious cult whose rites and ancestor worship were carried out in elaborate Confucian temples. The influence of Confucianism certainly waxed and waned over the centuries but it had become so ingrained in the Chinese attitude to everything that the communists have given up their earlier attempts to discredit Confucius. And Confucianism has spread abroad, carried by Chinese immigrants to such places as Taiwan, Hong Kong and Singapore, and borrowed for their own purposes by the Koreans and the Japanese.

Confucius has suffered the same fate as all great moral and religious teachers, basically the distortions and additions of the interpreters and, later, the politicans. From early times biographies mixed fact with apocryphal legend while various commentators rummaged disruptively among his philosophies. These included the later philosopher, Meng-tzu, known in the West as Mencius (*c.* 370-290 BC), whose own work was later to join the work of Confucius among the small number of official classics. These early commentators may have helped to preserve the teachings of Confucius. The real distortions started when Confucius became part of the machinery of government, in China and elsewhere, and the Confucian scholar became a recognised servant of the establishment.

It is a fascinating and important part of Asian history. It particular-ly fascinates me since I have lived for several years in Japan which remains a far more Confucian society than many Japanese seem to realise. It was this personal experience that put a special edge on my pilgrimage to Qufu, the philosopher's home. In *The Analects* Con-fucius left behind him a philosophy which lent itself to misinter-pretation and distortion. No doubt Confucius himself saw it as a single philosophy or way of life. Unfortunately, it falls all too conveniently into a moral code and a political philosophy, which when separated led eventually to the ritualisation of the moral code and the ossification of the political system. Over the centuries Confucian humanism was deprived of its humanity to become the most rigid form of bureaucracy in the world.

Confucius' political theory was conservative. He looked back to a Utopian and unrealistic golden age and laid great emphasis on a reverence for tradition. It would have been a blueprint for bureaucratic and despotic government had not Confucius tempered it with an exacting and most original standard of personal behaviour which should have made all despots benevolent and all bureaucrats the very model of a perfect English gentleman. It is a pity that Confucius could never have met Dr Arnold of Rugby. On the ethics of personal behaviour they would have been remarkably in accord. So many of Confucius' sayings read like the perfect text for a Sunday sermon in the school chapel.

It is worth reading *The Analects* of Confucius. They are inspiring, interesting and charming. It is also sobering to see how the simple words of the ancient master have been changed over the centuries, twisted and elaborated to suit every political purpose. Ironically, Confucius once said, when asked if he was trying to be flattering, 'I am not so impertinent as to practise flattery. It is just that I so detest inflexibility.' The Chinese imperial government succeeded in turn-ing Confucianism into the most inflexible system of bureaucratic administration in the world, buttressed by self-interest, schools of narrow-minded official scholars and a diabolical examination system that tested little except the memory. In seventeenth-century Japan, where Confucianism had already been in and out of favour for centuries, the newly established Tokugawa government encouraged a school of neo-Confucianism which they hoped would give a moral authority to their political institutions and a bureaucratic system of government which even attempted to ordain the length of an actor's hair, not to mention the colour and size of a Confucian scholar's umbrella. Small wonder that Swift based one of Gulliver's journeys on an early European account of this Tokugawa society. The tradition lingers on with considerable vigour in modern Japan; ancestor worship, blind respect for seniority, rigid bureaucracy, the 'examination hell' and the open corruption that has long been a part of this system of government.

Even in China Confucianism has not always enjoyed official favour. It is said that during the Qin dynasty in the third century BC, the emperor had the works of Confucius destroyed and put Confucian scholars to death. But over the last 2000 years what is now called Confucianism became a cornerstone of Chinese government and of the individual's outlook on life, an essential ingredient of the Chinese character, intermixed with Taoism and Buddhism but probably more important than either of them.

In the heat of revolutionary fervour the Chinese communists dismissed Confucius as a relic of the imperial past and his teachings came under further attack during the Cultural Revolution. But not even revolutions can shrug off something as deep-seated as Confucianism and since the end of the Cultural Revolution the government has shown an open respect for the teachings of Confucius. His political theory hardly threatens the People's Republic while much of his ethical teaching with its emphasis on respect for parents and those in authority is obviously a healthy antidote to the anarchy of the Cultural Revolution, not least because it is a teaching that millions of older Chinese already accept.

With such thoughts buzzing around in my mind we drove into the centre of Qufu. While Shakespeare might find his way around modern Stratford, Confucius would be lost in Qufu. The massive gateways, the high walls and the dominance of dark brick mark it out as another Ming restoration and most of the temples and official buildings in the town date from the Ming dynasty or later. Confucius' descendants acquired great wealth and power and were granted all the land around Qufu with exemption from taxation. The family mansion was probably the largest private dwelling in China and is like a not-so-small version of the Forbidden City. The seventy-sixth descendant of Confucius lived here until the 1940s when he and the remnant of the Kong family fled to Taiwan. Today it is said that 50 per cent of the population of Qufu claim to be descendants of the great philosopher.

Qufu has only about 50,000 inhabitants. It is a small country town and that is its greatest attraction. I enjoyed the monuments, the great Confucian temple, the sprawling Kong mansion with the charming hotel housed in one wing, but far more I enjoyed wandering around the rural edges of the town and out into the countryside to watch the harvest gathered in. After months of being confined in great industrial cities, seldom getting nearer to the countryside than through the glass of the bus window, Qufu was a new and exhilarating experience. Suddenly one was living in the country, birds singing outside the hotel window and ten minutes down the road open fields and woodland walks. Within hours I knew why everyone had recommended Qufu, and I promptly changed my programme to stay for four days.

Although I toured them religiously, I found the official sights of Qufu the least rewarding thing about it. The official buildings occupy the centre of the town, the temple and the family mansion side by side running north to south. The temple of Confucius stands to the west, an enormous rectangular compound with ancient cypress trees and many great halls. One or two of the smaller halls date back as far as the twelfth century but the sumptuous main sanctuary was built in 1724. This is the largest Confucian temple in China but I found it rather dull except for the crowds of eager Chinese sightseers and the bizarre 'Confucian souvenirs' sold on little stalls all along the outside wall. I was growing blasé about late Chinese religious architecture but who could resist a tray of cheap white porcelain figures of the sage all mixed up with china ducks and puppies?

I did enjoy the tour of the Kong family mansion, the complex said to contain 463 rooms, halls and courts. Like the Forbidden City it is entirely enclosed by walls and is laid out with a main central section flanked by an east and west section, the latter now largely converted into the tourist hotel. You enter the public area of the mansion, an extensive courtyard lined with offices which administered the Kong estates and carried out magisterial and other public offices. Beyond walls and gateways lie the private apartments, their present shabbiness only hinting at the past grandeur when the family lived here under the direct protection of the emperor. At the northern end are the bedraggled remains of the private garden, now mainly taken over by weeds and amateur photographers and friends. Despite the general air of dilapidation, perhaps more noticeable in a private house than in a public temple, it is obvious that a great deal of restoration has been carried out since the Cultural Revolution. This undoubtedly reflects partly an official change of heart by the authorities but perhaps even more shows that the enormous tourist potential of Qufu has been realised. A grand and imaginative modern hotel was just about to open immediately opposite the gateway into the Kong mansion. But if the older hotel housed in the mansion itself remains open, sacrifice a little comfort and stay there. It was one of the main pleasures of Qufu and one of my most pleasing memories of China.

It was rather like being back in an Oxford college. As I strolled across the courts to breakfast, the sharp autumn air put an edge on my appetite and stung the cuts on my badly shaven chin caused by a nostalgic lack of light and hot water. There the resemblance ended. The series of courtyards were small, joined by circular archways and full of trees, beds of flowers and clusters of stone or pottery garden seats and tables. Some of the courts were open with rooms all around, others were crossed by a large pavilion containing a grander suite of rooms. By ten or eleven in the morning the autumn sun was hot and it was pleasant to sit out reading or writing, soothed by the gentle curve of the tiled roofs which swept like great waves all around me. The sun made intricate patterns of shadow on the stone pavement as it played through the latticework or through the curving bamboo. Late in the afternoon it was so quiet that I could hear girls laying supper in the restaurant four courts away and two or three birds filled the trees with song. It would be sad if the old hotel were to be closed or allowed to decline when the grand new establishment opens opposite. Yes, there were a few scampering rats in the dining room, for some reason only at dinner, but it's not every day a visitor stays in the Kong family mansion, almost a guest of Confucius himself.

An American once said to me, as our boat approached Piraeus, 'I reckon I can get Greece *out of the way* in three days . . .' At the time I thought it rather a gauche remark. Having caught a few glimpses of the backstreets of Qufu I got the Confucian monuments *out of the way* as quickly as possible. That's not quite true. I did save the tomb until last. To the east of tourist Qufu lay a lively market town, surrounded by and supplying a large rural area. There was no division between town and country. The moment I left the centre the drying harvest was everywhere, the streets spread with grain, old women winnowing by the kerb and the mud houses festooned with strings of bright orange corn cobs, fat ducks stalking the yards with a proprietory air. The main road led out to the north through a heavy brick gateway and people and small carts streamed backwards and forwards from the fields to the town, plodding through the hot, dusty air of autumn.

Exploring down narrow, mud-walled side streets I started finding the local craftsmen and women. Outside a building that looked more like a stable than a workshop I noticed piles of rope and hanks of twine. Inside, a woman sat in front of a large wooden wheel patiently rolling a length of coarse rope. The place was full of rope, hanging in bundles from the walls and ceiling, and flowing out from the feet of the woman through the door and across the pavement.

In the next street metre-high wooden hoops leant against the open door of a low, white building. A circular woven bamboo sieve, or so it seemed, hung by a nail on the wall. For a moment I was defeated until I saw the finished article standing in the road: a five-storey circular Chinese dumpling steamer with a coolie-hat shaped lid. Before I left Qufu I found three craftsmen making these large steamers but strangely I never saw one Chinese dumpling in Qufu.

On the outskirts of the town in a space beyond the last cluster of houses I found three blacksmiths at work. Their forges were no more than a small hearth and a simple box-bellows pumped by a young assistant, the fire topped by a lopsided little brick chimney which jutted through a roof of woven bamboo which shaded the men from the sun. Each forge was surrounded by objects waiting attention from these versatile craftsmen; metal wheels, cart springs, ploughs, broken hinges and the bent fork of an old motor bike. A youngish man with short, bristling hair and a knowing grin hammered away, bending, heating, twisting, and straightening a piece of metal from the undercarriage of an ancient cart. Not much gets thrown away in China and no doubt ingenuity was the main tool of these metalworkers who kept Qufu on the road.

I was starting to make my way back to the hotel when I noticed two women and a small girl, each with a large basket, queuing at the door of a house set back from the road. It was the baskets I noticed first for they were particularly handsome, the rims bound with leather and the whole basket with the curving lines of a stumpy fishing boat. I realised later that they were the standard working basket of the area but though I searched hard, I never found anyone making them. Attracted by the baskets I then saw a rack near the house draped with innumerable lengths of white wool. Ah, I thought, it must be a wool-dyer. Wrong, it was the local noodle-maker and those were freshly made noodles drying in the sun. The middle-aged woman working in the front room at first looked severe but proved to be the most friendly and least camera-shy of all the craftsmen and women I found in Qufu.

On a table by the door a young girl mixed the dough. The queue outside the door were the customers who brought their own ingredients in their baskets which were then made up into noodles while they waited. The women with the short cropped hair worked a small machine driven by an electric motor. This machine performed two functions with great efficiency. First it rolled out the dough until it had transformed it into a wide, thin continuous band which was wound onto a roller. When this had been completed, a line of metal extruding teeth were slotted into the machine and the band of dough was passed through them. They emerged as noodles which the women chopped into long lengths, nimbly twisting a disordered bundle into a neat skein and draping it over the edge of the owner's basket. It looked so easy. I am sure it was not.

I still had to visit the tomb of Confucius which was in a park about 3 km north of the town. For the first half-kilometre I was occupied with shaking off some fifteen bicycle-rickshaw boys and two splendid mule carts got up to resemble ancient imperial carriages. By the time I got to the edge of the town everyone was convinced that I did intend to walk and they drifted off in search of another customer. Outside the old walls of Qufu the road stretched straight ahead, the sun was hot and I wondered if I had made the right decision. But the walk was pleasant. I watched the people working in the fields, three men pulling a clumsy plough through the heavy soil. At one spot two shy and charming girls were drying maize by the roadside, patiently shucking the golden grain off the cobs and spreading it out on a long mat. I stood and watched them, the one boyish with short black hair and a heavy line of front teeth, the other puckish and delicate, her hair pulled back and hanging over her shoulder in one long plait. My shadow fell across their mat and they looked up. Their brown faces crumpled into shy smiles and they ducked their heads. I walked on, under the white marble ceremonial arch and along the hot, dusty road to the gateway leading into the burial ground where Confucius lies at rest entombed beneath a mound fronted by a stone stele and, on a paved terrace, an altar and a bronze incense burner.

It was a suitably quiet and simple place for a man who had lived out his life in poverty, oblivious of the honours poured on his descendants. As I stood there gazing at the mound, shapeless under dense undergrowth, I couldn't help wondering if it really contained the dusty remains of Confucius. On grounds of common sense alone it seemed most unlikely that the exact place of his internment had remained known during those early centuries, let alone across a span of over 2000 years. It didn't really seem to matter. The tomb mound and the surrounding park were a beautiful and perfect place to pay one's respects to a moral philosopher who posthumously had bolstered most oriental governments while during his own lifetime had failed to sell a single idea to the neighbouring potentates. Without doubt it is a remarkable story, revealing in both its success and its failure.

The surroundings of the tomb are known as the Confucian Woods, the largest artificial forest in China. I walked for two hours among the old trees and the wild undergrowth, stele everywhere and, occasionally, grand tombs with rectangular marble arches and towering carved stone figures and grotesque animals. Coming out of the park, hot and weary, I weakened and hired a rickshaw for the ride back into town. It was like carefully debating whether to take a taxi or not when the fare was slightly less than tuppence. Nonetheless I heard my driver boasting to other rickshaw boys how he had overcharged me. I knew that already but the swaying ride through the fields with the touch of an early evening breeze was worth every fen.

It was possible to go from Qufu to the sacred mountain of Taishan either by train or bus. Either way it took about three hours. I chose to go by bus. It was a bad decision. It started well enough. I found the bus station and eventually the right bus which left Qufu on time. Superficially the bus was like other Chinese country buses; third hand, uncomfortable and slow up the hills. But this bus to Taishan had an additional feature which, combined with the rough road, made the journey almost unbearable.

In the roof, about half-way down the bus, was a metal trapdoor 1 metre square. Its fastening had broken and for three hours it banged and rattled up and down using the interior of the bus as a sound box to magnify the terrible noise a hundredfold. It was like being inside a theatrical thunder-machine; Covent Garden and *The Flying Dutchman*, say. Each second great axes of metallic vibration split my head in two. The Chinese shouted complaints to the driver who shrugged indifferently. At last an exceptionally burly Chinese walked forward and shook the driver by the shoulder. The driver stopped the bus and angry words were exchanged. The driver came back and struggled with the trap. There was a promising 'clunk' and he returned to his seat. Within seconds the thunder returned, worthy of the entrance of any demon king. By the time we reached Taishan I, and I should think everyone else on the bus, had a blinding headache.

New places often conjure up expectations that on arrival only prove to have existed in one's imagination. Taishan, China's most sacred mountain, suggested a remote and silent place with ancient monasteries among the peaks and drifting clouds. The reality was endless souvenir stalls and hordes of Chinese tourists riding to the peak in China's first large cable-car. It was interesting and fun but it was not *Lost Horizon*.

There are nine sacred mountains in China: five Taoist and four Buddhist. They have drawn pilgrims for centuries – emperors and peasants – but now they mostly draw holiday-makers. Taishan, the Exalted Mountain, is the holiest of the Taoist five, dedicated to an ancient god and his daughter, the Princess of the Azure Clouds, whose temple and tomb are the climax of the ascent. The emperors were supposed to make the long climb to offer sacrifices for the safety of the nation. Only five emperors actually undertook the pilgrimage though Emperor Qian Long climbed the mountain eleven times. According to legend Confucius made the pilgrimage and Chairman Mao made a suitable political epigram about the sunrise, 'The East is Red'. The Buddhists have also made the mountain their own, so every pilgrim is catered for.

Today one arrives at the town of Tai'an, for centuries the gateway to the mountain and, more recently, the home town of Mao's fourth wife, the notorious former film-actress and leader of the 'Gang of Four'. The mountains of central Shandong dominate the northern side of the town, spreading out in an irregular and towering wall of granite. Out of the centre of this Taishan rises to 1545 metres. Tai'an is the complete pilgrimage town, providing accommodation for visitors and centred on the huge Daimiao Temple from which the road runs north towards the 6000 stone steps which lead all the way to the mountaintop and which provide the pilgrim, or the tourist, with a genuine sense of achievement.

For the less devout and the faint-hearted there is now a bus service to Zhongtianmen, half-way up, and the cable-car from there. A good compromise is to walk all the way up and use the transport for the descent as the steps are more testing coming down. If you do not walk one way you will miss the changing mountain scenery, the many interesting buildings along the way and the amusing life of the 'pilgrim's' path. The advantage of walking both ways is that you can go one way by the main central route and the other by the quieter and beautiful western route. If you want to see everything along both routes, allow yourself a day for the ascent and a day for the descent as there are a number of deviations which take time. And although I started by saying that Taishan was not what I had expected, I am glad that I went there. The modern pilgrimage of young holiday-makers offers its own kind of experience and another glimpse of modern China.

By this final stage of my journey I was satiated with large temples but I felt a masochistic need to start my own pilgrimage from the Daimiao where you set out by passing under the Triumphal Portal of the Eastern Peak, the splendid name strengthening your resolve as you look out over the spreading roofs of the temple to the grey walls of granite steep against the sky. The temple is handsome, the main hall one of the largest in China, surrounded by tall, ancient stele, groups of old cypress and gingkos and in one corner a graceful bronze pavilion brought here from the summit of the mountain. And there is a local form of blindman's buff which endlessly delights the Chinese visitors. The player is blindfolded and must feel his or her way around a large pinnacle of rock, three times anti-clockwise and three times clockwise. Then they must step out some 10 metres to find an old cypress across the court. They never succeed but usually end up throwing their arms around a complete stranger to the unfailing delight of the crowd.

A road runs north from the temple for about 3 km passing under one or two ceremonial arches and by a variety of stalls selling food, souvenirs and renting walking sticks. Suddenly the road narrows by a frenetic bus park and ahead lie the first flight of steps. From here on a variety of buildings and monuments and changing glimpses of the mountains partly distracted me from the grumbling muscles in my calves. The cheerful parties of young Chinese also helped. The boys grumbled, the girls carried the luggage and the boys' jackets. Many of the boys had acquired American-style hats, a sort of fedora but executed in cardboard. Here and there I saw groups of old peasant women, real pilgrims, praying at wayside shrines and burning token money in small furnaces. The temple buildings were sadly dilapidated and the growing number of buildings along the path, many offering refreshments and souvenirs, is further spoiling both the atmosphere and the view.

As so often in China the way is marked by poetic names which don't always quite come up to their literary aspirations. As I passed through the Number One Archway Under Heaven, passed the Red Gate Palace and crossed the Bridge over the Clouds to pause at the Pavilion of the Five Pines I began to think I was wading my way through one of those 1000-page romantic Eastern novels so popular in the last few years. But frequently I was brought back to reality by the sight of the porters who daily carry food and drink up the mountainside, their loads balanced on either end of a long bamboo pole, their shoulders scarred with weals where the pole has rubbed for years as they trudge up and down the flights of steps. All these sights help to distract you through the long climb to the summit guest house and the hope that the cloud will lift to grant you the dawn sunrise and a distant view from the Summit for Contemplating the Sun.

From Tai'an I was due to return to Beijing to catch a plane back to Japan. It seemed fitting that I should spend my last night in China in a train and it prevented me from having to find a bed in Beijing. There was an overnight train which arrived in Beijing at eight and I could take a taxi from the station to the airport. It would mean a four-hour wait there but I was looking forward to such international facilities as a good breakfast and a bookshop selling newspapers and some Western fiction. But before all that I was praying that I could find a soft sleeper on the train.

Tai'an was one of those intermediate stations from which one could only buy a hard seat ticket and hope to negotiate something better once on the train. Before I even boarded the train, as it drew into the station, I could see that it was packed. I got into one of the soft sleeper carriages but was immediately herded towards the hard sleeper compartments. I shall always remember the young woman in charge. She was one of those rare Chinese officials who really care. She apologised that the hard sleepers were totally full but she thought she might find me one when we arrived at Jinan in just over an hour. She settled me with some tea on a tip-up seat in the corridor where I gazed at a wonderful vista of sixty pairs of twitching feet. The hard sleeper carriage recalls the morgue and battery hens, all at the same time. Sixty humans, of both sexes, are racked up three-deep, no compartments, no doors, no curtains. I got a top bunk at Jinan and once I had achieved the ascent and manoeuvred myself head-first into the narrow space between the roof and the bunk, it was comfortable. What it would be like in the heat of high summer is another matter. In late autumn the only obstruction that lay between me and sleep was the maddeningly unsyncopated snoring, a vibrant concerto for fifty-nine worn-out, weezing bassoons.

I was ready for a long wait in the taxi rank at Beijing station but as I took my place at the back of the queue a young driver leant over the barrier and asked me where I wanted to go. The airport meant a good fare and in a few minutes I was driving through the centre of Beijing for the last time and out through the dismal northern suburbs towards the airport. It says something about Beijing that driving from the central station we did not pass one notable landmark to which I could bid farewell. There were just the huge central avenues sweeping through a nothing-in-particular townscape until they thinned down into the narrower streets running through the sprawling housing estates and the heartless apartment blocks. And finally, back into the blind avenue of trees and dense shrubbery which led to the international airport.

It was international in the sense that aircraft took off here for other countries. In every other respect it was incurably Chinese. There was no newspaper, in any language, and certainly no books, not even a last flurry of propaganda booklets from the Beijing Foreign Language Press, the kind that explain things like 'the peaceful liberation of Tibet'. There were, however, a Western and a Chinese restaurant. Wanting breakfast, I headed for the Western restaurant. It was shut. I ended up with an approximation of a Western breakfast in the Chinese restaurant. The eggs were cold, the toast mostly untoasted, the coffee muddy and the waiters indifferent. It all made the perfect and predictable end to a perfect but frequently unpredictable journey. India had overwhelmed me, Japan had wooed me. Sometimes China overwhelmed me; occasionally it wooed me; and often it bludgeoned me, all adding up to the unforgettable and unique China experience.

Postscript: Shotgun Wedding, 1997

HONG KONG

North Star, Day Star, Shining Star, Morning Star, Solar Star – no, not a new constellation but the boats of the Star Ferry Company which still speed across the harbour of Hong Kong. I first rode the ferry twenty years ago. Then it was the only public transport between Kowloon and Hong Kong island. The service has survived the building of the harbour tunnel and the construction of the Mass Transport subway. Each time I visit Hong Kong I like to ride the ferry and enjoy what commercial development has left of the view, in a spirit of nostalgia and a gesture of protest. On the ferry, amidst the chipped green paint, the breath of garlic and the frenzy of whistles, bells and flashing red lights with the final crash of the barrier as the next ferry draws away, I can recapture something of an older Hong Kong before it was turned into the world's shopping centre and a commercial boom town.

It was always a scruffy, noisy place. Those Cantonese characteristics live on amidst the sleek shopping centres and the pretentious white, bronzed, gold or silver skyscrapers which have crowded out the harbour view, obscuring the Victoria Peak. The process had started twenty year ago and what I really wish for is a glimpse of Hong Kong one hundred years ago when the buildings were wooden and two-storeyed and each bay around the coast a private place. Today Kowloon is all raucous traffic and leprous concrete apartments, the windows barred and girls crouching over sewing machines late into the night. Across the water is little Manhattan by the sea, the good architecture badly sited, the bad architecture hardly more pleasing than rows of false teeth. The island is expensive and hums with money. On the mainland everything that is finished looks as if it is already falling to pieces and everything that is unfinished appears likely to remain that way.

It is a miracle that Hong Kong works at all and while commercial development has not respected the environment, it has provided jobs and a new life for millions of refugees from the mainland and the tourists of the world with their favourite shopping spree. In the lounge of a Hong Kong hotel one evening I watched weary Australians, Germans, British, Indians, all comparing their new watches, cameras and videos like trophies from some exacting safari. In more private places the senior officials of the Shanghai and Hong Kong Bank give lavish dinner parties, the rich Chinese assume more power from the British and, so it is said, the Chief Steward of the Jockey Club remains the leading figure of Hong Kong society.

In 1985, after ritualistic negotiations, the British government agreed to return Hong Kong to the People's Republic of China when the lease runs out in 1997. With a Chinese military band playing the British national anthem in Beijing's Tiananmen Square, Mrs Thatcher solemnly signed the treaty. For a number of reasons, not least that Hong Kong's water supply comes from mainland China, she had no choice. This was the beginning of the twelve-year engagement which will culminate in the shotgun wedding of 1997. It is irresistible to speculate on the course of the marriage since it involves not only the future of Hong Kong but is a pointer to the development of China in the twenty-first century.

Any country whose economy centres on a nervous money market is dependent on international confidence. Hong Kong's market plummeted when the Chinese made it clear that they were going to insist on a return of the colony and, for a time, money, and some rich Chinese flowed out of Hong Kong. Confidence is now restored for 1997 is a long way off. But how confident will the financial world feel around 1995? The answer lies more with the political and economic development of China than anything that will happen in Hong Kong. There is a wide gap between the average standard of living in Hong Kong and China. That gap is not likely to close significantly by 1997 but it may be tolerable if a sufficient part of Hong Kong's prosperity flows into mainland China.

Certain factors, in theory, should ease the absorption of Hong Kong back into China. Most Hong Kong Chinese come from the neighbouring Cantonese area with relations still in China but in certain ways they have taken on a distinct identity. When the refugees used to arrive in Hong Kong it took them two years to adjust to the demands of the colony's working standards. Across the border the Chinese government has begun to prepare a bridal bed but the economics are not going according to plan. The large development zone, established around Canton on capitalist lines, is intended as a link with Hong Kong's economy and is meant to earn vital foreign currency by its exports. Last year the zone exported 30 per cent of its products, pouring 70 per cent of its consumer goods into the hungry home market; an exact reversal of the government's equation. Even the pragmatic Deng Xiaoping was to state publicly that this capitalist *experiment* was always subject to revision. Such political shufflings allow one to observe only that the future is full of uncertainties.

While everyone has become nervous of making predictions about China's future, most people think it is unlikely that China will swing to the extreme left again, let alone lurch into the anarchy of another Cultural Revolution. Deng Xiaoping has clipped the wings of the army, always the great unknown quantity in Chinese communist politics. He has also pushed his own supporters, many of them young by politburo standards, into important positions in central and local government. There remains some opposition, mostly among the entrenched bureaucracy but they have been no match for Deng, even in his eighties. When he and the few other members of the old brigade die, there will certainly be some kind of emotional watershed but there is every hope that China will remain on its pragmatic course with Deng's disciples taking over control of the politburo. If that happens and their policies allow the continuing economic growth, China will make real progress into the industrial, technological world. If political stability is maintained then the main threat to China's increasing prosperity will remain the stranglehold of bureaucracy, of ancient tradition, which daily bleeds every activity in China. The petty frustrations that bedevil the individual traveller in China are one tiny symptom of this national cancer.

One can speculate but perhaps it is wiser to wait and see. The individual traveller, like myself, can only look back on the thousands of Chinese I saw in the streets and along the roadside struggling with a quiet desperation to improve their lives. I remember all the Chinese I had dealings with, some maddening, others lovable, but perhaps that is a fair summary of the Chinese character. China is unlike any other place. It is often called a Third World country but I find that a misleading description. China is mostly poor, largely dilapidated, with a vast number of the people uneducated but who, in an indefinable way, continue to reflect their long history and their rich culture, giving you a sense that you are in the presence of a great people.

Some Practical Information

These notes are intended primarily for the individual traveller but some of the information may help those going to China in a group. They are mostly pieces of information which I acquired through experience but which I wish someone had given me before I set out. In several cases the advice emphasises cautionary tales I have told in the book.

It is difficult to give wholly reliable advice on many subjects since the tourist situation in China is always changing, often with two steps forward and one step back. In the spring of 1985 we had no difficulty in getting to Lhasa from Chengdu. That summer, because of local celebrations, Tibet was suddenly closed to all tourists for several weeks. When it opened again, it was announced that tourists could now fly from both Chengdu and Xi'an. When I arrived in Xi'an that October, several people in the hotel were keen to go to Tibet and I assured them that it was easy. I was wrong. By the end of the week I met three foreigners who had been waiting in Xi'an for a flight for over two weeks. The golden rule is to go immediately if you have the opportunity to visit a *sensitive* area.

Experience has made me cautious about giving definite advice about anything in China. During my own travels I learned to be grateful for what I achieved and to shrug off my failures when I knew that the system had defeated me. I also learned to be sceptical about what other travellers told me, however sincere they may have been. Backpackers in particular tend to enthuse about the places they have been to but to scorn those they have not visited. Always one must realise that what the Public Security Bureau gave to someone yesterday, they may not give to you tomorrow. China is as variable as that.

1   Getting in and out of China

For individual travellers it is easier to enter China through Hong

Kong. Visas can be obtained at a reasonable price in twenty-four hours and you can go on to Canton by train or boat. In Japan it took me over two months and a large sum of money to obtain a visa. Remember that you will have to spend at least one night in Hong Kong waiting for your visa. There is a lack of budget hotels in Hong Kong but good and reasonable accommodation is available to anyone at the two YMCAs, the one on Salisbury Road being particularly central. Write and book in advance: YMCA, Salisbury Road, Kowloon, or 23 Waterloo Road, Kowloon.

Flights out of China can present problems. If you intend to work your way north and to fly home from Beijing, be sure that your homeward flight is booked in advance and don't rely on making a last-minute change, particularly in spring or autumn. Many people make a roughly circular tour of China intending to fly out from Shanghai, often back to Hong Kong. This is convenient but make certain that you arrive in Shanghai sufficiently in advance to book a flight. The simple answer is to go to Shanghai, book your flight and see the city and afterwards visit nearby Hangzhou and Suzhou for a few days, returning to Shanghai on the day of your flight.

The best months for travel in China are April and May, and September and October. Inevitably, these are also the most crowded months but with the popularity of China the tourist season is expanding. The summer is unpleasantly hot and over much of China the winter is unbearably cold.

2 Accommodation

Throughout the tourist season it is difficult to find a bed in Beijing and throughout the whole year it becomes harder to find a bed in Shanghai. I use the word 'bed' rather than 'hotel' or 'room' deliberately. Sooner or later the individual traveller will be grateful just for a bed. In many places travellers will get a simple but adequate hotel room but if you travel alone you must be prepared for the occasional dormitory-style accommodation, often basic. Now and then a hotel will claim to be full. I have never known it to be true and persistence will eventually produce a bed. I have also never heard of a foreigner left to sleep in the street. I wasted a lot of nervous energy in China worrying about where I was going to sleep. I always found a bed and although some were rough, they were always clean. All this is a part of the China adventure. If you don't want that kind of adventure, don't go to China or, go in a group leaving someone else to fret about which particular basic hotel you will be sleeping in that night.

3   What to take with you?

What clothing you take will depend on the season and where you are going but remember that at all seasons altitude affects temperature and play safe. In general I would advise you to take everything that you will need with you. In China, even in the main cities, you cannot rely on buying anything, particularly of reasonable quality. It is vital that you take all medicines that you will require even down to ordinary aspirin. If you fall seriously ill you will be well looked after but there are no Western-style chemist shops. The Chinese still make wide use of herbal medicines. These are normally excellent though often slow to take effect. Take all the film that you will require and keep it to be developed at home. Chinese coffee is usually disgusting and only available at breakfast in hotels. A jar or two of instant coffee and powdered milk are the best panacea for the discomfort of the hard seat. An enamel mug is essential and a pair of re-usable chopsticks are advisable if you intend to eat in the local restaurants. Their half-washed chopsticks have the reputation of transmitting hepatitis. A small knife is also useful for fruit. Take all the guide books you require together with an ample supply of reading. There are few bookshops in China which sell anything in English and the few government publications for tourists are of poor quality. In most of the large towns it is possible to buy a local map but not always in English. Beer is available everywhere but foreign wines and spirits are expensive. China is one of the few larger countries in the world where I would advise you to overpack rather than under-pack, with the vital stipulation that almost everywhere you will have to carry your own luggage and, on occasions, for long distances.

4   Health and security

If in any doubt about your basic fitness to go to China, consult your doctor. For the normally healthy person it is an exhausting but healthy country. The further you get off the beaten track, the greater your chances of an upset stomach and diarrhoea but in the ordinary tourist hotels the food is healthy and a thermos of boiled water is always to hand. Never drink water from the tap. Local restaurants and street stalls involve some risk but although Chinese restaurants are often superficially dirty the food is usually clean and sometimes delicious.

Everywhere in China, night and day, I felt as safe as I do in Japan, which means totally. The same is true for women. I never feared for my possessions or money except when I was in a dormitory with other foreigners where I did have my alarm clock stolen. Apart from Chinese standards of behaviour the penalties for stealing from foreigners are gruesomely discouraging. In a few places like Guilin the 'rip off' is developing but if you challange the tout he will back down.

5   Money

Internationally recognised traveller's cheques can be cashed at banks and the larger hotels which often contain a bank. It is advisable to stock up on cash when you are in a hotel offering this convenient facility. The tourist money, Foreign Exchange Certificates (FECs), is more and more becoming changeable with the ordinary Chinese currency, Renmibi (RMB), but the more official and the grander establishments will accept payment only in FECs. If that is your life-style beware of acquiring too much RMB since it cannot be converted when you leave China. If you are going to live at the cheapest level you will be able to use RMB most of the time and can take advantage of the blackmarket exchange of FECs for RMB at a bonus of at least 50 per cent offered by touts all over China. But this situation is changing and I would recommend sounding things out for your first few days before plunging into a big exchange deal. Always keep some FECs in hand in case you find yourself in a situation where RMB are not accepted.

Nearly every time you pay for anything in China you are given a receipt. Never throw away any receipt until you are completely finished with that transaction. In many hotels they insist that you pay one or more night's charge in advance and you get a receipt. I often found that when I came to check out they had no record of the payment I had made in advance and if I could not have produced the receipt I should have been forced to pay again. A wallet full of little bits of paper is a bore but so is paying twice.

6 Travel arrangements

The China International Travel Service (CITS) is the government agency responsible for tourism and they have an office in every tourist centre in China, often in the main tourist hotel. Their attitude ranges from helpfulness to indifference and, worst of all, offices that are mostly closed. If you use the CITS to book anything for you, a train ticket or a tour, you will pay the highest price. In certain cases you will be forced to use them and in other cases the convenience will make the additional cost worthwhile. It has become easier to buy your own train and bus tickets at the booking offices but you may spend hours in restless queues to save a few yuan, wasting precious time you could have spent sightseeing. You can purchase your own air tickets at any Civil Aviation Administration of China (CAAC) office where you may also have to wrestle with bureaucracy. But on more than one occasion the CITS told me that a certain flight was full but I was able to buy the ticket I wanted at the CAAC office. When making your travel arrangements in China, whatever they may be, you have to decide which is more valuable, time or money.

7 Length of stay

The length of your stay in China will be controlled by various personal factors. If you go in a group, the decision is made for you. If you go as an individual traveller you should remember that in each month of travel at least 20 per cent of your time will be taken up in administering your journey. Each person likes to travel at a different speed but if you wanted to see all the main places of interest in China you would need at least four months, ideally six months. China is a vast country and the three-week tour can only scratch part of the surface.

8 Language barrier

You will meet few Chinese who speak English fluently and less with a good ability to understand English. Language is often the cause of travellers' difficulties, usually when a Chinese gives the impression they have understood when in fact they have only the vaguest idea what you are talking about but are too proud to admit the fact. But in one way and another you will survive and there are a lot of CITS officials and hotel personnel who are both kind and helpful and speak reasonable English. One has to learn, as quickly as possible, when to keep one's temper and when to lose it.

9 Renewal of visas and obtaining special permits

Your initial visa is not likely to be for longer than two months. Visas can usually be extended at the local Public Security Bureau (PSB) though the length of the extension varies. It is impossible to give exact advice as the situation is changing all the time. Do not let your visa run out as your passport is often examined for one purpose and another. If you wish to stay in China longer than your first visa allows, make inquiries immediately you get to China at the nearest PSB.

They also issue special permits for controlled areas such as Tibet and towns such as Datong. Again the list of places requiring a special permit is constantly changing and recently shrinking but if you try to go to a controlled area without a special permit you will not be able to purchase an air, train or bus ticket. It is rumoured that certain PSBs are more lenient than others but it is no use knowing that they are lenient in Kunming if you are obliged to apply for a special permit in Beijing. Like everything else in China travel, you must accept an element of luck. On the whole I would make applications to PSBs in larger towns since they are more likely to know the latest regulations. Some PSB out in the sticks may not get the latest circular from Beijing for months and will not know that they have the authority to issue you with a permit to a newly opened area.

10 Group or individual travel?

Ultimately this is a decision that only you can make. The advantages of going in a group are obvious and for many people going to China in a well-organised group will be the sensible decision, particularly if you can spare only two or three weeks. But group travel is inflexible, usually over-hurried and more expensive once you are in China, though the cheaper airfare may offset that. To me the main drawback of group travel is that although you are conveyed in reasonable comfort from one sight to another, you will have almost no opportunity to walk the streets and get the real feel of China or to slip slightly off the tourist round. I actually saw group travellers taking photographs of the empty street in front of a hotel in the five minutes allowed them between breakfast and embussing.

I would warmly encourage you to go to China as an individual traveller providing:

(a) You already have some experience of travelling on your own in a country where you could not speak (or read) the language and where facilities were limited to primitive.

(b) You are reasonably fit and can comfortably walk 15 km in a day. You might also be forced to carry all your luggage for 3–5 km.

(c) You are prepared to rough it to the extent of sometimes sleeping in a dormitory. You must also be prepared to eat Chinese food all the time except for the Western breakfasts served in most hotels.

(d) You are able to take up to ten hours on a hard seat. From time to time you may have no other choice.

(e) You have a minimum of four weeks for your journey. In a month, by flying some of the longer distances, you could see quite a lot of either northern or southern China or get a more selective view of the whole country. If you consider going to Lhasa, allow yourself at least a week from start to finish.

You should go with a particularly sympathetic companion. Close friendship is more likely to survive the inevitable trials and tribulations of travel in China.

If you do decide to go individually I think the main essentials are a good pair of walking shoes which are non-slip whatever is underfoot; a backpack or bag with a shoulder strap which you can carry in comfort; an indestructible sense of humour.

Finally, you will need a guide-book. I strongly recommend a rather racy but wonderfully practical book called *China: A Travel Survival Kit* (Lonely Planet Press, 1984), available everywhere. Without it I should not have survived.

Select Bibliography

1 FOR THE TRAVELLER

Berlitz, *Chinese for Travellers*, Editions Berlitz, 1980.
China Guide Series, *All China; Peking; Xi'an; Shanghai; Hangzhou; Canton & Guilin*, and other volumes, Hong Kong, 1980–5.
G. Earnshaw, *On Your Own in China*, Century, 1983.
E. Garside, *China Companion*, André Deutsch, 1981.
F. Kaplan & A. de Keijzer, *The China Guidebook*, Eurasia Press, 1982/3.
R. Malloy, *Travel Guide to the People's Republic of China*, William Morrow, 1980.
E. Morrell, *A Visitor's Guide to China*, Michael Joseph, 1983.
Nagel's Encyclopaedia-Guide, *China*, Nagel, 1979.
A. Samagaiski & M. Buckley, *China: A Travel Survival Kit*, Lonely Planet Press, 1984.
B. Schwartz, *China Off the Beaten Track*, Harvill, 1985.

2 FURTHER READING

Anon, *China ABC*, New World Press, Beijing, 1985.
China Handbook Series, *History*, Foreign Language Press, Beijing, 1982.
China Handbook Series, *Tourism*, Foreign Language Press, Beijing, 1984.
Confucius (trans. D. Lau), *The Analects*, Penguin, 1984.
V. Cronin, *The Wise Man from the West*, Rupert Hart-Davis, 1955.
W. Eberhard, *A History of China*, Routledge & Kegan Paul, 1977.
J. Fairbank & E. Reischauer, *China: Tradition & Transformation*, Houghton Mifflin, 1973.
J. Feibleman, *Understanding Oriental Philosophy*, Mentor, 1976.
C. Fitzgerald, *The Birth of the Communist Party*, Penguin, 1970.
C. Fitzgerald, *China: A Short Cultural History*, Barrie & Jenkins, 1976.
J. Fraser, *The Chinese Portrait of a People*, Fontana, 1981.
R. Garside, *China After Mao: Coming Alive*, André Deutsch, 1981.

H. Giles, *A History of Chinese Literature*, Tuttle, 1974.

C. Hibbert, *The Dragon Wakes*, Penguin, 1984.

S. Karnow, *Mao and China*, Penguin, 1984.

Lao Tzu (trans. D. Lau), *Tao Te Ching*, Penguin, 1985.

Mao Zedong, *Selected Works* Vols 1–5, Foreign Language Press, Beijing.

Mencius (trans. D. Lau), *Works of Mencius*, Penguin, 1970.

J. Needham (abridged by C. Ronan), *The Shorter Science and Civilisation of China*, Cambridge University Press, 1978.

R. Newnham, *About Chinese*, Penguin, 1971.

Marco Polo (trans. R. Latham), *The Travels*, Penguin, 1982.

S. Schram, *Mao Tse Tung: A Biography*, Penguin, 1970.

F. Schurmann & O. Schell, *Imperial China; Republican China; Communist China*, Penguin, 1968.

D. Wilson, *The Long March*, Penguin, 1977.

3 INTERPRETATION

J. Ballingall, *A Taste of China*, John Murray, 1984.

D. Bonavia, *The Chinese*, Penguin, 1984.

F. Butterfield, *China: Alive in a Bitter Sea*, Times Books, 1982.

C. Dodwell, *A Traveller in China*, Hodder & Stoughton, 1985.

H. Harrer, *Seven Years in Tibet*, Granada, 1984.

H. Harrer, *Return to Tibet*, Penguin, 1985.

L. Heng & J. Shapiro, *Son of the Revolution*, Fontana, 1984.

S. Leys, *The Chairman's New Clothes*, Allison & Busby, 1977.

S. Leys, *Chinese Shadows*, Penguin, 1978.

A. Miller, *Salesman in Beijing*, Methuen, 1984.

T. Norbu & C. Turnbull, *Tibet*, Penguin, 1983.

P. Short, *The Dragon and The Bear*, Abacus, 1982.

E. Snow, *Red China Today*, Penguin, 1972.

E. Snow, *Red Star Over China*, Penguin, 1978.

H. Suyin, *The Crippled Tree; A Mortal Flower; Birdless Summer; My House Has Two Doors; Phoenix Harvest*, 5 vols, Triad Granada, 1982.

4 ARCHAEOLOGY, ART & ARCHITECTURE

M. Keswick, *The Chinese Garden*, Academy Editions, 1978.

S. Lee, *A History of Far Eastern Art*, Thames & Hudson, 1970.

M. Medley, *A Handbook of Chinese Art*, Bell & Hyman, 1977.

J. Rawson, *Ancient China: Art and Archaeology*, British Museum, 1980.

L. Sickmann & A. Soper, *Art & Architecture of China*, Penguin, 1971.

M. Sullivan, *Arts of China*, Thames & Hudson, 1973.
M. Tregear, *Chinese Art*, Thames & Hudson, 1980.
W. Watson, *Early Civilisation in China*, Thames & Hudson, 1966.
W. Watson, *Ancient Chinese Bronzes*, Faber, 1977.

5   CHINESE NOVELS & POETRY

C. Birch, *An Anthology of Chinese Literature*, Penguin, 1967.
D. Blair (ed.), *Rice Bowl Women*, Mentor, 1982.
Cao Xuequin (trans. D. Hawkes & J. Minford), *Story of the Stone*, 4 vols, Penguin, 1982.
A. Davis (ed.), *Penguin Book of Chinese Poetry*, Penguin, 1962.
A. Graham (trans.), *Poems of the Late T'ang*, Penguin, 1984.
D. Hawkes (trans.), *The Song of the South: An Anthology of Ancient Chinese Poetry by Qu Yuan & Other Poets*, Penguin, 1985.
Li Po & Tu Fu (trans. A. Cooper), *Poems*, Penguin, 1981.
Liu Jung-en (trans.), *Six Yuan Plays*, Penguin, 1977.
Li Yu, *The Before Midnight Scholar*, Arrow, 1985.
Shen Fu (trans. L. Pratt & Chiang Su-Hui), *Six Records of a Floating Life*, Penguin, 1983.
Wang Wei (trans. G. Robinson), *Poems*, Penguin, 1982.
Wu Ch'eng-en (trans. A. Waley), *Monkey*, Unicorn, 1984.
Wu-chi & I. Yucheng Lo (ed.) *Sunflower Splendour: 3000 Years of Chinese Poetry*, Anchor Books, 1975.

6   FOREIGN NOVELS ABOUT CHINA

J. Ballard, *Empire of the Sun*, Gollancz, 1984.
P. Buck, *The Good Earth*, Longman, 1963.
Y. Inoue, *Tun-Huang*, Kodansha, 1983.
B. Lord, *Spring Moon*, Sphere, 1983.
T. Mo, *Sour Sweet*, Abacus, 1983.
T. Mo, *The Monkey King*, Abacus, 1984.
C. New, *Shanghai*, Futura, 1985.
H. Suyin, *A Many-Splendoured Thing*, Triad Panther, 1985.
H. Suyin, *Till Morning Comes*, Bantam, 1984.

Index